Streetwise Chicago

CHICAGO

A History of
Chicago Street Names

Don Hayner and Tom McNamee

With a Foreword by John Callaway

Loyola University Press · Chicago

Loyola University Press
3441 North Ashland Avenue
Chicago, Illinois 60657

Library of Congress Cataloging in Publication Data
Hayner, Don.
     Streetwise Chicago: a history of Chicago street names/Don
  Hayner, Tom McNamee.
        p. cm.
     ISBN 0-8294-0597-6. ISBN 0-8294-0596-8 (pbk.)
     1. Street names—Illinois—Chicago—History—Dictionaries.
  2. Chicago (Ill.)—History—Dictionaries. 3. Streets—Illinois—
  Chicago—History—Dictionaries. I. McNamee, Tom. II. Title.
  III. Title: Street wise Chicago.
  F548.67.A1H38 1988
  917.73'11'0014—dc19   88-12922
                              CIP

Carl Whiting is a freelance illustrator in the Chicago area. A
graduate of the Center for Creative Studies in Detroit, Michigan.
He has worked for a wide variety of clients from advertising,
magazine, and newspaper illustration, to books and cards. He
plays a mean guitar and draws inspiration from his cat, "Max".

Designed by C. L. Tornatore

To our wives,
Dawn Russell Hayner and Deborah Leigh Wood

And to our children,
James Hutchison Hayner and John Ross Hayner,
and Caitlin Shara McNamee and Jared Ross McNamee.

Contents

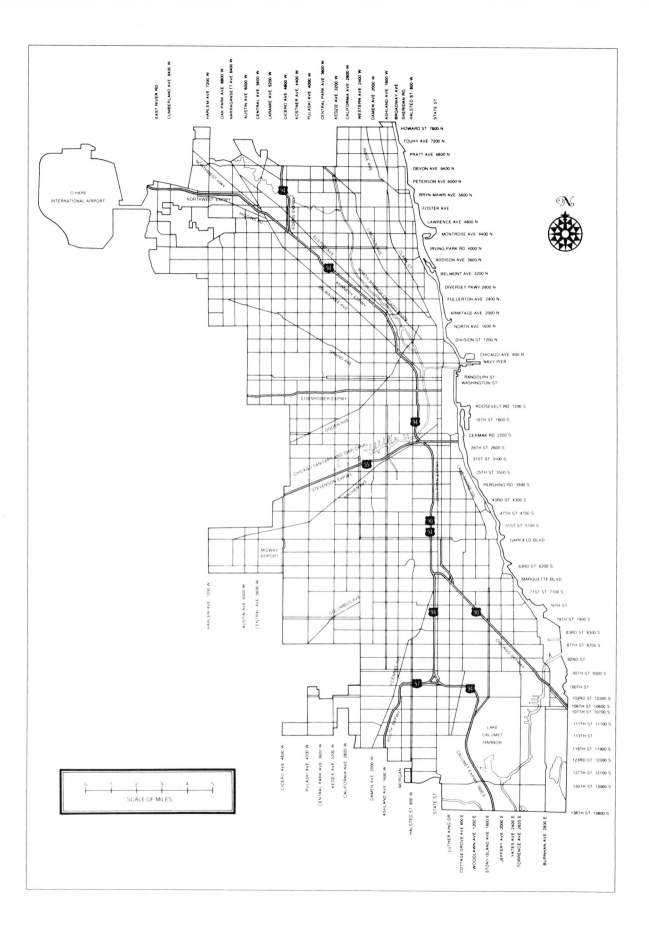

Foreword

by John Callaway

F ancy it.

"My darling, I'm now going to take you someplace you've always wanted to go."

"Where is that, dear?"

"Don't ask. Just trust and come with me."

And off you drive. Where do you go? Down Memory Lane. Literally. It is on Chicago's Far Northwest Side. More precisely, in the terminology of Chicago's streets grid (or is it street grids?) you drive to 5146 N, from 8000 W to 8158 W. That will take you down Memory Lane.

I've been walking and driving Chicago's streets and reporting from them since 1956, and I didn't know there was a Memory Lane. Now, thanks to this instructive, historically helpful, frequently whimsical volume, I came to learn that Chicago has a Memory Lane and many other streets, avenues, boulevards, places, and roads that I (and I'll bet you) didn't know about. In this urban geography, mystery-history story, our passionate street sleuths, McNamee and Hayner, are amazingly, almost perversely fanatical in tracking down the whys and hows of street names. Even as this Foreword is being written, they are begging their editor for more time so they can make one last stab at discovering the origin of that Loch Ness Monster of Chicago street names—Agatite Avenue (see their comments in the Preface and in the book on page XI. Will they ever sleep peacefully until Agatite yields to scientific, historically documented consensus?)

But they can rest well now that we know that Beaubien Court (120 E, from 150 N to 186 N) is named after "Jolly Mark" Beaubien, an innkeeper, ferryman, fur trader, and "truly wicked fiddle player." And we can relax now that we know that Beaubien was the father of twenty-three children and that his brother, Jean Baptiste Beaubien, fathered twenty children, and that between the two of them (and their incredible wives) they produced more children than the entire population of Chicago in 1829.

Now be warned that despite all of the superb scholarship and investigative journalism that resulted in the Beaubien revelations, the explanations for some of the street names end up being less than enthralling. To go back down Memory Lane: "More than likely, the whimsical man or woman who named this street was inspired by the saying, 'a stroll down Memory Lane.'" But if I know McNamee and Hayner, they probably spent a month double-checking to see if it were possible that an ancient Indian or alderman or real estate developer's last name weren't "Memory."

This book is nothing like the first street guide I was issued as a cub police reporter for the City News Bureau of Chicago in June of 1956. That was the "little black book"--*Leonard's Street Guide*. Only with *Leonard's* in my pocket could I survive the transition from walking the few maple-lined streets of my small hometown of New Martinsville, West Virginia, to chasing fires and murders in the countless big city streets of Chicago. *Leonard's* just told the name

of the street and how far north it was and how far east to west it ran. This volume is a feast, but not terribly moveable unless you happen to have a coffee table in your automobile.

As a young, practically penniless newcomer to Chicago, walking city streets was my pastime. I got to know the hustlers, Gypsies, and street walkers of South Wabash, the Italian street fairs at 23rd and Oakley, the bargains on Maxwell Street, the slums of 63rd and Woodlawn, the seemingly endless ethnic diversity of Devon. I walked the length of West Madison Street years before the riots of 1968 turned it partially into a no-man's land. I walked all the way up and down Chicago's lakefront. As a police reporter, death and destruction on the streets burned their names into my consciousness: a murder-suicide on Flournoy; a terrible multiple-fatality fire on Dorchester; an el crash at Wilson Avenue; the tear-gassed streets of the Democratic convention of 1968. I became street-smart.

But this book is street-wise. In digging for why Chicago's streets have the names they do, the authors provide us with a series of historical developments and personal sketches that add up to much, much more than a street guide. And we really get a sense of the self-interest which built Chicago—it is no small fact that a huge number of our streets are named after real estate developers. I can hardly wait for the naming of Rubloff Drive. You can bet on it.

And we learn that people take their

streets seriously in this town. McNamee and Hayner remind us that a twenty-year court battle ensued over the changing of Crawford Avenue to Pulaski. Some people still call it Crawford.

A personal note: It was just the week before that 1968 Democratic convention in Chicago that I covered the story of the defacing of the new Dr. Martin Luther King, Jr. Drive signs that replaced the signs for South Park Avenue. And I was stunned to learn in this book that in the first six months after a one-mile stretch of 43rd Street was renamed Pope John Paul II Drive (to commemorate his 1979 visit to Chicago) that twenty-three of the new street signs were stolen!

This book has inspired me to make one modest and one ambitious suggestion for our city fathers and mothers. My modest proposal—if you want to rename

a street without igniting huge controversy, try something like Dawson Avenue (3432 W, from 2800 N to 2962 N). It was named, we learn from our authors, for John Brown Dawson, a barber, Methodist minister, and real estate operator of the 1860s. Who would object if we someday hold a ceremony and update the naming of Dawson Avenue in honor of Cubs' star Andre Dawson? My ambitious proposal—do away with vanity addresses so that the fire department dispatchers will quickly know where to send their units when people are trapped in high-rise fires. In doing away with vanity addresses such as on Michigan Avenue, provide new names for the various streets that are created in the huge new downtown developments. What the hell, name one Rubloff Drive.

We really are serious about street names, but mostly this volume is just

great fun. The late Sidney Harris, who wrote those famous "things I learned en route to looking up other things" columns, would have gone wild with this book. I'm sure Sidney knew (but I didn't) that Academy Place was and still may be the city's narrowest street (ten feet wide) and that Grand Avenue was called "Whiskey Point Road" when it was an Indian trail. Oh, for the joy of broadcasting a live mini-cam news report from Whiskey Point Road!

Well, I've stalled as long as I can. Maybe McNamee and Hayner have by now dicovered the true origins of the name Agatite Avenue and have phoned it in to their editor. If they succeed, I hope they both have streets named after them.

Preface

Nobody in Chicago, at least nobody we know, knows how Agatite Street got its name. Heaven knows, we tried to find out.

We began our search at City Hall, where the Department of Maps and Plats maintains an index card file on street names. According to the index card for Agatite Street, agatite is a type of tree, more commonly called the "pea tree," indigenous to the West Indies. Sounds reasonable. But we made a double check at the Chicago Historical Society, which maintains a similar card file on Chicago street names. The Historical Society offered the same explanation, word for word.

Adhering to the old City News Bureau addage of "If your mother says she loves you, check it out," we triple checked the meaning of *agatite* by thumbing through several tree and shrub dictionaries. We found several pea trees, but no agatite. So we phoned the Morton Arboretum in DuPage County, the Chicago area's leading authority on arboreal matters. A taxonomist there, after digging through several authoritative volumes, assured us that agatite is in no way a type of tree. "Sounds more like a rock to me," he said.

Good enough. We phoned the Department of Geology at the University of Chicago. A geologist there, who himself had often wondered about the origin of the street name Agatite, said, no, agatite is neither a rock or mineral, although agate is. Maybe, our geologist speculated, some non-scientist in naming the street had added the common Latin suffix "ite" to agate. Or maybe, he ventured further, that same layman had misspelled the word *apatite*, a calcium phosphate found in teeth and bones.

Now why, you might ask, would anyone name a street in Chicago for a mineral in the teeth? Who knows? But then this is the same town in which somebody apparently named a street for a milk can in a field—Canfield.

We tell this story of our search for Agatite to demonstrate the efforts we made, usually successful, to learn the meaning of each street's name, and also to illustrate the impossibility of nailing down the definite meanings and exact sources of many of the street names, those meanings being lost in history. The best we can do in such cases is offer the various possibilities, myths, and legends. For a relatively few names we cannot even offer that much. We must admit defeat—for the time being anyway—and say, "Source unknown."

Often in this book, we have had to make judgment calls. According to the City Hall index file, for example, Racine Avenue was named in honor of Jean Baptiste Racine, the classical French writer. We doubt this. The compiler of the City Hall file, we have found, frequently seized upon some famous man, such as the writer Racine, when he was stumped on a street name. We think a more likely explanation, given the intertwined histories of Chicago and other Midwestern towns, is that Racine Avenue was named for Racine, Wisconsin. The town, in turn, was named for the Racine River. And the river, in turn, was called *racine*—the French word for "root"—by French explorers because tangled tree roots in the water made navigation there nearly impossible.

Our blueprint for writing this book was the City Hall street-name card file, compiled by Howard C. Brodman, superintendent of the Bureau of Maps and Plats from 1933 to 1958. The file, based on the scrapbooks of Edward J. Brennan (see our Introduction), newspaper clippings, local histories, and other sources, is incomplete and has many errors, but it offers at least a stab at the meanings of most of the names. Without access to this valuable file, research for this book would have been virtually impossible.

A second source of information was the street-name file in the Chicago Historical Society, essentially a duplication of the City Hall file with extra tidbits of information gleaned from 1930s' newspaper articles. The Historical Society was of great help in other ways too, providing us with a treasure trove of old Chicago history books, city records, newspaper clippings, and original manuscripts.

Chicago historian Virgil Vogel's research on Midwestern Native Americans provided us with at least a few words of explanation on almost every street with an Indian name. Vogel's 1955 magazine article for the *Chicago Schools Journal*, "The Indian Origin of Some Chicago Street Names," was invaluable.

For information on Chicago Park District street names we turned to Steve Herman, an archivist for the District, who guided us in our search through several early Park District volumes.

We found several dozen other local and national reference books and histories to be of considerable assistance, particularly A.T. Andreas' three-volume *History of Chicago*, the University of Illinois at Chicago's *Local Community Fact Book, Chicago Metropolitan Area*, Kenan Heise's *Hands on Chicago*, as well as Dominic Pacyga's and Ellen Skerrett's *Chicago, City of Neighborhoods*. In addition we would like to thank the Newberry Library, a large number of neighborhood historical societies, and various folks who just live on the streets—sometimes they knew the origin of a street's name when nobody else did.

We owe our greatest debt of gratitude to the *Chicago Sun-Times*, our "mothership" on our research journeys. Some of the entries in this book first appeared, in different form, as short articles in the *Sun-Times*. And the *Sun-Times* librarians, especially Judith Anne Halper and Terri Golembiewski, always seemed to know where to turn to verify the most elusive of small facts.

Finally we'd like to thank *Sun-Times* City Hall reporter Ray Hanania, who was our computer maven on the project, local historian Ellen Skerrett, and our editor Father George Lane.

And we know we are not finished. We know hundreds of neighborhood historians are out there, and we would love to talk to them all. For future editions of this book, we would welcome additional facts about Chicago's street names. Especially Agatite.

Introduction

Lose yourself on the streets of Chicago and you may find yourself among spiritualists, tugboat heroes, a bear hunter in the "Loop," and a ball player who wanted his epitath to read: "Here lies a man who batted .300."

Drive down Artesian Avenue. You may be surprised to learn it was named for an artesian well drilled by a group of spiritualists who thought God had led them to oil on Chicago's West Side. Don't look for magnolias on Magnolia Avenue. The *Magnolia* was a tugboat used to save hundreds of lives in the Chicago Fire of 1871. If you happen upon George Street, tip your hat to Sam George, the man who shot the last wild bear in the "Loop." And never mind that Cap Anson was once a city clerk. Anson Place honors his heroics with the Chicago White Stockings, now known as the Chicago Cubs.

Through the city streets a twisting tale of a town is told. Each street name tells a story. Piece together the lore of the curbs and corners and you have a streetwise history of a streetwise town. It is a crazy-quilt history, one upon which no historian has imposed a design or theme, one guided only by the street signs themselves.

Begin, if you like, in 1830. Nowadays, most Chicagoans believe a cow was the first four-legged creature to play a critical role in the city's history. Actually, it was a horse. The sale of a lone mare in 1830 closed the deal that literally put Chicago on the map.

In that year, when Chicago consisted of fewer than 300 souls squatting in a marsh, a downstate map-maker named James Thompson came to town and laid the cartographic cornerstone of a great American city. Thompson, employed by a federal commission that planned the digging of the Illinois and Michigan Canal, mapped Chicago's first streets. Working with straight lines and right angles, the rigid geometry of a practical man, he imposed an efficient man-made order on the curves and undulations of the glacially formed land. His would be a straightforward town, a businesslike town. And so Chicago is today. Then he labeled his sensible streets, naming them for the wealthy, the famous, and the powerful, while pretty much ignoring the common man. And so Chicago does today.

Thompson mapped a compact little settlement, less than a square mile of pioneers and Indians, bounded by Kinzie, Jefferson, Washington, and Dearborn streets. But from these modest beginnings grew the Chicago of today, an expansive Midwestern transportation hub crisscrossed by train tracks, river routes, airplane runways, and 3,677 miles of streets.

A fine surveyor, but only a so-so visionary, Thompson evidently saw little promise in this muddy land laced with swamps and split in thirds by a sluggish river. In return for mapping the settlement of Chicago, the canal commission offered him some prime "downtown" real estate. Thompson instead chose a mare, a well-bred mare.

Chicago, to be sure, had its share of transportation byways before Thompson came along. There were crooked horse paths and meandering river paths, Indian trails and narrow coach roads, almost all of them known by names that declared a highly specific purpose.

Vincennes Trace was an Indian trail. Walk it long enough and a foot-weary traveler would arrive in Vincennes, Indiana. The Green Bay Trail worked its way north to Green Bay, Wisconsin. And South Water Street, perhaps the city's oldest street, hugged the south bank of the Chicago River from Fort Dearborn to the river's fork. South Water was a self-explanatory name, one that would never confuse an early nineteenth-century visitor.

Naming streets for their destinations was the common-sense practice throughout the world for centuries, as cities and roads evolved slowly to fulfill people's needs. The Good Samaritan came to the aid of a stranger on the Road to Jericho. Saul converted to Christianity and assumed the name of Paul on the Road to Damascus. And every tourist seeking the Tower of London knows you take Tower Road to get there.

In early Chicago, a town so impatient to grow that it mapped out streets on the empty prairie, Thompson changed all that. He named his streets for people of fame, stature, clout, and power—most importantly power. Among his choices were two presidents, a local landowner, a couple of explorers, and, by association, himself. His home was in Downstate Randolph County, which tells us how Randolph Street got its name.

Powerful Chicagoans ever since have named city streets for themselves, their friends, their relatives and, in rare flights of fancy, a favorite poet or two. How else could Chicago find itself with street names such as Maud, Grace, Cornelia, and Gladys? They were all lucky relatives. Maud Long was the daughter of an alderman. Grace was the daughter of a mayor. Cornelia was a mayor's granddaughter, and Gladys was the granddaughter of a major West Side real estate speculator.

Even U.S. Presidents could find

themselves powerless to merit a Chicago street name. John Adams, a member of the Federalist Party, was at first snubbed because a majority of the city council belonged to a different political party, and John Tyler was rejected because he was judged to be a standard-bearer of mediocrity. As Theodore Roosevelt once put it, "Tyler has been called a mediocre man, but this is unwarranted flattery. He was a politician of monumental littleness."

And yet, dozens of exceptions exist to this rule of power in Chicago street nomenclature. The many exceptions touch upon the flip side of the city's history, a history of Indians and immigrants, heroes and henchmen, do-gooders and dreamers, the pious and the penniless. Blackhawk Street honors an Indian warrior. Emerald Avenue honors those who spoke with a brogue. McDowell Street celebrates a social worker. Cabrini Street honors a saint. Still other names tell of beer riots and obscure mayors, teetotalers and stockyard hands. Read Chicago's history through its street names, and you will inevitably stray from the heavily-traveled main roads and down paths long forgotten.

Thompson, the map-maker, got Chicago off on the right foot. He gave the future city an easily navigable grid system of mostly parallel streets. But as Chicago grew, annexing huge neighboring towns and settlements, getting around town came to be a major hassle. Chicago's problem wasn't so much traffic congestion, as it was street-name congestion. Too many streets shared the same name. By 1893 Chicago had seventeen Lincoln streets, avenues, or places; while some streets had six or seven different names in different places. The street one block west of Halsted Street, for instance, was simultaneously known as Green Street, Lime Street, Dayton Street, Florence Avenue, Craft Street, Reta Avenue, and Newberry Avenue.

By 1900, Thompson's handy street plan had been confounded by enormous land grabs, politely called annexations, that burdened Chicago with hundreds of additional street names and several conflicting street-numbering systems. Between 1889 and 1893, Chicago annexed sixteen areas, including the Towns of Jefferson and Lake, the Village of Hyde Park and the City of Lake View. Chicago's physical size jumped by 362 percent in 1892.

Further undermining Thompson's orderly blueprint were the aldermen in Chicago's city council. Chicago's aldermen have always demonstrated an unfailing fondness for naming whole streets or small parts of streets for any man, woman, or thing that might make them, the aldermen, look like swell guys. Unfortunately, notes one turn-of-the-century history book, *Chicago and Its Makers*, these same aldermen are "frequently not of the highest intelligence," and are guided more by "political or financial interests" than by "esthetic requirements" when choosing new street names.

Into this street-naming chaos in 1901 walked Edward P. Brennan, a regular guy from Holy Family parish on the Near West Side. Brennan, a building superintendent for Lyon and Healy, was the first to envision Chicago as a giant piece of graph paper. In a letter to the *Record Herald* newspaper, he proposed that Chicago adopt a uniform street-numbering system and designate State and Madison streets as the base lines, their intersection becoming ground zero.

"A man had to spend half his time studying street guides in order to be able to find his way around town," Brennan said, in a *Chicago Daily News* article in 1936. "I recalled the old saying, 'All roads lead to Rome.' It seemed to me that it could be brought down to date and made to apply locally by rewriting it to 'All streets lead to State and Madison streets.'"

The new numbering system, Brennan said, should indicate how far an address is from the State and Madison baselines, and odd and even numbers should be used to indicate the side of a street on which a house is located.

The *Chicago Tribune*, reporting on the Brennan plan in 1908, deemed it a good idea, but predicted the city council would never go for it because too many constituents, especially small businessmen, would object. An address change would require, at the very least, new business stationery. "Here is a task for the Council Committee on Street Nomenclature," the *Tribune* wrote. "It also may be another job for the undertaker, as its fate is likely to be early death and burial."

Remarkably, the council, led by Brennan's cousin, an alderman, passed Brennan's suggestions into law in 1908. Specifically, the council ordained that State and Madison would, indeed, be the baselines for a street numbering system under which each 800 in an address would indicate a mile. Thus today, a home in the 1600 block of north Maplewood Avenue is about two miles north of Madison Street, and a business on the 2400 block of west Pershing Road is about three miles west of State Street. On the South Side the numbering system is slightly less precise because certain streets, such as 12th Street (now Roosevelt Road), were not renumbered when the Brennan plan went into effect. Roosevelt Road is only one mile—not a mile and a half—south of Madison Street. In fact, east-west streets on the South Side do not conform to the city's 800-to-a-mile address system until south of 31st Street, when the distance between 31st Street and Pershing Road (39th Street) is exactly one mile.

Along east-west streets today, thanks to Brennan, even numbers are on the North Side and odd numbers are on the South Side. Along north-south streets, even numbers are on the west and odd numbers are on the east. In addition, every city block is divided, for addressing purposes, into numbered 20-foot segments. A house is given the address of the 20-foot segment within which its front door is located.

In 1913 Brennan, by this time a respected member of the exclusive Chicago Club, magnified his vision. He urged the city council to give just one name to all portions of any street interrupted in its course through the city. Again, remarkably, the city council did so.

It was also Brennan who first proposed naming Chicago's streets alphabetically, with all streets located within one mile of the Chicago-Indiana border beginning with the letter "A," all streets within the second mile west of the border beginning the the letter "B," and so forth. As a result, many north-south streets running between Pulaski Avenue and Cicero Avenue today have names that begin with the letter "K," such as Kostner, Kilpatrick, and Kenton, and names further west begin with the letters L, M, N, and O. On the city's most western edge are the streets Pontiac, Plainfield, Pittsburgh, Pioneer, Paris, Panama, Page, and Pacific.

Brennan himself named more than three hundred Chicago streets, oftentimes renaming streets with duplicate names. In the 1930s, the City Club pushed through the renaming of more streets. And in 1936, the city council, at the urging of Howard C. Brodman, then superintendent of the city's Department of Maps and Plats, renamed another 138 streets that had more than one name or duplicated other street names. That saved businessmen an estimated $500,000 annually by simplifying mail and merchandise deliveries.

Today, largely because of Brennan's and Brodman's efforts, Chicago's simple street system is uncluttered with repetitive or unnecessary names. Chicago has 1,145 street names, thousands fewer than at the peak of the city's street-name confusion. But in 1947, five year's after Brennan's death, the city council violated Brennan's cardinal rule of less-is-more when it created one more Chicago street name: Brennan Avenue.

In the most broad-stroke terms, Chicago street nomenclature has been for more than 150 years the province of politicians, land owners, and the very wealthy. They have named streets for themselves, for their families, and for their hometowns. John L. Cochran, the developer of Chicago's Edgewater community, for example, named six streets for stops along the Main Line, a commuter rail line going out of Philadelphia, his hometown. And why not? He owned the streets. Chicago has, in fact, over 170 streets named after local real estate developers and their relatives, but only a handful named for Polish heroes. Chicago has over thirty streets named after English towns, the ancestral homes of many of Old Chicagoans, but only a dozen or more streets named for the immigrant Irish. And Chicago has forty-four streets named for aldermen and mayors, but fewer than a dozen for blacks and Puerto Ricans.

Way down on the bottom of the list are poets, artists, and writers, especially those of local birth. Chicago has a Dunbar Avenue, named for the black poet and novelist Paul Laurence Dunbar, and a Sandburg Terrace, named for the poet Carl Sandburg. But that is about it. There are no streets named for Chicago writers Theodore Dreiser, James T. Farrell, or Nelson Algren.

There was, to be precise, almost an Algren Street. For a few months in 1981, upon Algren's death, city crews replaced old signs on Evergreen Street with signs that read "Algren Street." It seemed appropriate. Algren had lived in a third-floor walkup on Evergreen for many years. But just about nobody living on Evergreen wanted to live on Algren, what with the hassles of getting a new driver's license and all. So they taped cardboard "Evergreen Street" signs over the new signs and threatened to dump their alderman. Who was this Algren anyway? What land did he own? The city council backed off.

But for all the tales of spiritualists, tugboat heroes, bear hunters, and ballplayers, Chicago's street signs are simply streetcorner memorials, named by folks seeking a modest form of immortality, for themselves and for others.

And so if one day you find yourself on, say, Catherine Street, consider that Albert J. Schorsch, a Northwest Side real estate developer, wanted his wife Catherine to be remembered.

CHICAGO

MARX BROS. IN PERSON
ANN SHERIDAN - JEFFREY
LYNN "IT ALL CAME TRUE"

Chicago, 1940, State and Lake Streets, looking south on State Street from the State and Lake Chicago Rapid Transit Co. elevated train platform. (The subway was still under construction, as seen in the far southwest part of the photograph. The streetcar was operated by the Chicago Surface Lines. Both companies later became the CTA.)

Henry Wald

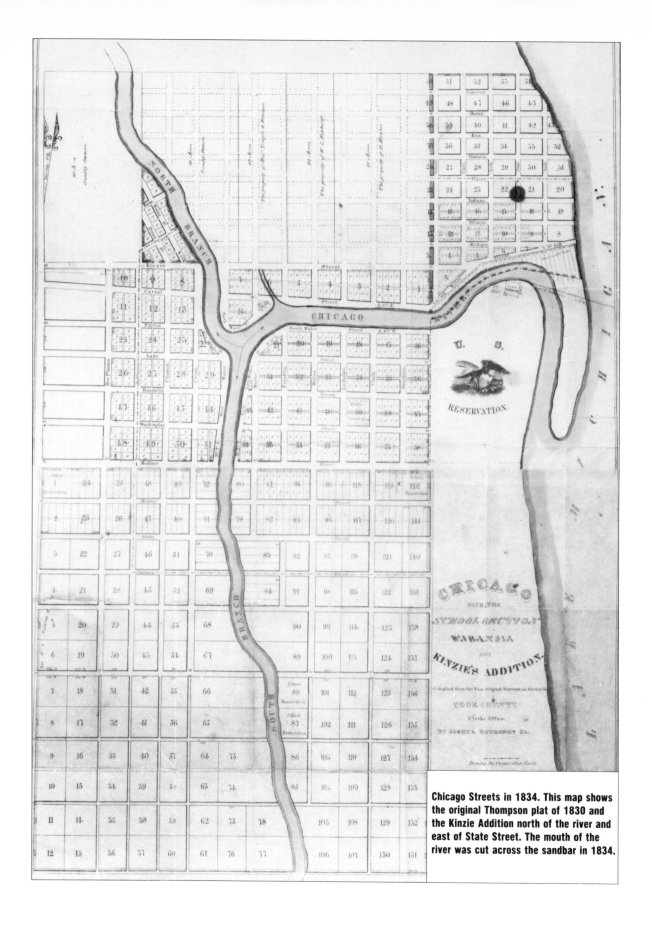

Chicago Streets in 1834. This map shows the original Thompson plat of 1830 and the Kinzie Addition north of the river and east of State Street. The mouth of the river was cut across the sandbar in 1834.

A

Abbott Avenue
210 W, from 9041 S to 9058 S

Named for Robert Sengstacke Abbott, who founded the *Chicago Defender* in 1905. By 1915 it was the largest Negro-owned business in the country. To this day it is Chicago's leading black newspaper.

Aberdeen Street
1100 W, from 722 N to 12256 S*

Aberdeen, Scotland's third largest city, for which this street was named, is on the North Sea coast.

Academy Place
812 W, from 42 N to 40 S

A mere ten feet wide, Academy Place was once—and may still be—the narrowest street in Chicago.

Ada Street
1324 W, from 1698 N to 12258 S*

Ada Sawyer Garrett was the granddaughter of J.A. Butterfield, one of Chicago's foremost real estate subdividers in the 1830s. In 1924, Ada Garrett sold the Logan Square Ball Park for $650,000 to developers. This provided land for what became a $12 million development and a major expansion of the Logan Square neighborhood.

Adams Boulevard
144 S, from 5600 W to 5980 W

Adams Street
200 S, from 100 E to 5600 W*

Named for John Adams (1735-1826), the second president of the United States, who served from 1797 to 1801.

Addison Street
3600 N, from 500 W to 8400 W*

Dr. Thomas Addison (1793-1860) of Guy's Hospital, London, was the first to describe a disease of the endocrine glands and the anemia now named for him—Addisonian anemia.

Administration Drive
5620 S in Washington Park

This street runs alongside a Chicago Park District administration building in Washington Park.

Agatite Avenue
4432 N, from 800 W to 8642 W*

This street's name is a mystery. "Agatite" apparently is not a word, and there seems to be no famous, infamous, or obscure person by that name in Chicago history. It may be a mispelling of "apatite," a calcium phosphate found in teeth and bones. Or, it may be a layman's variation on the mineral name "agate."

Wrigley Field at Clark and Addison, home of the Chicago Cubs since 1916.
G. Lane

One common explanation, that agatite is a type of tree, appears to be false.

Ainslie Street
4900 N, from 806 W to 5874 W

In Chicago's earliest days, Ainslie was a small community in the area near the lake through which this street runs. The street was named for a real estate subdivider of that name. In 1848, after his death, his widow, Mary Ainslie, married an alderman, John S.C. Hogan. The newlyweds soon left Chicago for California to pan for gold.

The asterisk indicates a non-continuous street.

Albany Avenue
3100 W, from 7600 N to 11300 S*

Albany Drive
3100 W in Humboldt Park

An early real estate developer, DeLancey Lauderbach, was a founder in the 1880s of the community of Albany Park, now a Chicago neighborhood. He named the community and the street for his hometown, Albany, New York.

Albion Avenue
6600 N, from 1012 W to 7224 W*

Named for the town of Albion, England.

Aldine Avenue
3300 N, from 400 W to 870 W

Named for Aldine, England, by Uzziel P. Smith, a Chicago real estate developer in the 1870s.

Equestrian Indian figure by Ivan Meštrović at Congress and Michigan.

G. Lane

Alta Vista Terrace, 1900-1904, a Chicago landmark district.

G. Lane

Alexander Street
2246 S, from 200 W to 268 W

John T. Alexander was a prominent land owner in what is now Chicago's Morgan Park community.

This street might also have been named for Dr. Alexander Wolcott, one of Chicago's earliest settlers.
See Wolcott Avenue.

Algonquin Avenue
5600 W, from 6416 N to 6950 N

The Algonquin were a large language group of Indian tribes which included most of the Indians east of the Mississippi River.

Allen Avenue
3500 W, from 2900 N to 3054 N

O.H. Allen was a partner in the real estate development firm of Story & Allen. This street cuts through one of the firm's earliest subdivisions.

Allport Street

1234 W, 1600 S to 2158 S

Walter W. Allport (1824-1893) started with almost nothing, but vowed he would one day be Chicago's very best dentist. His was a classic Chicago success story.

When Allport was fourteen, his father lost the family farm in Lorraine, New York, and pushed the boy into the world. With a bundle of clothes on his back, two silver half-dollars in his pocket, and his mother's blessings, Walter set out on his own. He took odd jobs here and there, and he studied dentistry along the way.

In 1854, Allport came to Chicago, saw the future, and decided to stay. He would, he declared, be Chicago's very best dentist. So he rented a seven-by-eight foot space above a Lake Street shop, installed a barber's chair, and called it a dentist's office. In his first month he made all of $20.50.

But within five years, Allport had the largest dental practice outside of New York City. In 1860 he was elected the first chairman of the American Dental Association, an honor that bestowed civic-leader status upon him in old Chicago.

Alta Vista Terrace

1054 W, 3800 N to 3846 N

Alta Vista means "high point," and it marked the spot where the Rock Island Railroad crossed the watershed between the Kansas and Neosho rivers. Historians speculate that the name Alta Vista was brought to Chicago by Rock Island officials who settled here.

Designated Chicago's first historic district in 1973, Alta Vista is a one-block street of forty striking homes. They are notable for their design, careful upkeep, and old Chicago elegance.

Sometimes called the "Street of Forty Doors," Alta Vista was developed by Chicago real estate developer Samuel Eberly Gross, who modeled it after London's Maypole Street. The ornate facades of the forty houses are paired, one on each side of the street, starting from opposite directions. In the middle of the block are four three-story houses, each with an upstairs ballroom.

These homes, by the way, presented quite a contrast to the frame workers' cottages Gross had erected on the South Side in such communities as Canaryville and Back of the Yards.

Altgeld Street

2500 N, from 800 W to 7200 W*

John Peter Altgeld (1847-1902), the Illinois governor who pardoned the Haymarket bombing defendants, was rejected by the voters for following his conscience. When asked later why he had granted the pardons—to do so was political suicide—he replied, "No man's ambition has the right to stand in the way of performing a simple act of justice."

Altgeld, the son of an illiterate German immigrant, had little formal education, but he read law, was admitted to the bar in 1871, and went on to become chief justice of the Superior Court of Cook County.

***John Peter Altgeld* by Gutzon Borglum in Lincoln Park near Diversey, dedicated on Labor Day, 1915.**

G. Lane

Elected governor in 1892, one of his first tasks was to consider an appeal for clemency on behalf of the three Haymarket defendants still living. They were among eight alleged anarchists who, after a deadly bombing in Chicago's Haymarket Square on May 4, 1886, were convicted of conspiracy to incite a crowd to murder. Four of the men were hanged. A fifth committed suicide.

John "Pardon" Altgeld pardoned the remaining three, calling their trial a frame-up. Three years later, when he ran again for governor, he was burned in effigy and he was defeated at the polls by the Republican candidate, John R. Tanner.

Ancona Street

654 N, from 812 W to 1368 W*

Ancona is an Italian city on the Adriatic Sea.

Adrian "Cap" Anson, first baseman for the Chicago White Stockings, predecessors of the Cubs.

Courtesy, *Chicago Sun-Times*

Anson Place
418 N, 2200 W to 2258 W

This short street is named after a man who wanted his epitaph to read, "Here lies a man that batted .300."

Anson was a first baseman, captain, and manager for the National League's Chicago White Stockings, predecessors of the Cubs. In twenty-two seasons with Chicago, he indeed tallied a batting average over .300, .331 to be exact.

Born on April 17, 1852 in Marshalltown, Iowa, Anson was first recognized as a standout ballplayer for the Forest City Team of Rockford. In 1872 he played for the Philadelphia Athletics, and in 1876 he signed with Chicago. As manager and player, he guided Chicago to five league championships and always ranked among the top six batters. Only twice did he hit below .300.

Anson never drank or smoke, and he bet only on his own team. Some credit Anson with the idea for spring training, apparently after he was almost killed by a falling beer keg.

It was sometime in the late 1880s, and Anson was concerned that his players weren't taking proper care of themselves. So he ruled out carousing after nightfall. This seemed to work well enough as long as Anson stood guard outside the hotel where his players were lodged. But one night someone tossed a beer barrel out a window, and it landed perilously close to where Anson was standing guard. It seemed the players were drinking barrels of beer in their hotel rooms. All that changed in 1886 when Anson ordered the White Stockings to spring training in Hot Springs, Arkansas.

After baseball, Anson retired with a fortune of $300,000, but he eventually lost it all in various business ventures.

Despite hitting over .300 in days when the pitcher was only forty-five feet from the plate, Anson was said never to have been hit by a pitched ball.

In the end, Anson's epitaph simply read, "He played the game."

Anthon Avenue
8534 W, from 4539 N to 4742 N

Wallace R. Anthon was supervisor of the Chicago Department of Maps and Plats in the middle 1960s. The Schorsch brothers, a family of Northwest Side realtors, came to know and respect Anthon in the course of their business dealings, and they named this street for him. *See Schorsch Street.*

Anthony Avenue
400 E at 6800 S to 3000 E at 9404 S

Elliott Anthony (1827-1898) was a distinguished jurist with a knack for getting in on the ground floor. He was a founder of the Republican Party in Illinois, a founder of the Chicago Public Library, and an architect of the 1862 and 1870 Illinois Constitutions.

Anthony was born on the frontier in Onondaga County, New York. He was admitted to the bar at the age of twenty-four and moved to Chicago the next year. He served as Chicago's city attorney and as general solicitor for the Galena & Chicago Union Railroad, and for twelve years he was a Chicago Superior Court judge.

Anthony lived through the Chicago Fire of 1871, and apparently never forgot the experience. When he built his dream home in Evanston, he installed a fireproof library with iron doors. In later life he traveled the world, spending months at a time in Europe and Russia.

Arbour Place
368 N, from 1362 W to 1566 W

At the time this street was named, parts of the Near West Side were still wooded. An arbor is a leafy, shady recess formed by trees and shrubbery.

Arcade Place
20 S, from 120 W to 1758 W*

This street, beginning in the heart of the Loop's financial district, is just what its name implies, an arch-covered passageway between buildings. A wrought-iron arch graces the entrance to this cobblestoned street of old-fashioned street lamps and red awnings.

The arcade, where Arcade Place begins on LaSalle Street.

Arch Street
1316 W, from 2900 S to 3048 S
(source unknown)

Archer Avenue
1 W at 1900 S to 6400 W at 5500 S

Archer Avenue
5500 S, from 6400 W to 7160 W

Col. William Beatty Archer, an abolitionist and civil engineer, was shunned at first by Bridgeport's immigrant Irish whan he supported the Union cause in the Civil War. Some Irish feared freed slaves would take their jobs, but eventually they came around to the Union cause.

Archer gave hundreds of jobs to Bridgeport's Irish while supervising construction of the Illinois & Michigan Canal, begun in 1836. He was a popular guy. And in 1856 he nominated Abe Lincoln for vice president, and later he supported the new president's declaration of civil war.

"To Lincoln's call for volunteers, the sons of Chicago gave an instant warm response," wrote historian Joseph Hamzik. The Chicago Irish formed Mulligan's Brigade and the Irish Legion and fought valiantly for the Blue.

Going back yet another thirty years along Archer Road, history records the first stirrings of Chicago's continuing city-suburban feud.

The rustics of Hickory Creek, a defunct settlement on Archer about a half-day's ride from Fort Dearborn, had invited the fort people to a dance. Three young dandies accepted, arriving in sparkling boots atop sleek horses.

"Their polished manners and ability to execute the Pigeon Wing and Double Shuffle, while the fiddler played, awed the beautiful belles of the ball," Hamzik reports. The local girls danced with the dandies all night, but the farm boys drifted away.

Dawn arrived and the three fort dandies prepared to go home. But upon entering the stable, they found their horses had been shorn of their flowing manes and tails. The city slickers had gotten their comeuppance out on Archer Road.

In the 1890s Archer Avenue was the setting for Finley Peter Dunne's Mr. Dooley. Dooley was the great philosopher–bartender and "the first truly memorable Irish character in American literature" according to Charles Fanning. Archey Road and Bridgeport, according to Fanning, "is the first fully realized ethnic neighborhood" in American literature.

Ardmore Avenue
5800 N, from 934 W to 7828 W*

John L. Cochran, the developer of the Edgewater community, named this street after the suburb of Ardmore, one of the towns on the Main Line, a commuter rail line running west out of his home town of Philadelphia. *See Berwyn and Edgewater Avenues for more on Cochran.*

Argyle Street
5000 N, from 822 W to 8600 W*

James A. Campbell, an alderman and real estate speculator of Scottish descent, named this street in honor of Archibald Campbell, Marquis, who was the first Duke of Argyle in 1701.

Arlington Place
2444 N, from 400 W to 658 W

Arlington, Virginia, on the south bank of the Potomac River opposite Washington, D.C., was the home of Confederate General Robert E. Lee.

Armitage Avenue
2000 N, from 300 W to 7190 W

Named for Thomas Armitage (1819-1896), an American clergyman who was a founder of the American Bible Union in New York in 1850.

A second possible namesake was Edward R. Armitage, a Northwest Side alderman from 1919 to 1923.

Armory Drive
5200 S in Washington Park

This street, as the name suggests, skirts the edge of the National Guard Armory, 5200 S. Cottage Grove Avenue, on the edge of Washington Park.

Armour Street
1500 W, from 400 N to 756 N

George Armour, who is in no way related to the meatpacker Philip Armour, was a real estate speculator, grain merchant, and financier. He was a director of the city's chamber of commerce in 1858 and 1859, a partner in the grain elevator firm of Armour, Dole & Co. in 1860, a member of Chicago's first War Finance Committee during the Civil War, and a trustee of the Merchants' Loan & Trust Corporation at the time of the Chicago Fire of 1871.

Philip Danforth Armour, 1811–1881

Armstrong Avenue
5660 N, from 5300 W to 5550 W

Thomas Armstrong, a Chicago landowner, was recording secretary of the Chicago Historical Society in the period just after the Civil War.

Artesian Avenue
2432 W, from 7458 N to 11856 S*

This street owes its name to a nineteenth century spiritualist who fell into a trance and proclaimed he'd struck oil on Chicago's West Side.

On a Sunday in October, 1863, Abraham James, a trance medium, accompanied several oil scouts for the Chicago Rock Oil Co. to the outskirts of town, near Western and Chicago avenues. According to Adaline Buffum, a member of the Spiritual Philosophers sect that founded Rock Oil, James and his companions walked around for about a half hour and were about to leave when James "became suddenly entranced" and marked three spots with heaps of stones.

He ran to a large tree and fell down, "apparently exhausted, still being in the trance state." His companions "learned from him, by signs, not speaking, that at the places indicated the oil would be found." Drilling began. Finally, in 1865, at a depth of 1,200 feet, Rock Oil struck a gusher of water. Rock Oil had dug an early Chicago artesian well. A few Spiritual Philosophers hastened to clarify the original revelation. Both oil and water had been prophesied, they explained. And this, after all, was a truly heavenly elixir.

"Pure and sweet" artesian water is untainted by "the charges of disease and death that now lie at the door of the present Chicago Water Works," said George A. Shufeldt Jr., a charter member of Rock Oil. "When this water is once in common use, erysipelas, boils, and eruptive diseases will disappear, and that bane of our Western cities, low typhoid fever, will be abated in Chicago."

"This living well of water will be the poor man's friend for all time to come, and the doctor's enemy for eternity."

But Buffum took Shufeldt to task. Nobody, certainly not Shufeldt, had mentioned a prophesy of water until water had been found, she said. "Water and oil," she insisted, "will never mix." Over the next twenty years, artesian wells were drilled all over town. Nineteen wells, yielding a million gallons of water every ten hours, were drilled in the stockyards alone. Even the packer barons, apparently, had gotten religion.

Arthington Street
900 S, from 500 W to 5958 W*

Realtor Henry D. Gilpin named this street in about 1859 for his hometown, Arthington, England.

Arthur Avenue
6500 N, from 1200 W to 7144 W*

Arthur T. Galt was the son of a real estate subdivider, Azarlah Galt, who once owned much of the land that later became the Edgewater Golf Club. Arthur used part of his inheritance to purchase a valuable ancient Greek manuscript for the city's library.

THIS IS GOOD, RIGHT?

Ashland Avenue
1600 W, from 7742 N to 12259 S*

Ashland Boulevard
1600 W, from 6800 N to 7426 N

This street, formerly known as Reuben Street, was named in honor of the Kentucky estate of Henry Clay, which was surrounded by ash trees. It was named by either one of two Chicagoans from Kentucky. Ashland runs through land that was first developed by Henry Hamilton Honore (see Honore Street), and some credit him with naming the street. Others, however, claim that Samuel A. Walker, a Kentucky native who developed the land in the vicinity of Ashland and Harrison Street around 1864, named the street after the same estate.

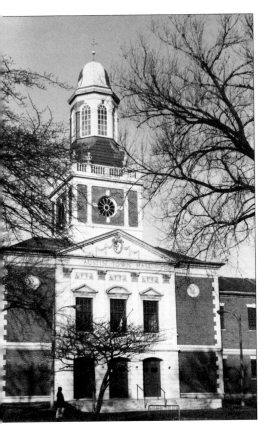

Astor Street
50 E, from 1200 N to 1554 N

John Jacob Astor (1763-1848), a German immigrant, used his profits from frontier fur trading to build a real estate empire. He was the sole owner of the American Fur Company, which used Chicago as a major base. At the time of his death, he was the richest man in America, leaving a fortune of more than $20 million.

Attrill Street
2200 N, from 2600 W to 2638 W

Henry Attrill was a real estate speculator and builder.

Augusta Boulevard
1000 N, from 1200 W to 5968 W*

Augusta Carpenter was the daughter of Philo Carpenter, Chicago's first druggist. *See Carpenter Street.*

Austin Avenue
6000 W, from 6172 N to 6458 S*

Austin Boulevard
6000 W, from 1158 S to 1557 N

Henry W. Austin was the major force behind the development of the Austin neighborhood on Chicago's Far West Side. In 1865 he purchased about 280 acres from another speculator, Henry L. DeKoven (see DeKoven Street), and laid out a community of wide streets and parkways. He enticed a New England clock manufacturer to his new town, Austinville, by offering the company free land. The clock company was destroyed by fire in 1868, and most of the workers returned to Connecticut.

Austin Town Hall (1929), a Chicago Park District facility at Central and Lake, a replica of Independence Hall, Philadelphia.

G. Lane

Avalon Avenue
1232 E, from 7530 S to 9858 S

The Isle of Avalon is thought to be the burial place of England's legendary King Arthur.

Avenue A
All the alphabet streets were named by Frank J. Lewis who laid out this Southeast Side area around 1918 as a huge subdivision with streets, alleys, and sidewalks, but no homes. His land was between 108th and 114th streets, and between Avenue O and the Illinois-Indiana state line. Lewis apparently thought a rapid transit line would be built out to 106th and Indianapolis, which would serve his new subdivision. But this never happened. The subdivision did not develop with homes until after World War II. He probably gave the streets alphabet names simply for convenience sake until the area developed; at least that's one guess.

Frank J. Lewis (1867–1960), the son of immigrant Irish parents, was born in Chicago where his parents once ran a farm on the site of the Merchandise Mart. He became a real estate developer, director of several companies, and he owned the F. J. Lewis Manufacturing Co., a tar products company. On his death, Lewis bequeathed $15 million to Roman Catholic charities and institutions. He once said, "I'm in partnership with the Lord."

Avenue B
4032 E, from 10500 S to 11156 S*

Named for the letter.

Avenue C
4000 E, from 10100 S to 11156 S*

Named for the letter.

Avenue D
3932 E, from 10130 S to 11156 S*

Named for the letter.

Avenue E
3900 E, from 10400 S to 11158 S*

Named for the letter.

Avenue F
3832 E, from 10142 S to 11758 S*

Named for the letter.

Avenue G
3800 E, from 9800 S to 11758 S*

Avenue G Drive
3800 E in Calumet Park

Named for the letter.

Avenue H
3732 E, from 9700 S to 11758 S*

Named for the letter.

Avenue J
3700 E, from 9600 S to 11658 S*

Named for the letter.

Avenue K
3624 E, from 13300 S to 13536 S

Named for the letter.

Avenue L
3600 E, from 9500 S to 13536 S*

Named for the letter.

Avenue M
3532 E, from 9500 S to 13536 S*

Named for the letter.

Avenue N
3500 E, from 9500 S to 13536 S*

Named for the letter.

Avenue O
3432 E, from 8900 S to 13746 S*

Named for the letter.

Avers Avenue
3832 W, from 6354 N to 10834 S*

Frederick Henry Avers, born in 1831 in Buffalo, New York, was a contractor who built the Sherman House and the Palmer House before the Chicago Fire of 1871. After the fire he was a major figure in the city's rebuilding.

Avondale Avenue
1800 W at 2026 N to 7800 W at 6794 N
John L. Cochran, a real estate developer from Philadelphia, created a community called Avondale that is bounded roughly by Addison, Diversey, the Milwaukee Road tracks, and the North Branch of the Chicago River. He named the community and the street after Avondale, Pennsylvania. Cochran also developed the community of Edgewater.

The two-thousand-year-old Balbo Monument in Burnham Park near the south end of Soldier Field, a gift to the City of Chicago from Benito Mussolini in 1933.

G. Lane

B

Baker Avenue
3014 E at 8300 S to 3158 E at 8436 S

Named for D.W. Baker, a director of the Chicago Board of Trade in the early 1870s.

Balbo Avenue
700 S, from 1 E to 86 E

Balbo Drive
700 S in Grant Park

In 1933, on the occasion of the Century of Progress Exposition, General Italo Balbo, an Italian aviator, visited Chicago with his flying armada. The city was so flattered that it named a street in his honor.

Baldwin Avenue

1900 E, from 7400 S to 7458 S

John Baldwin was a South Side real estate developer in the late 1870s. This street ran through one of his subdivisions.

Balmoral Avenue

5400 N, from 1000 W to 8364 W*

John L. Cochran, a real estate developer of Scottish descent, came to Chicago from Philadelphia in 1881. He named ~~streets in his Edgewater~~

Barron Drive, Edward S.

4100 E in Calumet Park

(source unknown)

Barry Avenue

3100 N, from 316 W to 7600 W*

Commodore John Barry (1745-1803), an Irish immigrant, settled in Philadelphia in 1760 and headed the U.S. Navy. He is sometimes called the "father of the American Navy."

Beach Avenue

1422 N, from 1600 W to 3554 W*

Elli A. Beach, born in 1842, was a grain merchant and a real estate developer on both the North and South Sides. He was most active in the 1870s.

Beacon Street

1338 W, from 4400 N to 4758 N

This street in the Uptown neighborhood was named after the street of the same name in Boston, Massachusetts.

[Beaubien] ~~ourt~~

~~...~~ 150 N to 186 N

~~...~~ such a toddling town, then ~~...~~' Beaubien, his twenty-three ~~...~~d his fun-loving French ~~...~~ credit for setting the tone. ~~...~~ Beaubien (1800-1881) was an ~~...~~erryman, fur trader, and truly ~~...~~le player. In his own words, ~~...~~dle, "like ze debble." While ~~...~~ folk slept, he drank and ~~...~~ fiddled.

~~...~~6 at what now is the corner ~~...~~d Wacker, Beaubien opened ~~...~~ash Hotel, described in 1833 ~~...~~ish visitor, Charles Latrobe, as ~~...~~-story barrack" filled with the ~~...~~lling confusion, filth and ~~...~~eaubien would sit on his hotel's ~~...~~, surrounded by a few or more ~~...~~ty-three children, and shoot ~~...~~he Chicago River.

Beaubien arrived in Chicago in 1826, coming off an Indian trail from Detroit. He and his brother, Jean Baptiste Beaubien, who fathered twenty children, produced more children than the entire population of Chicago in 1829.

When he came to the frontier, Mark later explained, he saw there were few people and decided, "I populate it."

Mark Beaubien, 1800-1881

Belden Avenue

2300 N, from 300 W to 7190 W*

Belden F. Culver, born in New York State in 1829, settled in Chicago in 1855 and established, with his brother Charles, the grain commission firm of Culver & Co. He was a member of the Chicago Board of Trade from 1855 to 1879.

Bellevue Place looking west from Lake Shore Drive, c. 1913. Inscription reads, "This is the Harold McCormick corner. Mrs. McCormick is John D. Rockefeller's daughter."

C.R. Childs, courtesy G. Schmalgemeier

Bell Avenue
2232 W, from 7568 N to 11870 S*

Lt. George Bell in 1861 led the 37th Regiment of Illinois Volunteers, which was mustered into service in Chicago.

A second possible origin was Alexander Graham Bell (1847-1922), the inventor of the telephone.

Belle Plaine Avenue
4100 N, from 800 W to 8356 W*

The words are French for "beautiful field."

Bellevue Place
1030 N, from 4 W to 134 E

Bellevue Castle, near Kassel, West Germany, is renowned for its collection of rare paintings by old masters. The word means literally a "beautiful scene or vista."

Belmont Avenue
3200 N, from 400 W to 9000 W

Belmont Harbor Drive
3600 N in Lincoln Park

Named for the Civil War's Battle of Belmont on November 7, 1861, in which General U.S. Grant led 3,000 Union troops down the Mississippi and then marched to the village of Belmont, Missouri, some fifteen miles south of Cairo, Illinois. Grant's men were driven back by rebel forces under General Leonidas Polk. There were 607 Union casualties and 642 Confederate casualties.

Bennett Avenue
1900 E, from 6700 S to 9556 S*

John Ira Bennett was a Civil War colonel, Chicago lawyer, suburban village president, and federal court judge. Bennett was born in 1831 on a Quaker farm in Otsego County, New York, graduated Phi Beta Kappa from Union College, and in 1857 was admitted to the Tennessee Bar. Fifteen years later, after serving as a Union recruiter in the Civil War and practicing law downstate, he moved to Chicago with his wife, Maria.

In 1879 he was appointed one of the masters in the chancery division of the U.S. District Court for the Northern Illinois region. That same year, he served as president of Hyde Park, which was then an independent village.

Bensley Avenue
2500 E, from 9526 S to 13758 S*

A.F. Bensley was a South Side real estate subdivider known for his work in 1886 in the Cleaverville area.
See Cleaver Street.

Benson Street
1400 W, from 3100 S to 3278 S

Charles E. Benson was a landowner who laid this street through his subdivision in 1874.

A second possible origin was Francis H. Benson (1823-1898), a founder of Rosehill Cemetery in the Ravenswood neighborhood on the North Side.

Benton Place
172 N, from 1 E to 72 E

Named for Thomas Hart Benton (1782-1858), a U.S. Senator from Missouri from 1821 to 1851.

Berenice Avenue
3832 N, from 1800 W to 6358 W*

Charles F. Ford, a real estate subdivider in the late 1880s, named this street for his daughter.

Berkeley Avenue
1024 E, from 4114 S to 5244 S*

Named for a principal Boston thoroughfare, Berkeley Street. It was a Chicago landowner's way of saying thanks to Boston for donating $10,000 to Chicago after the Chicago Fire of 1871.

Bernard Street
3434 W, from 2400 N to 6242 N*

J.L.S. Bernard was a builder of large homes in Oak Park and on Chicago's Northwest Side.

Berteau Avenue
4200 N, from 1400 W to 8356 W*

F.G. Berteau was an early, prominent French resident of Chicago. He was a charter member of the Societé Francaise de Bienfaisance d'Illinois, which was organized by French immigrants and Chicagoans of French extraction in 1863.

Berwyn Avenue
5300 N, from 916 W to 8758 W*

John L. Cochran, the developer of the Edgewater community, named this street and several others for stations along the Main Line out of his hometown, Philadelphia. Berwyn is one of those streets, as is Ardmore, Bryn Mawr, Rosemont, Wayne, and Devon avenues.

Besly Court
1408 W, from 1600 N to 1864 N

E.D. Besly, born in 1838, was the manager of the Chicago branch of the Besly Waukegan Brewing Company, which had been started in Waukegan by his father, William Besly. E.D. Besly settled in Chicago in 1869.

Best Drive
6090 S in Washington Park

William Best, born in Canterbury, England in 1841, was president of Chicago's South Park Board of Commissioners from 1887 to 1891. He immigrated to Chicago with his parents when he was eleven. Later he became a partner in a wholesale tobacco house.

Beverly Avenue
2000 W at 8700 S to 1030 W at 11026 S*

Beverly Glen Parkway
9934 S, from 1600 W to 1754 W

These streets were named for the Southwest Side community of Beverly Hills, which in turn was named for Beverly, a town in Yorkshire, England.

According to another story, the name was first suggested by an early settler after her childhood home in Massachusetts.

Bingham Street
2518 W, from 2000 N to 2148 N

Henry W. Bingham was a real estate subdivider in 1875.

Birchwood Avenue
7500 N, from 1310 W to 7762 W*

Named for the forest of birch trees that grew in this Rogers Park area before 1909.

Belmont Harbor, 3200 N on the lakefront.
David A. Miller

Birkoff Avenue

648 W, from 8300 S to 8417 S

In 1887 George Birkhoff, Jr. laid out the subdivision through which this street runs. He was a member of the first Chicago Board of Real Estate, chartered in 1883.

Bishop Street

1438 W, from 824 N to 12258 S*

Henry W. Bishop was a trustee of the will of John Crerar, who left $2.5 million to build the John Crerar Library, a science-engineering-medicine library now housed on the University of Chicago campus.

A second possibility is that Bishop Street honors Lt. Col. Joel S. Bishop, temporary commander of Fort Dearborn for about three weeks in the fall of 1809 and for about nine weeks in the summer of 1810.

Bissell Street

832 W, 1630 N to 2258 N

William Henry Bissell, a pre-Civil War governor of Illinois, was best known for accepting a challenge to a duel from Jefferson Davis, the future president of the Confederacy.

Bissell, born into a poor family in Yates County, New York, was a physician and lawyer. He fought in the Mexican-American War and was elected to Congress in 1848 and 1850. He made a name for himself when he took exception to a Virginia congressman's assertion that a Mississippi regiment had saved the day at the Battle of Buena Vista on February 23, 1847. In fact, Bissell insisted, that regiment had been more than one and a half miles from the action.

In defense of Mississippi's honor, Davis challenged Bissell to a duel. Bissell accepted. But President Zachary Taylor stepped in and averted bloodshed.

Bissell, governor of Illinois from 1857 to 1860, died while in office.

The Blackstone Library, 4904 S. Lake Park Avenue in Hyde Park, dedicated in 1904.

G. Lane

Bittersweet Place

4100 N, from 600 W to 6228 W

Bittersweet, this street's namesake, once was a common Midwestern wildflower.

Blackhawk Street

1500 N, from 400 W to 1658 W*

Black Hawk (1767-1838) was a Sauk Indian chief who fought for his homeland and paid for it—even after his death. He was born in the great Sauk village on the Rock River, near the present-day city of Rock Island. In 1804, all the land east of the Mississippi—including his village—was ceded to the U.S. government. But Black Hawk refused to recognize the treaty, claiming correctly that it had been entered into without tribal consent by chiefs who were drunk.

In 1831 and 1832 Black Hawk and his followers fought federal troops unsuccessfully in the Black Hawk War. Black Hawk was taken prisoner. He was transported to Washington to meet the president, Andrew Jackson, and then returned to the Midwest to live out his life in Iowa. He had lost his homeland forever.

In 1839, one year after his death, Black Hawk's tomb was invaded. His head was severed from his body, and the head and skeleton were carried away and placed on exhibition.

Blackstone Avenue

1436 E, from 4900 S to 10350 S*

Named for Timothy Beach Blackstone (1829-1900), one of many early Chicagoans who latched onto the railroads and took a ride to riches. He oversaw construction of two of Chicago's most important rail lines, was elected president of the Chicago & Alton Railroad, and founded the Illinois city of Mendota.

Blackstone, born in Branford, Connecticut, was a descendant of Sir William Blackstone, author of *Commentaries on the Laws of England*, published in the 1760s, one of the most influential treatises of Anglo-American law.

At eighteen, Timothy Blackstone started out as an assistant to the surveyors of the New York & New Haven Railroad. He supervised construction of the Illinois Central Railroad between Bloomington and Dixon in 1851, and supervised construction of the entire Joliet & Chicago Railroad, later merged into the Chicago & Alton in 1856.

Blackstone's wife, Isabella F. Norton, donated a neighborhood library, the Blackstone Branch Library, 4904 S. Lake Park Avenue, to the Chicago Public Library.

Blake Street

2208 W, from 3600 S to 3636 S

Patrick Blake was a real estate subdivider of the McKinley Park neighborhood.

Blanchard Court

20 E, from 2412 S to 2440 S

Probably named for Samuel Blanchard Chase (1823-1896), the developer of an area near Belmont Avenue and Lake Michigan.

Bliss Street

1100 N, from 900 W to 928 W

M.M.S. Bliss was a real estate subdivider in the 1890s. This street runs through one of his original subdivisions.

A less likely possibility is that the street was named for Sylvester S. Bliss, a young druggist who was treasurer of the Chicago College of Pharmacy in 1859.

Bloomingdale Avenue

1800 N, from 1500 W to 7190 W*

Bloomingdale was an early western suburb of Chicago. This street's name is otherwise self-explanatory—a dale of blooming flowers.

Blue Island Avenue

1068 W at 1200 S to 2400 W at 2598 S

In Chicago's pioneer days a six-mile ridge, running between 87th Street and 130th Street, appeared like an island of blue above the mists of the swamps east of the ridge. The suburb of Blue Island took its name from the ridge, and the street took its name from the suburb.

Bonaparte Street

1400 W at 2998 S to 1320 W at 2948 S

Named for Napoleon Bonaparte (1769-1821), the emperor of France from 1802 to 1814.

Bond Avenue

3134 E, from 8344 S to 8410 S

Shadrach Bond (1773-1832) was the first governor of Illinois, serving from 1818 to 1822. He was a farmer who lived near Kaskaskia.

Bonfield Street

1300 W, from 2700 S to 3096 S*

Captain John Bonfield led 176 Chicago policemen at Haymarket Square the night of the tragic riot of May 4, 1886. During the labor strikes of that year, Bonfield was criticized for practicing and encouraging police brutality.

Bosak Avenue

10200 S, from 2434 W to 2444 W

Chicago Police Officer William Bosak (1946-1979), an undercover narcotics investigator, was shot to death on the South Side on March 3, 1979, by a man filled with anger because he had been arrested by the police three months earlier. Bosak's partner, Roger Van Schaik, was also slain. See Van Schaik Street.

Bosak was a dedicated cop. He worked when he was sick. He worked on his lunch hour. He had 135 honorable mentions for service beyond the call of duty. In the words of a fellow officer, "Bill always had a bad guy to chase." At his funeral, attended by almost 900 Chicago-area police officers, he was described as "a noble officer who was also a good dad, a good husband, a good son, and a good brother."

Bosworth Avenue

1530 W, from 1200 N to 7656 N*

H.P. Bosworth was a real estate subdivider in 1860, associated for a time with the Ravenswood Land Company.

Boulevard Way

2942 W, from 2422 S to 2456 S

This is a short street that ends at Marshall Boulevard on the Lower West Side.

Bowen Avenue

4134 S, from 400 E to 844 E

Joseph T. Bowen was a real estate subdivider around the turn of the century.

A second possibility is that this street was named for another subdivider, George S. Bowen.

Bowler Street

746 S at 2100 W to 921 S at 2194 W

Named for James B. Bowler (1875-1957), who served as alderman of the 25th Ward for more than twenty-five years between 1906 and 1937. He was born and raised on the Near West Side, was a six-day bicycle racer in his youth, and was serving as a U.S. Congressman when he passed away.

Bowmanville Avenue

2342 W at 5300 N to 2000 W at 5498 N

Jessie B. Bowman sold a town he didn't own. He created the community of Bowmanville on the Northwest Side in 1850. His town was bounded by Foster, Western, California, and Lawrence avenues. Those who purchased lots in Bowmanville later discovered that Bowman's title to the area was not legal, and they had to pay for the lots a second time. Bowman, in the meantime, had skipped town.

Bradley Place

3732 N, from 800 W to 2640 W*

Named for Captain Hugh Bradley, who arrived at the mouth of the Chicago River in 1816 to rebuild Fort Dearborn.

Dr. Daniel Brainard, founder of Rush Medical College.

Courtesy Rush-Presbyterian-St. Luke's Medical Center

Brainard Avenue

2700 E at 13048 S to 3400 E at 13746 S

Dr. Daniel Brainard (1812-1866), who practiced medicine in Chicago and founded Rush Medical College, hit town looking more like a quack than a doc.

"Dr. Brainard rode up to my office, wearing pretty seedy clothes and mounted on a little Indian pony," his good friend, John Dean Caton, once wrote. "He reported that he was nearly out of funds and asked my advice as to the propriety of commencing a practice here."

Brainard, who aspired to mingle with Chicago's elite, practiced medicine in Chicago from about 1835 to 1860. He gained recognition when he successfully delivered the child of a sickly vagabond woman who had become something of a charity project among the society set. After that, his practice among the wealthy flourished.

He was born in Oneida County, New York, and died in the Sherman House hotel.

Brandon Avenue

3200 E, from 7900 S to 13548 S*

Stephen A. Douglas, the Illinois statesman, was also a South Side landowner, and he named this street for his birthplace, Brandon, Vermont. *See Douglas Boulevard.*

Brayton Street

12562 S, from 52 E to 178 W

Brayton L. Richards was a partner in the construction firm of Boyer & Richards, which built all of the homes in the South Side neighborhood called Brayton Manor.

Brennan Avenue

2300 E, from 9600 S to 9772 S

Edward P. Brennan (1866-1942) was the mastermind behind Chicago's orderly street numbering system.

An employee first in his father's grocery store and then, from 1893 to 1929, in the Lyon & Healy music store, it was Brennan who suggested in 1901 that Chicago's streets be numbered like lines on a sheet of graph paper. The intersection of State and Madison streets, he suggested in a letter to a newspaper, should be ground zero in Chicago's street system. He wrote, "Here is a task for the Council Committee on Street Nomenclature. It also may be another job for the undertaker as its fate is likely to be early death and burial."

Remarkably, he was wrong. The city council in 1908 passed an ordinance calling for his simplified numbering system.

Five years later Brennan suggested Chicago do away with the confusion of having several streets with the same name and single streets with many names. Remarkably, the city council took him up on the idea again.

In that same year Brennan dreamed up names for about 300 new city streets, most of them names that in some way relate to Chicago's own early history.

Briar Place

3138 N, from 328 W to 758 W

A subdivider from back East named this street for Briarcliff Manor, a village in Westchester County, New York.

Brighton Place

2700 W, from 3954 S to 4058 S

Brighton Park, this street's namesake, was an unincorporated subdivision as early as 1840. The village of Brighton Park, a livestock trading center, was incorporated in 1851. Brighton was the traditional name for livestock markets in Britain and the eastern United States. In the early 1850s a Chicago mayor, John Wentworth, built the Brighton Park Race Track near Archer and Western avenues. Today, McKinley Park is on the site of the old race track.

Broad Street

1500 W at 2928 S to 1400 W at 3066 S

Named for Lewis P. Broad, of Broad & Pitney Co., a real estate subdivider in Bridgeport.

Broadway

600 W at 2800 N to 1200 W at 6358 N

Broadway, formerly known as Evanston Avenue, was named after New York City's famous theater district.

Brodman Avenue

4416 N, from 8400 W to 8659 W

Howard C. Brodman (1885-1961) was, after Edward P. Brennan, the man most responsible for simplifying the system of Chicago's street names. As superintendent of the Chicago Department of Maps and Plats from 1933 to 1958, Brodman quietly but persistently reduced the number of street names by eliminating the various names for different stretches of the same street. *See Brennan Avenue.*

Brompton Avenue

3535 N, from 500 W to 766 W*

Brompton is a district of London, England, south of Hyde Park.

Bross Avenue

3200 S, 2200 W to 2442 W

William "Deacon" Bross (1813-1890) was an old-time newspaperman, businessman, and politician. Yet, he was thought to be an honorable man.   As Illinois lieutenant governor, Bross urged the state legislature to back the 13th Amendment, making Illinois the first state to vote to free the slaves.

Bross also helped found the *Chicago Tribune*, and in his memoirs he later recalled that the *Tribune* was supremely self-confident, even then. Born in a log house in New Jersey, "Deacon" Bross moved to Chicago in 1846. He opened a bookstore, but soon found the city's reading population to be tiny. So he started a religious newspaper, the *Prairie Herald.*

In 1852 Bross joined forces with John L. Scripps and founded the *Democratic Press.* This paper was merged with the *Tribune* in 1858. From that day on, Bross worked closely with the *Tribune*, influencing its editorial decisions and writing financial reports.

In 1864, he was elected lieutenant governor, a post he held for four years.

Buckingham Fountain, in Grant Park at Congress Street, a gift to Chicago in 1927 to honor Clarence Buckingham.

G. Lane

Bross was also a major patron of the arts at a time when Chicago had almost no arts. So he saw the same shows over and over. He saw "Faust" five times in one year.

Browning Avenue

3548 S, from 500 E to 586 E

Orville H. Browning (1806-1881), U.S. senator from Illinois in 1861 and 1862, was one of Abraham Lincoln's best friends until the president proposed the Emancipation Proclamation, something Browning considered a calamity.

Browning, a Republican, was appointed to the senate by Governor Richard Yates, but lost the seat to the Democrats a year later. He returned to Washington in 1863 to establish what was ostensibly a law firm. Actually, he and his partners traded on their influence with Republican leaders in securing special favors for contractors.

Or, possibly the street was named for Capt. O. Browning, a black soldier from Chicago who was killed in World War I.

Bryn Mawr Avenue

5600 N, from 936 W to 8800 W*

John L. Cochran, the subdivider of the community of Edgewater, named this street and several others for railroad stops along the Main Line, the commuter rail line leading out of his hometown, Philadelphia. *See Berwyn Avenue.*

Buckingham Place

3332 N, from 600 W to 888 W

Ebenezer Buckingham (1829-1912) was a Chicago businessman and banker for whom Buckingham Fountain is not named. He was born in Zanesville, Ohio, and moved to Chicago in 1859 to join his brother, John, in the grain elevator business. He made a fortune by buying and managing several Illinois Central

Railroad grain elevators at the mouth of the Chicago River. Twenty-five years later he was named president of the Northwest National Bank.

After the Chicago Fire of 1871, Buckingham joined Chicago's new-money elite on Prairie Avenue, a street of imposing mansions.

But for all his personal success, Buckingham's name is linked in Chicago history with the beautiful Buckingham Fountain in Grant Park. The fountain was modeled after the Latona Fountain in Versailles, France, and was given to Chicago in 1927 by Ebenezer's daughter, Kate. It measures 280 feet across, holds 1.5 million gallons of water, and shoots water 135 feet high.

Kate commissioned the fountain to honor her brother, Clarence, a director of the Art Institute.

Buena Avenue
4200 N, from 636 W to 1030 W

Buena Circle
4200 N, from 1042 W to 1050 W

Possibly named for Buena, a borough of New Jersey, by Edward C. Waller, a real estate subdivider from New Jersey. The Buena Park neighborhood on Chicago's North Side was named after Waller's sixty-acre estate in the Lake View township in the 1860s.

Buffalo Avenue
3300 E, from 8232 S to 13662 S*

Named for Buffalo, New York, and also for the buffalo that once roamed the American plains.

Burkhardt Drive
In Douglas Park

Henry S. Burkhardt was a commissioner of the West Park District from 1884 to 1891.

Burley Avenue
3234 E, 8232 S to 13558 S*

Augustus Harris Burley (1819-1903) was a man of varied interests, all of them more or less good for Chicago.

Born in Exeter, New Hampshire, Burley moved to Chicago in 1837 to work as a stockboy and clerk in the bookstore of his half brother, Stephen F. Gale. Burley eventually bought his brother out. In 1856 he became an officer in the new Merchants' Savings, Loan & Trust Co. at South Water Street and LaSalle, and served on the bank's first board of directors.

In his lifetime, Burley also served as an alderman, a state legislator, president of the Chicago Board of Public Works, and superintendent of Lincoln Park. He was instrumental in laying out an extension of Lincoln Park from Fullerton to Diversey.

Burling Street
728 W, from 1532 N to 2932 N*

Edward J. Burling (1819-1892) was Chicago's second architect. Most of his buildings have been destroyed, but one of his finest works, St. James Episcopal Cathedral at Wabash and Huron streets, still stands.

Born in Newburgh, New York, Burling came to Chicago as a carpenter's apprentice in the early 1840s. Chicago's only architect at the time was John M. Van Osdel. Though Burling had no formal training, he soon began designing buildings himself.

Chicago was booming, and Burling met with immediate success. Eighteen of his buildings, including a church and three hotels, were constructed in a single year, 1855. He designed the first *Chicago Tribune* building, the first Chicago Music Hall, and the first masonry building of Holy Name Church.

Most of Burling's buildings were destroyed by the Fire of 1871, but St.

James survived, though badly damaged. It was restored according to his original plan and rededicated in 1875.

Burnham Avenue
2800 E, from 7640 S to 8658 S*

Daniel H. Burnham (1846-1912) gave Chicago a fine front yard. He was the architect and city planner who established the principle of a lakefront park in his master plan for Chicago of 1909.

No other plan so influenced Chicago's growth. The Burnham Plan of 1909 resulted in the creation of a series of lakefront parks and beaches, including Grant Park at the lakefront, a greenbelt of forest preserves on the city's periphery; the construction of Chicago's main post office; and the siting of the present Eisenhower Expressway.

Burnham is probably best known for saying: "Make no little plans; they have no magic to stir men's blood and probably themselves will not be realized." He may not have actually said those words, but he lived them. He and his partner, John Wellborn Root, designed some of Chicago's most celebrated buildings, including the Rookery and the Monadnock buildings.

Burnham was chief of construction for the World's Columbian Exposition in 1893. At a time when Chicago was bursting with architectural boldness, he adopted a classical style of architecture for the world's fair.

Burnside Avenue
234 E at 9134 S to 800 E at 9462 S

General Ambrose E. Burnside (1824-1881) was a Union general in the Civil War and a treasurer of the Illinois Central Railroad. Colonel W. W. Jacobs, who subdivided this area in 1887, named his subdivision and this street in Burnside's honor.

Daniel H. Burnham, premier Chicago architect who gave the city its famous 1909 plan.

Courtesy *Chicago Sun-Times*

Burton Place

1500 N, from 62 E to 172 W

In 1845, John Burton, a real estate subdivider, owned all of the land bounded by Dearborn Street, Clark Street, North Avenue, and the Chicago River. Burton was known for his elaborate English gardens.

Busse Avenue

6710 W, from 5000 N to 5026 N

Fred A. Busse was the first mayor of Chicago to serve a four-year term, from 1907 to 1911. Chicago's population at that time was about two million people.

Butler Drive (Pvt.)

1250 E, from 12500 S to 12858 S

(source unknown)

Byron Street

3900 N, from 1000 W to 8356 W*

The English poet George Gordon Noel Byron, sixth Baron Byron (1788-1824), was one of the most important figures of the Romantic Movement.

Exterior of the Monadnock Building (Burnham & Root, 1891) and lobby of the Rookery (Burnham & Root, 1886), remodeled by Frank Lloyd Wright in 1905.

C

Cabrini Street
828 S, from 500 W to 1334 W*

St. Frances Xavier Cabrini (1850-1917), the Italian-born founder of the Roman Catholic Missionary Sisters of the Sacred Heart, came to be known as the "Saint of the Immigrants" during nearly thirty years of missionary work in America's big cities. In Chicago, she founded Columbus Hospital in 1905, she was the first U.S. citizen to be canonized by the Catholic Church, and the low-rise public housing projects on the Near North Side were named in her honor in 1941-42.

Caldwell Avenue
4500 W at 5700 N to 6437 W at 7163 N*

Billy "Sauganash" Caldwell was so respected in his day that he received the ultimate Chicago honor, a tavern in his name.

The Sauganash, one of Chicago's first drinking establishments, was named for Billy Caldwell shortly after his death in 1841. Saloon keeper Mark Beaubien (see Beaubien Street) wanted to name his new hotel and tavern for a great man. And who, he reasoned, was greater than Billy Caldwell?

St. Frances Xavier Cabrini, first American citizen to be declared a saint by the Roman Catholic church.

Courtesy Missionary Sisters of the Sacred Heart

Caldwell, a tall and powerful man, was born in 1780 to a Potawatomie woman and an Irish officer in the British army stationed in Detroit. Among white settlers he was known as Caldwell. Among Indians, he was known as Sauganash, "the Englishman."

Today, Billy Caldwell is best remembered for securing peace between the Fort Dearborn settlers and the Indians, culminating in the treaty of 1835. It was Caldwell, together with Shawbona, who pioneered shuttle diplomacy in 1827 to prevent war between the whites and the Potawatomies and Winnebagoes. Again, in 1832, it was Caldwell who dissuaded the Potawatomies from joining with Black Hawk in his raids on the white settlements. After the Treaty of 1835, Caldwell helped to assemble nearly 2,500 Indians, mostly Potawatomies, in Chicago for the last time. They accepted government payments and marched off to a new home at Council Bluffs, Iowa.

Caldwell never returned to Chicago. *See Sauganash Avenue.*

Calhoun Avenue
2526 E, from 9526 S to 13622 S*

Calhoun Place
24 N, from 50 W to 234 W*

Chicago's first newspaper was the *Chicago Democrat*, launched by John Calhoun (1808-1859) on November 26, 1833, a few months after Chicago's incorporation as a village. Calhoun was a 25-year-old Jacksonian Democrat from New York State. The paper was later edited by one of Chicago's more colorful mayors, "Long John" Wentworth.

California Avenue
2800 W, from 7558 N to 11059 S*

California Boulevard
2800 W, from 1200 S to 3056 S*

California Terrace (Pvt.)
3122 N, from 716 W to 756 W

Named for the State of California.

Calumet Avenue
334 E, from 1800 S to 13571 S*

Calumet Expressway
20 E at 9800 S to 1800 E at 13800 S

Calumet Skyway
645 E at 7100 S to 3332 E at 9800 S

Calumet was a form of the Norman-French word "chalumet," meaning a shepherd's pipe. More specifically for French explorers engaged in trade with the Indians, calumet meant "pipe of peace."

Cambridge Avenue
506 W at 800 N to 526 W at 3178 N*

Cambridge Avenue (Pvt.)

529 W, from 2348 N to 2358 N

Named after Cambridge University, which was founded in Cambridge, England, in the eleventh century.

Campbell Avenue

2500 W, from 7458 N to 11856 S*

Campbell Park Drive

708 S, from 2200 W to 2258 W

Campbell Place

540 N, from 100 W to 128 W

Alderman James L. Campbell (1832-1916), in the long tradition of Chicago statesmen, mixed politics, natural disaster, and land speculation to pile up a fortune.

Campbell was born in Caledonia, New York, and joined the Iowa bar in 1862. He moved to Chicago that same year, and before the decade was up he was elected alderman of the West Side's 12th ward, a post he would hold for the next twenty-seven years.

In the days after the Great Chicago Fire, Campbell stood back and surveyed the rubble. He fixed his eye on the hundreds of homeless people wandering among the smoking ruins, and he decided then and there on a career change: real estate. Within the next few years, Campbell, hustling between City Hall and his real estate office, bought up huge tracts of land on the Near West Side, erected more than 1,000 buildings, and got rich.

Canal Street

500 W, from 372 N to 4358 S*

A little more than 150 years ago the federal government dug a long ditch that made Chicago.

The Illinois and Michigan Canal, begun in 1836 and completed in 1848, linked Lake Michigan to the Mississippi via the Illinois River. Many historians claim the canal fueled the growth of Chicago and kept the city from becoming a part of Wisconsin.

The canal ran from Bridgeport to LaSalle-Peru, and its route is now designated as the Illinois and Michigan Canal National Heritage Corridor. None of it, except an archeological dig in Bridgeport, at Ashland Avenue and the Chicago River, remains in Chicago. Most of its Chicago length is covered by the Stevenson Expressway.

Sometime before 1818, when the boundaries of the future state of Illinois were drawn, the northern border was pushed north of the southern tip of Lake Michigan to make sure Chicago and the entire canal would all be in one state. In 1830, an engineer named James Thompson was ordered by the U.S. government to map out two towns along the future canal's route: Ottawa and Chicago. Lots in these towns were to be sold to finance the canal's construction. And this was how Chicago came into being.

The digging of the canal brought 5,000 workers to Chicago (mostly Irish immigrants) and garnered the city coast-to-coast advertising.

An old Illinois and Michigan Canal lock near Lockport, 1947.

Courtesy *Chicago Sun-Times*

Canalport Avenue
500 W at 1748 S to 1000 W at 2190 S

This area of the Near South Side is crossed by finger-like slips or ports jutting into the South Branch of the Chicago River.

Canfield Avenue
7900 W, from 5130 N to 6359 N

The most likely source for this street is that it was named for a bunch of milk cans in a field. Supposedly, a stop on the Illinois and Wisconsin Railroad, now the Chicago & North Western line, was called Canfield in the 1850s because it consisted of nothing more than a wooden platform for milk cans in the middle of a farmer's field. When the area was platted, the subdivision took its name from the train station, and the street took its name from the subdivision.

John G. Cannon Drive
400 W at 2800 N in Lincoln Park

John G. Cannon Drive
25 E at 1800 N in Lincoln Park

John G. Cannon was the superintendent and secretary of the Lincoln Park District from 1917 to 1920.

Carmen Avenue
5100 N, from 830 W to 8652 W*

The opera *Carmen* was the masterpiece of the French composer Georges Bizet (1838-1875).

Carondolet Avenue
3032 E, from 12200 S to 13436 S

The Baron de Francisco Luis Hector Carondolet (1748-1807) was governor and Spanish commander of Louisiana and West Florida from 1791 to 1797.

Carpenter Street
1032 W, from 850 N to 12256 S*

Philo Carpenter was typical of those hundreds of people who came to Chicago from someplace else, arriving by boats and by foot, in search of something better—like more money.

Carpenter, a young widower with some training in pharmacology, traveled to Chicago from Troy, New York, in 1832 by mail coach and Indian canoe. Among the shacks on the settlement's river banks, he opened a log-cabin drug store at what now is Lake Street. And he made good.

Just two years later, now a wealthy merchant with extensive real estate holdings, he returned to New York State and married Ann Thompson of Saratoga County. He rode with his bride back to Chicago in a fine one-horse shay, the first pleasure vehicle to roll through the gates of Fort Dearborn.

In his later life, Carpenter, a descendant of New England pilgrims, was a director of the Chicago Theological Seminary, managing director of the Chicago Bible Society, and a founder of the Relief and Aid Society, which came to the aid of burned-out Chicagoans after the Chicago Fire of 1871. Carpenter died in 1886. Elizabeth Street may have been named for Carpenter's daughter, Elizabeth Carpenter Sawyer.

Carroll Avenue
328 N, from 44 W to 4758 W*

Carroll Drive
(In Garfield Park)

Charles Carroll (1737-1832), American Revolutionary patriot, member of the Continental Congress, a wealthy Catholic landowner, and U.S. Senator from Maryland, was the last surviving signer of the Declaration of Independence.

Carver Drive
1200 E, from 13000 S to 13200 S

Named for George Washington Carver (1864-1943), who started his life as the child of recently emancipated slaves and ended it as a world renowned agricultural chemist. He was a specialist in crop rotation and soil conservation.

Castleisland Avenue
4540 N, from 8422 W to 8532 W

Named for the town of Castleisland on the River Maine in County Kerry, Ireland.

Castlewood Terrace
4862 N, from 800 W to 956 W

Charles W. Castle, a North Side subdivider, platted this wooded area as the Castle subdivision in 1896.

Philo Carpenter, 1805-1886

Catalpa Avenue
5500 N, from 1000 W to 8758 W

The catalpa is a tree. The Edgewater subdivider John L. Cochran named this street after Catalpa Street in his hometown, Philadelphia.

Catherine Avenue
5400 N, from 8109 W to 8649 W

Named for Catherine Schorsch (1902-1965), the wife of Albert J. Schorsch, one of seven brothers who engaged in real estate development on Chicago's Northwest Side.
See Schorsch Street.

Caton Street
1652 N, from 2100 W to 2162 W

John Dean Caton (1812-1895) was one of Chicago's first lawyers and a chief justice of the Illinois Supreme Court. He was born in Monroe, New York, arrived in Chicago in 1833, and was admitted to the Illinois bar two years later. He opened what may have been Chicago's first law practice.

In 1842 Caton was appointed associate justice of the Illinois Supreme Court, and in 1855 he became Chief Justice. He was praised by his peers as an excellent judge, one who decided cases more on the basis of principles than precedent.

Retiring from the bench in 1864, Caton settled down in the country near Ottawa, Illinois, and wrote extensively. Among his books were, *Matter and Supreme Intelligence, The Antelope and Deer in America,* and *The Early Bench and Bar in Illinois.*

Mayor Anton J. Cermak (right) pictured with Gov. Franklin D. Roosevelt, as the nominee for president throws out the first ball at a Cubs-Yankees Series game, October 1, 1932.
Courtesy Chicago Sun-Times

Cedar Street
1120 N, from 2 E to 94 E

Named for the cedar tree.

Central Avenue
5600 W, from 6964 N to 6500 S*

This street runs through the center of the community of Austin, hence its name.

Central Park Avenue
3600 W, from 6400 N to 11700 S*

Central Park Boulevard
3600 W, from 449 N to 400 S

Central Park Drive (In Garfield Park)

The street runs north and south of Garfield Park, which formerly was called Central Park, evidently because it was located half way between the Loop and the city's western limits.

Cermak Road
2200 S, from 338 E to 4600 W

Named for Mayor Anton J. Cermak (1873-1933), who lived in South Lawndale at 2348 S. Millard. Some people credit Cermak with putting together the first ethnically balanced election slate, thus

minimizing ethnic backbiting and allowing for the creation of the powerful Democratic organization in Chicago. Cermak, mayor from 1931 to 1933, was elected in a Prohibition year on a "wet" ticket. He died in Miami, Florida, on March 6, 1933, three weeks after being struck by an assassin's bullet, apparently intended for President Franklin D. Roosevelt.

Chalmers Place (Pvt.)
900 W, from 2300 N to 2358 N

George Chalmers, who immigrated to American from England in 1852, erected scores of the most prominent buildings in Chicago in the 1870s. He specialized in building tunnels and aquaducts.

Champlain Avenue
634 E, from 4200 S to 11946 S*

Champlain Avenue (Pvt.)
634 E, from 13029 S to 13099 S

Samuel de Champlain (1567-1635) was a French navigator and colonizer who founded the city of Quebec and discovered Lake Champlain.

Chanay Street
2132 N, from 2720 W to 2738 W

This street possibly was named for Chaney, Maryland, although the spelling varies slightly.

Chappel Avenue
2032 E, from 6700 S to 13800 S*

Eliza Emily Chappel Porter (1807-1888) was Chicago's first school teacher. She ran a school that was underfunded, poorly staffed, and crippled by high dropout rates.

Arriving in Chicago from Mackinaw, Michigan in 1833, Eliza Porter opened her school with $67 and twenty-five students. Classes were held in a one-room cabin, with a calico curtain separating the classroom from her living quarters. The school had benches and one small table, but no desks, and its only supplies were a globe, a map of the world, a map of the United States, a Bible, and a few hymn books.

In 1835 Eliza turned the school over to several of her best former students and moved with her new husband, the Rev. Jeremiah Porter, to a mission in Green Bay, Wisconsin.

During the Civil War, Mrs. Porter ministered to both Union and Confederate soldiers. "We are told," one old friend said at her funeral, "that her hand closed the eyes of 1,300 soldiers in both armies."

Charles Street
1700 W at 9400 S to 1400 W at 10500 S

Oscar Charles, a landowner and subdivider, most likely named this street for himself in about 1895. A second possible origin was Charles Jouett (1772-1834), the federal Indian Agent in Chicago from 1805 to 1811 and from 1815 to 1818.

Charleston Street
2100 N, from 2000 W to 2548 W

Named for Charleston, the capital of West Virginia.

Chase Avenue
7300 N, from 1200 W to 7728 W*

Samuel Blanchard Chase (1823-1896) was a subdivider of the North Side. He lived on Belmont Avenue.

Chelsea Place
11040 S, from 1600 W to 1730 W

Named for Chelsea, Massachusetts.

Cheltenham Place
7878 S, from 3000 E to 3118 E

Named for the Philadelphia suburb of Cheltenham, Pennsylvania, by R.W. Bridge, a subdivider, who grew up in that town.

Cherry Avenue
928 W at 1100 N to 1100 W at 1564 N

Named for the cherry tree.

Chester Avenue
8500 W, from 4400 N to 5556 N

(source unknown)

Chestnut Street
860 N, from 292 E to 1558 W*

Chestnut Street (Pvt.)
854 N, from 436 W to 532 W

Named for the chestnut tree.

Chicago Avenue
800 N, from 385 E to 5968 W*

Chicago Skyway
1 E at 6600 S to 4044 E at 10600 S

These streets were named for the city of Chicago. It is an Indian name for something powerful or big, possibly a wild onion.

Chicago Beach Drive (Pvt.)
1624 E, from 4900 S to 4936 S

This street ran alongside the old Chicago Beach Hotel, later 5th Army headquarters, destroyed c. 1970.

Chicora Avenue
5700 W, from 6500 N to 6972 N*

The *Chicora* was a steamboat, navigated by a man named Graham Morton, that sank in Lake Michigan in 1895. The word was used by Spanish explorers to refer to two groups of Indians in South Carolina.

Chippewa Avenue
2000 E, from 11600 S to 12158 S

The Chippewa Indians once were common throughout northern Michigan, Wisconsin, Minnesota, and North Dakota. They also were called the Ojibway.

Christiana Avenue
3332 W, from 6150 N to 11226 S*

Christiana Avenue (Pvt.)
3332 W, from 4700 S to 4858 S

Oslo, the capitol city of Norway, was called Christiana until 1924.

Church Street
1500 W at 10300 S to 2038 W at 11878 S

Thomas Church (1801-1871), a New Yorker who came to Chicago in 1824, built the first building on Lake Street. He invested in real estate on Lake Street, South Water Street, and Michigan Avenue. He was the first president of the Chicago Firemen's Insurance Company.

Churchill Street
1832 N, from 2000 W to 2156 W

M.E. Churchill subdivided this area in the West Town neighborhood in about 1893.

A view to the southeast from Clark and Washington Streets in 1858. The Methodist Episcopal Church block is being erected, lower center. Photo from tower of Court House.

Alexander Hesler, courtesy *Chicago Sun-Times*

Charles Cleaver, 1814-1898

Cicero Avenue
4800 W, from 6352 N to 8657 S*

Marcus Tullius Cicero (106 B.C. to 43 B.C) was a Roman statesman, lawyer, scholar, and writer. Remembered as Rome's greatest orator, he tried in vain to uphold republican principles in the final civil wars that destroyed the republic of Rome.

Claremont Avenue
2332 W, from 7568 N to 10658 S*

On August 17, 1807, Robert Fulton's steamboat, the *Clermont,* traveled up the Hudson River from New York City to Albany in 62 hours. *See Fulton Street.*

Clarence Avenue
6234 N, from 6500 W to 7756 W

Some historians say this street was named for the Clarence River in Australia. The river is 245 miles long and flows southeast to the Pacific Ocean.

Clarendon Avenue
800 W, from 3928 N to 4756 N

Edward Hyde (1609-1674), first Earl of Clarendon, was the first minister of King Charles II. He served Charles in exile and then in England until 1666.

Clark Street
100 W at 2138 S to 1800 W at 7553 N

Formerly Green Bay Road, this street was named for General George Rogers Clark (1752-1818), a Revolutionary War hero who captured much of the Northwest Territory, including the present state of Illinois, from the British.

Cleaver Street
1432 W, from 1126 N to 1458 N

Charles Cleaver (1814-1893) built a little town, Cleaverville, south of early Chicago.

Born in London, England, Cleaver moved to Chicago in 1833 and ran a smelly soap and lard rendering works in a swampy area between present-day 37th and 39th streets. His only neighbors were a few tolerant fishermen and woodchoppers. In 1851 he began to build a company town south of his factory, buying up ninety-three acres and spending $60,000 in one year on the construction of wooden housing. He established a grocery, a general store, a religious meeting house, and a town hall. He paid the Illinois Central Railroad $3,800 for a year's worth of passenger train service to Chicago and *Voila!,* a commuter suburb. As Cleaverville's centerpiece, he built a mansion for himself in 1857, Oakwood Hall, on a large lot at Oakwood Boulevard and Ellis Avenue.

The Cleaverville settlement marked the beginnings of Chicago's Oakland community.

Cleveland Avenue
500 W, from 800 N to 2358 N*

Cleveland Avenue (Pvt.)
445 W, from 814 N to 954 N

While most Chicagoans assume this street honors U.S. President Grover Cleveland, who served from 1885 to 1889 and from 1893 to 1897, it appears it went by the name of Cleveland before the president ever took office. More likely, the street was named for Franklin A. Cleveland, a subdivider in the 1880s.

Clifford Avenue
5000 W, from 5734 N to 5780 N

Named for William J. Clifford, a landowner and subdivider, who was a partner in the firm of Clifford & Wadleigh in the early 1870s.

Clifton Avenue
1226 W, from 1900 N to 4758 N*

Named after Clifton, New Jersey, a city on the Passaic River.

Archibald Clybourn, 1802-1872

Clinton Street
540 W, from 372 N to 1854 S

DeWitt Clinton (1769-1828) was a mayor of New York City, a governor of New York, and a sponsor of New York's Erie Canal, which led to the rapid settlement of Illinois.

Clover Street
4614 W, from 4000 N to 4068 N

The prairies of Chicago once were rich with clover.

Clybourn Avenue
426 W at 1200 N to 2400 W at 3174 N

Archibald Clybourne (or Clybourn) (1802-1872) was the first and perhaps the only man to build a twenty-room mansion next to a Chicago stockyard—his own, built in 1829.

He was also very likely the first man to build a Chicago stockyard (1829). His house, called "pretentious" for its day, was built on Elston Road (see Elston Avenue) with bricks made by Francis C. Sherman, founder of the Sherman House hotel and a Chicago mayor.

Clybourne and his father, Jonas, also had the distinction of being two of the earliest Chicago butchers. During the Blackhawk War of 1832, the Clybournes and another family of butchers helped feed the pioneers who took refuge at Fort Dearborn.

Archibald Clybourne was the first constable of the Chicago region, in addition to being a justice of the peace and a school trustee. But his primary contribution to the lore of Chicago was his stockyard. Little did he know in 1829 that he was setting the scene for the city that would be known as "hog butcher for the world."

Clyde Avenue
2100 E, from 6700 S to 13758 S*

Before 1900, the area bounded by Cicero Avenue, Austin Boulevard, 59th Court, and 61st Avenue was called Clyde. The Burlington Northern Railroad still stops at the Clyde Station on Austin Boulevard. The name dates back at least to 1867. The street took its name from the old community.

Coast Guard Drive
2030 E in Jackson Park

This street once led to a U.S. Coast Guard station in Jackson Park. The station is no longer in use.

Coles Avenue
2500 E at 7100 S to 3100 E at 8258 S

Edward Coles was an Illinois governor and former slaveholder who helped stop slavery in Illinois.

Coles hailed from Albemarle County, Virginia. In 1808 he inherited a plantation and slaves from his father, Col. John Coles, a well-connected landowner who fought in the Revolution.

Presidents were among Coles' friends and acquaintances. He was a private secretary to President James

Madison, and was sent by him to Russia on a diplomatic mission in 1816. He also corresponded with Thomas Jefferson on the slavery issue.

Called by one friend, "an experimental philosopher," Coles became obsessed with the slavery question. Eventually he decided to move to "free soil" and free his slaves. The "free soil" he chose was Illinois. He settled in Edwardsville, freed his slaves, and helped them in their new life.

Coles came to Chicago in 1819, one year after Illinois became a state. He found slavery here and people who were trying to expand it. In 1822 he was elected governor of Illinois on an anti-slavery platform.

In his first message to the General Assembly, Coles called for the abolition of slavery in Illinois. But the pro-slavery forces countered by calling for a referendum that could have resulted in a constitutional convention to legalize slavery. During this struggle, which could have changed the history of Illinois, Coles wrote to a friend, "I assure you, I never before felt so deep an interest in any political question. It preys upon me to such a degree that I shall not be happy or feel at ease until it is settled." The pro-slavery forces were defeated at the polls in August, 1824. Coles, however, lost in a bid for the U.S. Senate that same year, and in 1831 he lost in a bid for Congress. Shortly after that he moved to Philadelphia. There he married, got out of politics, and lived long enough to see the realization of his dream, an end to slavery. He died in 1868, three years after the Civil War.

Colfax Avenue
2600 E, 7400 S to 9638 S*

Schuyler Colfax (1823-1885) was a Republican vice president of the United States (1869-1873) whose career ended in scandal. He grew up in New Carlisle, Indiana, and began his public life as editor of the *St. Joseph Valley Register*, the leading Whig organ of northern Indiana. He served in the U.S. House of Representatives from 1855 to 1869, where he was a vocal proponent of Negro suffrage. His political career ended when he was found to have improperly accepted stock in a company seeking government favors.

Columbia Avenue
6734 N, from 1040 W to 7758 W*

The realtor A.W. Wallen named this street for his alma mater, Columbia College in New York. In 1912, the school's name was changed to Columbia University.

Columbia Drive
1782 E in Jackson Park

Columbia Drive
5858 S in Jackson Park
Named for the Columbian Exposition of 1893, the Chicago world's fair that played a major role in the development of the South Side and Jackson Park in particular.

Columbia Malt Drive
3960 E, from 10456 S to 10548 S

The Columbia Malting Company, a brewery on this South Chicago street, shut down in 1964. The Falstaff Brewing Corporation of St. Louis purchased Columbia's 4.8-acre plant.

Columbus Avenue
7400 S at 2400 W to 8656 S at 4022 W

Columbus Drive
In Grant Park and north to 530 N

Named for Christopher Columbus (1451-1506), the explorer from Genoa, Italy, who discovered the New World in 1492.

Commercial Avenue
3000 E, from 7900 S to 13358 S*

Commercial Court
2948 W, from 8000 S to 8100 S

These busy streets are centers of commercial activity in South Chicago.

Commodore Whalen Drive
2200 E in Jackson Park

William P. Whalen, yachting editor of the *Chicago American* newspaper for twenty years, was a veteran of twenty-nine Mackinac races.

He fell in love with yachting while still in his teens and gave fifty years to the sport. He participated in virtually every Chicago yachting event as owner and skipper of the Audax I, II, and III.

Although Whalen was five feet, eight-and-a-half inches tall and weighed only 160 pounds, he also played center for the Chicago Cardinals football teams of 1924, '25 and '26.

Commonwealth Avenue

340 W, from 2300 N to 2936 N*

Named after a street of the same name in Boston, Massachusetts.

Concord Lane (Pvt.)

1632 N, from 200 W to 244 W

Concord Place

1632 N, from 300 W to 5174 W*

Named for Concord, New Hampshire, the state's capital.

E. Congress Drive

500 S in Grant Park

Congress Parkway

500 S, from 100 E to 5574 W*

E. Congress Plaza Drive

400 S in Grant Park

Named for the U.S. Congress.

Conservatory Drive

3600 W in Garfield Park

This street runs alongside the Garfield Park Conservatory in Garfield Park on Chicago's West Side.

Constance Avenue

1832 E, from 6700 S to 9565 S*

Constance, West Germany, where the Rhine River flows out of Lake Constance, began as a Roman fort.

Corbett Street

958 W, from 2424 S to 2554 S

Named for James M. Corbett (1869-1949), who founded a construction and engineering company that specialized in the construction of large sewer projects in Chicago.

Corcoran Place

400 N, from 5501 W to 5969 W

(source unknown)

Corliss Avenue

800 E, from 10300 S to 13448 S*

Corliss Avenue (Pvt.)

800 E, from 13100 S to 13382 S

Named for the great steam engine that powered George Pullman's railroad car manufacturing works. The Corliss engine was built in 1876 by the Corliss Engine Company of Providence, Rhode Island, to drive the mechanical exhibits at the 1876 U.S. Centennial exposition in Philadelphia.

George Pullman, the Chicago inventor and manufacturer of the railroad sleeping car, purchased the 700-ton, 2,400 horsepower engine in 1880 and had it hauled to Chicago in thirty-five railroad cars. It continued in use until 1910.

These avenues are in the vicinity of the South Side neighborhood of Pullman.

Cornelia Avenue

3500 N, from 500 W to 8324 W*

Cornelia Dyer was seven years old when her grandfather, the subdivider Walter S. Gurnee, named this street for her. Gurnee was mayor of Chicago from 1851 to 1853.

Cornell Avenue

1600 E, from 4818 S to 9326 S*

Cornell Drive

1632 E in Jackson Park

On the day Paul Cornell arrived in Chicago, somebody stole his suitcase. But he had $1.50 in his pocket and some business cards, so he stuck around. Cornell (1822-1904) founded Hyde Park and promoted the development of Chicago's celebrated lakeside park system. He practiced law, speculated in real estate, founded a cemetery and insurance company, and even started the bronzing company that would cast the lions that stand guard today before the Art Institute of Chicago.

***Colossal Lion* by Edward Kemeys in front of the Art Institute, installed in 1894.**

G. Lane

Cornell was born in White Creek, New York. At the age of nine he moved with his family to Schuyler County, Illinois, and worked as a farmhand to pay for his schooling. Admitted to the bar in 1847, he came to Chicago on a stagecoach to seek his fortune. In 1853, he purchased 300 acres of lakefront property near 53rd Street and laid out the suburb of Hyde Park and arranged for Illinois Central commuter train service. Along 1½ miles of lake frontage in his new suburb, he developed a pleasure park for the general public.

Cornell was a tireless promoter of parks, predicting that they would give "lungs to the great city and its future generations." He was instrumental in getting a state bill passed that founded the South Parks system.

Cornell also founded the Republic Life Insurance Company and the American Bronze Company. He is buried in Oak Woods Cemetery, which he helped to found, on the South Side.

Cortez Drive
3200 W in Humboldt Park

Cortez Street
1032 N, from 1200 W to 5540 W*

Hernando Cortez (1485-1547) conquered the Aztec empire in Mexico and became the most famous of Spanish conquistadors.

Cortland Street
1900 N, from 1200 W to 7190 W*

Named for Cortland, New York, which lies thirty miles south of Syracuse.

Cottage Grove Avenue
200 E at 2218 S to 1020 E at 12958 S*

Charles Cleaver (see Cleaver Street) named this street for a grove of trees that surrounded a cottage on his land. It was a popular meeting place for early settlers. The street was originally an Indian trail.

Couch Place
170 N, from 50 W to 740 W

Ira Couch (1806-1857), proprietor of the old Tremont House hotel, is best known today as the man whose bones lie in the gray mausoleum that stands near the Chicago Historical Society in Lincoln Park.

The Couch mausoleum, near North and LaSalle streets, dates from 1857, when the area was a cemetery. But Couch contributed much more to the city than a well-made tomb.

Couch traveled from New York State to Chicago in 1836 and rented a hotel called the Tremont, a wood-frame, three-story building at Lake and

Dearborn. It burned to the ground in 1839, and Couch, with help from his brother James, built a second hotel within the year. But in 1849, that hotel also burned to the ground.

The brothers then built a third hotel, an enormous 5½-story brick building. Folks called it "Couch's Folly." But Chicago was booming in 1850, and the new Tremont was so overbooked that guests had to sleep in the halls. Within three years Couch was a rich man. He rented the hotel to two men from Boston and retired on his riches.

As for that mausoleum, nobody knows who, if anybody, is in there with Ira. The 100-ton crypt cost $7,000 to construct and was meant to hold as many as eleven bodies. Ira may be in the crypt alone, or he may be in there with as many as five other Couches and a family friend.

So why does the mausoleum still stand in the park? Nobody is sure, but the best bet is that there were no funds or no permission to move it when the cemetery was moved, part to Ravenswood (Rosehill Cemetery) and part to Evanston (Calvary Cemetery), in 1859.

Coulter Street
2000 W at 2336 S to 2266 W at 2500 S

Named for James B. Coulter, a real estate subdivider in the early days.

Court Place
125 N, from 144 W to 740 W*

Chicago's courthouse once stood where the Cook County Building and City Hall now stand. This street runs to City Hall, where the courthouse used to be.

Coyle Avenue
6932 N, from 2400 W to 7342 W*

A.S. Coyle was a land developer associated with the National City Realty Co.

Crandon Avenue
2300 E, from 6700 S to 13758 S*

Frank P. Crandon was a prohibitionist candidate for congress from Chicago in 1882. He got 663 votes. His opponent, Republican George E. Adams, got 11,686 votes.

DeWitt Clinton Cregier,1829-1898

Cregier Avenue
1800 E, from 6700 S to 9358 S*

De Witt Clinton Cregier (1829-1898) came to Chicago as a water pump expert and ended up as mayor. His water work here, his guidance in making Chicago the second largest city in the country, and his work in bringing the Columbian Exposition to Chicago, all helped to get a street named in his honor.

An orphan at age thirteen, Cregier was educated in the public schools of New York. He later worked in the steamboat business, where he picked up a knowledge of engineering.

In 1853, Chicago officials selected him as chief engineer of Chicago's North Side pumping station. Cregier so impressed City Hall with his designs for such things as pumps and the double-valve fire hydrant that he was appointed city engineer in 1880 and commissioner of public works in 1882. Seven years later he was elected mayor for a term that included some of the most important events in the city's history.

Cregier was instrumental in setting the stage for the World's Columbian Exposition of 1893. He lobbied Congress for it and served on several committees and boards which brought it to reality.

His face even appeared on the bonds ($5 million worth) used to finance the fair.

He was mayor for only three months when the city expanded its borders to include 220,000 new residents. On June 29, 1889, Chicago annexed Lake View, Hyde Park, Jefferson, Lake, and part of Cicero. This increased the number of wards in the city from twenty-four to thirty-four.

In 1889 the Illinois legislature created sanitary districts. Chicagoans voted to establish such a district, and they elected nine trustees to run it. And from this board came the decision to begin the Chicago drainage canal that linked Lake Michigan and the Mississippi Basin and replaced the old Illinois and Michigan canal. This project, which reversed the Chicago River, opened in 1900.

As the city's twenty-seventh mayor, Cregier left office in 1891 to return to work as a civil engineer. In 1894 President Grover Cleveland appointed him Superintendent of the U.S. Indian Warehouse in Chicago and Special Disbursing Agent of Public Funds.

Crest Line Street
8144 S, from 4100 W to 4192 W

(source unknown)

Crilly Court
224 W, from 1700 N to 1766 N

Crilly Drive
3900 E in Calumet Park

Daniel Francis Crilly, a real estate developer, joined with meatpacker Philip D. Armour and a state legislator, Dave Shanahan, to construct a large park in the 1890s on the site of the old Brighton Park Race Track. They named it McKinley Park. Crilly was also a commissioner of the South Park District from 1900 to 1906.

Crosby Street
600 W, from 922 N to 1190 N

Isaac Crosby was a South Side and North Side subdivider in the 1870s. One of his largest subdivisions, begun in 1874, was bounded by 91st Street, 95th Street, Ashland and Vincennes avenues.

Crowell Street
1200 W, from 2700 S to 2736 S

Named for S.B. Crowell, a Chicago merchant and landowner in 1868.

Crystal Street
1232 N, from 1300 W to 5540 W*

This street was probably named for the glass or mineral.

Cullerton Street
2000 S, from 336 E to 4358 W*

Named for Edward F. Cullerton (1842-1920), a Near West Side alderman from 1871 to 1920.

Cullom Avenue
4300 N, from 900 W to 6056 W*

Shelby Moore Cullom (1829-1914), a two-term governor of Illinois, held one political office or another for fifty-two years and boasted about it. His marathon political career, he said late in life, "exceeded in length of unbroken service that of any other public man in the country's history."

Cullom was a somewhat colorless man, even-tempered, conservative, and a tee-totaler. If he is remembered at all today, it is for the leading role he played as a U.S. senator in the creation of the Interstate Commerce Commission.

Born in Kentucky and reared on an Illinois farm, Cullom studied law in Springfield, was admitted to the bar, and jumped into politics. Between 1860 and 1913 he was a state representative, a United States representative, an Illinois governor (1876-83), and a U.S. senator.

Cumberland Avenue
8400 W, from 3200 N to 5950 N

(source unknown)

Cuyler Avenue
4032 N, from 800 W to 6358 W*

Edward J. Cuyler, born in Essex County, New York in 1829, came to Chicago in 1855 as construction paymaster for the Chicago & North Western Railroad and stuck with the job until the railroad was laid to Janesville, Wisconsin, three years later. He worked most of his life for the railroad.

Cyril Avenue
1964 E, trom 7128 S to 7154 S

Cyril (c.827-869) and his brother, Methodius, were apostles of the Slavic peoples. Preaching Christianity in the native language, they brought the Slavic countries firmly into the sphere of the Christian church. They were recognized as saints of the Roman Catholic Church in 1881.

Rev. Arnold Damen, S.J., who founded Holy Family Church in 1857.

D

Dakin Street
3932 N, from 800 W to 6758 W*

Named for R.L. Dakin, a Chicago real estate subdivider.

Damen Avenue
2000 W, from 7546 N to 10058 S*

Formerly known as Robey Street, Damen Avenue was named for Father Arnold Damen (1815-1890), a Jesuit priest and founder of Holy Family Catholic Church (1857), St. Ignatius High School, and Loyola University (1870).

Father Damen managed a near-miracle during the Chicago Fire of 1871. He was in New York City the day the great fire struck, and he fell to his knees and prayed. He vowed that, should God spare his parish church from the fire's flames, a light would be kept burning forever in the church.

His prayers were answered. The fire began within blocks of the church, but the southwest wind turned the flames toward downtown. And seven lights, recently electric bulbs, have burned for more than one hundred years before the image of Our Lady of Perpetual Help in Holy Family Church at Roosevelt and May streets.

Given clout like that, the City Council in 1927 wisely named a street for him.

Daniel Drive (Pvt.)
300 E, from 13000 S to 13116 S

(source unknown)

Dan Ryan Expressway
764 W at 600 S to 1600 W at 11900 S

This crowded stretch of I-94 was named for Daniel B. Ryan, president of the Cook County Board of Commissioners from 1954 to 1961. Ryan (1894-1961), a graduate of De LaSalle Institute and Kent College of Law, was a successful insurance broker and son of another powerful county board member, Dan Ryan Sr. When the elder Ryan died in 1923, his son assumed his seat on the board. The Dan Ryan Expressway is one of the busiest roads in the world.

Dante Avenue
1432 E, from 6330 S to 9158 S*

Named for Dante Alighieri (1265-1321), the great Italian poet of the Middle Ages, who wrote the *Divine Comedy* and other classical works.

Dauphin Avenue
888 E, from 8700 S to 10806 S*

This street was named after Dauphin County, Pennsylvania, by the real estate developer Samuel E. Gross in 1873.

Davlin Court
3946 W, from 3000 N to 3154 N

John Davlin was a partner in Davlin, Kelly & Carroll Subdividers, a firm that developed the area bounded by Belmont, Pulaski (then called Crawford), Diversey, and Central Park Avenues in 1848.

Davol Street
1620 W, from 11234 S to 11470 S

Joseph A. Davol, born in 1835 in Rhode Island, was a Chicago jeweler, a wholesale drug merchant, a commodities trader, and finally a land speculator. He opened a jewelery store in Chicago in 1856, but went bankrupt in the panic of 1857.

Davol was treasurer and secretary in 1878 of the Blue Island Land & Building Company, which developed the Morgan Park community where this street is located.

This bas relief, *The Defense* by Henry Hering, on the Michigan Avenue Bridge (1928), is located a few feet from the site of Fort Dearborn. It depicts the Fort Dearborn Massacre of 1812.

Dawson Avenue
3432 W, from 2800 N to 2962 N

John Brown Dawson was a barber, Methodist minister, and real estate agent in the 1860s and 1870s. He turned to the ministry after his barber shop was destroyed in the Chicago Fire of 1871.

Dayton Street
832 W, from 1400 N to 4346 N*

William Lewis Dayton (1807-1864) was the first vice presidential candidate of the new Republican Party in 1856. He was a U.S. senator from New Jersey in 1842.

Dean Street
1700 W, from 1334 N to 1380 N

This street was named after either Judge John Dean, a Chicago landowner and civic leader as early as 1830, or after Munson D. Dean, a contractor and builder in 1855 and subdivider in the 1870s. Munson Dean was a highway commissioner in suburban Wheeling in 1860.

Dearborn Parkway
36 W, from 1500 N to 1556 N

Dearborn Street
36 W, from 1454 N to 5458 S*

General Henry Dearborn (1751-1829) was President Thomas Jefferson's secretary of war and a Massachusetts congressman. But Chicagoans best remember him for the historic fort named in his honor. Fort Dearborn, which stood where Michigan Avenue now meets Wacker Drive, was built by blue-coated U.S. soldiers in 1803.

General Dearborn organized a company that took part in the battle of Bunker Hill on June 17, 1775, and as Jefferson's war secretary he helped plan the removal of the Indians west of the Mississippi River. Largely because of his indecisiveness in the War of 1812, Detroit fell to the British. He was relieved of his command and honorably discharged.

DeKoven Street
1100 S, from 540 W to 570 W

There are many Chicago streets named for people, places, and events related to the Chicago Fire. DeKoven Street is not one of them, even though the fire started on the corner of DeKoven and Jefferson streets.

John DeKoven (1833-1898) was twenty-one when he came to Chicago in 1854 to make his mark in business. He was the grandson of a Hanoverian army ensign captured by the Americans around 1779. It was then, as a prisoner of war in Connecticut, that the elder DeKoven had married.

The grandson became a director of railroad companies and banks. He was a founder of the Northern Trust Company and a founder of another bank that later became part of the Continental Illinois National Bank and Trust Co.

But at the time of the Chicago Fire in 1871, DeKoven Street was hardly a prosperous place. Joseph E. Chamberlin, a *Chicago Evening Post* reporter who covered the fire, later wrote, "I was at the scene in a few minutes. The fire had already advanced a distance of about a single square through the frame buildings that covered the ground thickly north of DeKoven Street and east of Jefferson—if those miserable alleys shall be dignified by being denominated streets."

DeKoven was part of a poor neighborhood, a street crowded with wooden shanties. The fire began in a barn behind Patrick O'Leary's house. Today the Chicago Fire Department's training school stands on the site of the O'Leary barn.

Map showing the extent of the Chicago Fire, October 8 and 9, 1871.

Courtesy *Chicago Sun-Times*

Delaware Place

900 N, from 280 E to 130 W

Delaware Place (Pvt.)

944 N, from 516 W to 532 W

The name Delaware was given by the English to the Lenni-Lenape Indians who lived in the river valley of the same name. The state took its name from the valley. The valley, in turn, was named for Lord De La Warr, governor of the Virginia colony.

Delphia Avenue

8600 W, from 4500 N to 5646 N*

(source unknown.)

Deming Place

2534 N, from 400 W to 5358 W*

Frederick Deming was a landowner and subdivider on the Near North Side in the 1850s. He was an associate of the three Wright brothers who developed much of what now is the community of Wrightwood. *See Wrightwood Avenue.*

Denvir Avenue

2526 W, from 500 S to 532 S

In his own small way, James C. Denvir (1870-1974), the oldest politician in Chicago at the time of his death, helped Mayor Richard J. Daley get his start.

Denvir joined the Democratic Party in 1890, worked as a West Side precinct captain from 1914 to 1966, and played a bit role in transforming Chicago from a heavily Republican town to a heavily Democratic town.

He held a variety of political patronage jobs in his day, including deputy county treasurer and assistant Cook County sheriff. And as president of the Cook County Civil Service

Commission for a time, he administered a test to a particular young man interested in a job as clerk in the county controller's office.

"I sets up the test for him, and I don't think no more about it," he later recalled. "Nice Irish boy he was. Name of Richard J. Daley. He passed."

Depot Place

1544 S, from 500 W to 742 W

This street fronts a depot of the Chicago, Burlington & Quincy Railroad.

De Saible Street (Pvt.)

3756 S, from 236 W to 258 W

Jean Baptiste Point De Saible (1745-1818), nowadays more frequently spelled DuSable, was Chicago's first settler. He was a black man of Haitian origin who came to Chicago around 1780 as a fur trader and built his house at the mouth of the river. *See Jean Street.*

Desplaines Street
630 W, from 530 N to 2018 S*

Des Plaines River Road
9400 W, from 5200 N to 5212 N

The word is French for "the plains" and first was used by French explorers of the pioneer West. Both streets take their name from the river. Des Plaines River Road runs alongside the Des Plaines River.

Devon Avenue
6400 N, from 1200 W to 7758 W*

Named by John L. Cochran, the developer of Edgewater, for one of the stops along the Main Line, a commuter rail line running west out of Philadelphia, Cochran's hometown. Devon, Pennsylvania, was probably named for the English county of Devonshire.

Dewitt Place
238 E, from 830 N to 920 N

This street was named for either John De Witt, a subdivider in 1881, or for De Witt Clinton, governor of New York. See Clinton Street.

Dickens Avenue
2100 N, from 300 W to 7190 W*

Dickens Drive
2100 N in Lincoln Park

Dickens Boulevard
2100 N, from 300 W to 314 W

Named for Charles Dickens (1812-1870), the famous English novelist, who was popular throughout this country in the years that Chicago was developing into an important American city.

On Diversey at Lakeview Avenue, the Elks' Memorial to their World War I dead and the national headquarters of the Benevolent and Protective Order of Elks.

Courtesy B.P.O.E.

Dickinson Avenue
4944 W at 4100 N to 5000 W at 4168 N

Arthur W. Dickinson, a North Side subdivider in the 1880s and 1890s, developed parcels of land all over the North Side and just west of the Loop.

District Boulevard (Pvt.)
4220 S, from 4000 W to 4558 W

This street runs through the community of Archer Heights, which before 1900 was known as the Archer Road District. It was annexed by Chicago in 1889.

Diversey Avenue
2800 N, from 2230 W to 7158 W*

Diversey Parkway
2800 N, from 244 W to 2228 W

Diversey School Court
2756 N, from 1100 W to 1140 W

Michael Diversey has not one, but three Chicago streets named after him. He was an important man in town. He was a brewer.

In 1841 Diversey bought an interest in what was Chicago's first brewery. He bought it from William B. Ogden, Chicago's first mayor (1837-38). Diversey's partner was William Lill (*see Lill Avenue*), an English immigrant who walked to Chicago from Louisville, Kentucky, in 1835.

The Lill and Diversey brewery, at Chicago Avenue and Pine (now Michigan Avenue) was so successful, Chicago historian A.T. Andreas said, that by 1857 it "was the most extensive establishment of its kind in the West." It shipped brew down the Mississippi and up north to Wisconsin. In 1861 the brewery—by then sprawling over two city blocks—produced 44,750 barrels of ale, stout, and porter.

Anybody who made a purchase might get with it a drink of twenty-year-old bourbon, a barrel of which was kept in each of the brewery's stores.

Michael Diversey was also a Chicago alderman and a noted philanthropist. He donated land for the McCormick Theological Seminary, was a founder of St. Joseph Catholic Church, now at Hill and Orleans streets, and

donated land for St. Michael's Church at Eugenie and Cleveland streets. St. Michael's was named in honor of his patron saint.

Diversey died in 1869, but Lill continued to operate the brewery until 1871, when fire wiped it out and Lill lost $650,000.

Division Street
1200 N, from 90 E to 6000 W*

There seems to be no satisfactory explanation for how this street got its name, but one story is that it was so named because it divides Goose Island, an industrial island in the city, in half.

Dobson Avenue
1032 E, from 7100 S to 13400 S*

Named for R.W. Dobson, a subdivider on the South Side.

Dominick Street
1430 W at 2037 N to 1522 W at 2242 N

William F. Dominick was a director of St. James Hospital, which later became St. Luke's Hospital and now is part of the Rush-Presbyterian-St. Luke's Medical Center. With Charles R. Larrabee, he operated a foundry in the 1840s and 1850s. He was also a subdivider.

Dorchester Avenue
1400 E, from 4732 S to 8958 S*

Dorchester Avenue (Pvt.)
1400 E, from 9500 S to 9858 S

A part of Boston, Dorchester is five miles south of the center of that city. On March 4, 1776, colonial forces occupied Dorchester Heights, a hill overlooking Boston Harbor, forcing the evacuation of British troops from Boston on March 17.

The Stephen A. Douglas house at 636 East 36th Street in 1913.
Courtesy *Chicago Sun-Times*

Doty (West) Avenue
1200 E, from 10700 S to 13000 S

Doty (East) Avenue
1750 E at 10300 S to 1600 E at 13000 S

Named after Duane Doty (1834-1902), a civil engineer who laid out the town of Pullman in 1880. George Pullman, the founder of this original company town, named the street for Doty. In 1893 Mrs. Duane Doty wrote a book about the town of Pullman, describing in glowing terms the workers' paradise that never really was. The book was reprinted in 1974 by the Pullman Civic Organization.

In 1875, Duane Doty came to Chicago from Detroit, where he had been the superintendent of schools. He became Chicago's superintendent of public schools in 1877. He died in 1902.

Douglas Boulevard
1400 S, from 3100 W to 3758 W

Douglas Drive
1400 S in Douglas Park

Douglas Drive, Stephen A.
3500 S, from 735 E to 751 E

U. S. Senator Stephen Arnold Douglas (1813-1861) was the Democrats' pre-Civil War leader and Abraham Lincoln's rival for the presidency. But his lasting contribution to Chicago was to bring the Illinois Central Railroad to town and develop elegant South Side communities.

As a U.S. senator in 1850, Douglas pushed through the Illinois Central Railroad bill, a map for the railroad between Chicago and Mobile, Alabama.

Stephen Douglas was a resident of Chicago, and he owned much of the South Side community that bears his name today.

In 1852, Douglas purchased seventy acres of land along the lake between 33rd Street and 35th Street and laid out the two communities known as Groveland Park and Woodland Park. *See Oakenwald Avenue.*

Dover Street
1400 W, from 4400 N to 4756 N

Named for the capital of the state of Delaware.

Dowagiac Avenue
5400 W, from 6700 N to 6970 N

The word is Potawatomie for "scoop up," apparently referring to the abundance of fish in certain lakes and rivers. There is a city and also a river by this name in Michigan.

Drake Avenue
3532 W, from 6334 N to 11460 S*

John Burroughs Drake (1826-1895) liked to take chances. While the Chicago Fire was raging, Drake was looking for a deal. With flames engulfing the buildings across the street from the Michigan Avenue Hotel at Michigan Avenue and Congress Street, Drake thought it a fine time to buy the threatened 79-room structure. He made an offer, slapped down a payment, and waited for the smoke to clear. The hotel proved to be the only one on the South Side that didn't burn. It was even used to mark a border of the fire. Drake renamed it the Tremont House and began making money.

This wasn't Drake's only hotel. The most famous of his hotels, at least in his time, was the Grand Pacific, which became the unofficial western headquarters for the Republican Party. Here, some of Drake's friends, such as Abe Lincoln, U.S. Grant, and Stephen A. Douglas, jotted their names in the hotel registry. And here, the taste buds of the wealthy and powerful got a workout. Royalty, cattlemen from the West, statesmen and diplomats dined on buffalo steak, bear steak, venison, prairie chicken, and wild pigeon.

Not bad for a hotel owned by a young man who started out as a clerk in Ohio. As one of six children, Drake went to work as a store clerk at age eleven after his father died. Later, as a hotel clerk, he sent his mother money, and yet he was able to save enough to buy a stake in a Chicago hotel.

Drake came to Chicago in 1855. His heirs later controlled the Drake and Blackstone Hotels.

Draper Street
2540 N, from 1200 W to 1258 W

Lyman Copeland Draper (1815-1891) was a historian and biographer of Daniel Boone. A specialist in frontier history, he was the secretary of the Wisconsin Historical Society from 1854 to 1886.

Drew Street
1700 W, from 10500 S to 10838 S

Charles W. Drew, president of the Chicago Fire Underwriters in 1885, lived above his storefront offices after the Chicago Fire of 1871 destroyed his home. Being a prudent man, his business records were in a vault and were saved from the fire.

Drexel Avenue
900 E, from 5100 S to 9858 S*

Drexel Avenue (Pvt.)
900 E, from 13000 S to 13098 S

Drexel Boulevard
900 E, from 3900 S to 5052 S

Drexel Square Drive
5130 S, from 800 E to 857 E

The land for this street was donated to the city by the sons of Philadelphia banker Francis M. Drexel (1792-1863). In 1865, the Drexel family owned all the land bounded by 63rd Street, 67th Street, Ashland Avenue, and the Pennsylvania Railroad tracks, the core of the present West Englewood neighborhood.

Drummond Place
2632 N, from 530 W to 5558 W*

Named for Thomas Drummond, a judge of the U.S. Court for the Northern District of Illinois from 1850 to 1884.

Dunbar Avenue
246 E, from 9200 S to 9254 S*

Paul Lawrence Dunbar (1872-1906), an American poet and novelist from Dayton, Ohio, was the first black author to gain national recognition and a wide popular audience.

E

Early Avenue
5700 N at 1200 W to 5840 N
at 1358 W

This street was named for J.H. Early, a subdivider of this area in 1877.

East Circle Avenue
7034 W, from 5700 N to 5978 N

The name says it—this street and West Circle Avenue form a circle.

East End Avenue
1700 E, from 4900 S to 9358 S*

When Paul Cornell subdivided this area in Hyde Park in about 1852, this street was the east end of his subdivision.

Eastlake Terrace
1320 W, from 7500 N to 7760 N

This street runs very close to Lake Michigan, Chicago's eastern boundary.

Eastman Street
1440 N, from 800 W to 1122 W*

Abolitionist newspaper editor Zebina Eastman (1815-1883) was to the anti-slavery movement in the Midwest what the great William Lloyd Garrison was to the movement in the Northeast.

From 1842 to 1856 in Chicago, Eastman was editor of the *Western Citizen* and its successor, the *Free West*. In fiery editorials, he railed against the evils of slavery and called for its gradual and peaceful abolition.

Though he was considered a moderate among abolitionists, many of whom called for the institution's immediate end, he was coldly received by his fellow Chicagoans. Some threatened to destroy his press. Among the common folk in Chicago back then, abolition was an unpopular cause.

Eastman was born in North Amherst, Massachusetts, and was orphaned at the age of six. As a young man, he became convinced slavery was wrong and moved west to join the veteran abolitionist, Benjamin Lundy, in publishing the anti-slavery sheet "Genius of Universal Emancipation." In 1842, he moved to Chicago and published the *Western Citizen*, the leading abolitionist newspaper west of the Appalachians.

One obituary in the old *Chicago Inter-Ocean* described Eastman as "hot-headed," but full of "discretion and practical foresight."

East River Road
8800 W, from 4400 N to 5958 N

This street marks the eastern boundary of a forest preserve through which the Des Plaines River flows.

East-View Park (Pvt.)
1728 E, from 5400 S to 5450 S

This street runs along the edge of a private park, East View Park, near Lake Shore Drive in the Hyde Park neighborhood. The park offers a view of Lake Michigan to the east.

Eastwood Avenue
4632 N, from 800 W to 6354 W*

This street was named by the Northwest Land Association, subdividers of Albany Park, for a pine wood on the site of Ravenswood Gardens.

Eberhart Avenue
500 E, from 3128 S to 13328 S*

John F. Eberhart (1829-1914), an early Chicago school administrator, did his best to promote public school education among the rural folk of Cook County.

Born on a farm in Mercer County, Pennsylvania, Eberhart started out teaching penmanship to Pennsylvania farmers. As a young man he was strong enough to lift a 900-pound brass cannon on a dare, but he was sickly enough to have to move to Chicago in 1855 for the fresh prairie breezes. In 1859, he was elected superintendent of Cook County schools, a job he held for ten years. He started a school for teachers in Blue Island and established free kindergartens in all the county's public schools.

But as Eberhart rode the circuit of the county's rural schools, he often discovered more petty corruption than education. "In one district," he once recalled, "one of the directors was paid $50 per month to superintend the erection of a two-room schoolhouse, his son got $5 per week as janitor, and his daughter $50 per month as teacher, without a certificate."

In later life, Eberhart was an ambitious real estate developer, playing a role in the creation of Norwood Park, West Lawn, and Chicago Lawn.

Edbrooke Avenue
134 E, from 10500 S to 12650 S*

Edbrooke Avenue (Pvt.)
140 E, from 13330 S to 13360 S

Willoughby J. Edbrooke, born in Chicago in 1843, was an architect whose firm of Edbrooke and Burnham designed whole blocks of homes, business buildings, and public buildings.

Eddy Street
3532 N, from 1100 W to 6360 W*

D.C. Eddy was a quiet and unassuming man who was born in New York State in 1812. He settled in Chicago in 1841 and practiced law and banking. He ran for the state legislature on the Democratic ticket in 1870 and lost; he ran for the state senate in 1872 and lost again.

Edens Expressway
4700 W at 4600 N to 4900 W
at 6400 N

Edens Parkway
4812 W, from 5400 N to 5500 N

Named for William G. Edens (1863-1955), a man who never owned or drove a car, but was know as the "father of the Illinois good roads program."

Edens, who began his career as a railroad brakeman and retired as a Chicago banker, headed the Illinois Highway Improvement Association, a group that in 1918 convinced the state legislature to issue $60 million in bonds to improve the state's roads.

In 1953, two years after the Edens Expressway—then called the Edens Superhighway—officially opened, Edens told a reporter, "It's a shame. After the engineers built such a good road, darn fool drivers go out and kill themselves on it." The Edens was the first expressway built in the Chicago area.

Edgebrook Terrace
5924 W, from 6700 N to 6752 N

This street is in the Edgebrook neighborhood.

Edgewater Avenue
5732 N, from 1400 W to 1676 W

John L. Cochran, the man who developed and named the community of Edgewater, purchased land in the area in 1885. He laid out wide streets, stone sidewalks, and a sewer system. Advertisements in the late 1880s celebrated Edgewater as "the only electric lighted suburb adjacent to Chicago." *See Berwyn Avenue for more on Cochran.*

Edgewater Beach Drive (Pvt.)
936 W, from 5400 N to 5424 N

This street ran alongisde the Edgewater Beach Hotel, demolished in 1970.

Edmaire Street
11300 S, from 1655 W to 2022 W

The Edmaires possibly were a farming family in this Morgan Park area.

The Edgewater Beach Hotel; north tower, 1916, south tower, 1924; the buildings were demolished in 1970.

Courtesy Edgewater Historical Society

Edmunds Street
5000 N, from 5445 W to 5574 W

George Franklin Edmunds (1828-1919) was a lawyer and a Republican U.S. senator from Vermont from 1866 to 1891.

Edward Court
749 W, from 2100 N to 2158 N

Ninian Edwards (1775-1833), an early Illinois governor, once made the wise observation that loud talk and bold words are harmless, but "anyone might be whispered to death."

Edwards, a Kentucky lawyer, was commissioned by President James Madison in 1809 to be the first governor of the Illinois Territory. He was president of the convention which drafted the state's first constitution, and he served as governor of Illinois from 1826 to 1830.

Eggleston Avenue
432 W, from 5900 S to 12946 S*

Charles B. Eggleston, born in 1850 in Cincinnati, came to Chicago in 1871 and operated grain elevators. He was a South Side land developer and a member of the Chicago Board of Trade.

Eisenhower, Dwight D., Expressway
200 W at 436 S to 6000 W at 658 S

General of the Army Dwight D. Eisenhower (1890-1969) was supreme commander of the Allied forces in Europe in World War II and the thirty-fourth president of the United States, serving from 1953 to 1961.

Elaine Place
700 W, from 3400 N to 3460 N

Elaine Hundley was the wife of Elisha E. Hundley, a big builder in Lake View Township in the 1850s. With his partner, James H. Rees, Hundley built the Lake View House Hotel in 1854, north of Grace Street near the lake. The hotel, which was quickly filled by cholera refugees, was one of the first residences in the suburban Lake View area.

Elbridge Avenue
3600 W, from 3000 N to 3100 N

Elbridge Hanecy, born in Trenton, Wisconsin, in 1852, was a wealthy lawyer who spent his summer Saturdays at the old Washington Park Race Track in Washington Park.

Eleanor Street

1200 W, from 2500 S to 2872 S

Eleanor Kinzie was the wife of John Kinzie, one of Chicago's first settlers. *See Kinzie Street.*

Elias Court

1200 W, from 2900 S to 2978 S

Named for Elias K. Kane (1794-1835), a U.S. senator from Illinois from 1825 to 1835.

Elizabeth Street

1232 W, from 928 N to 12258 S

The most likely explanation is that this street was named for Elizabeth May Curtiss, the daughter of Mayor James Curtiss, who held office from 1847 to 1848 and from 1850 to 1851.

Elk Grove Avenue

1400 N at 1800 W to 1548 N at 1900 W

In 1831, Elk Grove in this West Town area was a popular meeting place for Chicago area settlers. It was a grove, and it did have elk.

Ellen Street

1282 N, from 1714 W to 1916 W

Ellen Kinzie, the first white child born in Chicago, was the daughter of John Kinzie, one of the earliest settlers. *See Kinzie Street.*

Elliott Avenue

1836 E, from 8112 S to 8160 S*

Elliott Anthony was a partner in 1874 in the real estate development firm of Anthony & Harvey. He was an attorney for the city in 1858 and an organizer of Union forces in Chicago during the Civil War. *See Anthony Avenue.*

Ellis Avenue

600 E at 2600 S to 1000 E at 13526 S*

Ellis Avenue (Pvt.)

954 E, from 13016 S to 13292 S

Ellis Park

600 E, from 3600 S to 3644 S

In 1835, Samuel Ellis, who ran a tavern called the Ellis Inn on 35th Street near Vincennes Avenue, owned all the land bounded by 31st Street, 39th Street, South Park Boulevard (now Dr. Martin Luther King Jr. Drive), and the Lake Michigan shore.

Ellsworth Drive

400 E in Washington Park

James W. Ellsworth was a commissioner of the South Park District from 1889 to 1899.

Elm Street

1142 N, from 96 E to 664 W

Named for the elm tree.

Elmdale Avenue

6000 N, from 1200 W to 1554 W

Named for the city of Elmadalen, Sweden.

Elmhurst Road

12800 W, from 6645 N to 6759 N

This street at one time originated in west suburban Elmhurst. It runs within Chicago's city limits only for a couple of blocks along the western edge of O'Hare International Airport. The road was named for the suburb. The suburb, in turn, made up the name in 1869 and dropped the name Cottage Hill.

Elsdon Avenue

3610 W, from 5415 S to 5445 S

Elsdon was a small railroad workers' settlement before World War I in what is now Gage Park.

Elston

1132 W at 824 N to 6214 W at 6175 N*

One-time alderman Daniel Elston was said to have lived beyond "the northern limits of civilization in Chicago." And the road that bears his name was the site of a Chicago-style Boston Tea Party.

Ellis Park, looking south from 36th Street, c. 1910.

C.R. Childs, courtesy G. Schmalgemeier

Elston (continued)

Elston lived in the wilderness off a crooked wagon track parallel to what is now Milwaukee Avenue. The road ran north from Kinzie to the northern part of Niles.

E.O. Gale in his *Reminiscences of Early Chicago* described an inn marking the northern limits of civilized life on this road. There were no settlers "as far as our vision extends, although we are informed that along the Indian Trail, yonder, Daniel Elston is living."

Elston came to Chicago from London where he was a well-to-do merchant, although he lost most of his goods when his ship foundered off the coast of Newfoundland.

Befitting a future alderman, he had an eye for real estate speculation. He bought land in what would become the Niles and Jefferson areas.

Elston became an alderman in 1837, when there were only six wards, and he founded the Daniel Elston Bank. But the road he lived on generated more interest than Elston himself did. In his early days there, it was a toll road owned and operated by Amos J. Snell.

There was one toll gate at Division Street, a second one south of Lawrence Avenue, and a third at the intersection of Elston and Milwaukee. In 1840 Snell was charging 2½ cents a mile to travel this plank road.   So heavy was the traffic that William Ringer, an old toll keeper, once collected $790 on a single Sunday. This didn't set well with the local farmers who, dressed as Indians, chopped down the toll gates and burned them.

Emerald Avenue

732 W, from 2019 S to 12932 S*

Emerald Drive

724 W at 6200 S to 746 W at 6438 S

This street runs through a number of South Side communities which once had large Irish populations—Bridgeport, Canaryville, Englewood, Auburn Park, and Gresham. As early as 1853 the Irish constituted twenty-five percent of all Chicago public officials. This street's name reflects Irish ethnic pride.

Emmett Street

3200 W at 2600 N to 3232 W at 2646 N*

John N. Staples, a subdivider, named this street for his friend and occasional business partner, John Emmett, in 1883.

The asterisk indicates
a non-continuous street.

Englewood Avenue
6232 S, from 246 W to 756 W*

Henry B. Lewis, an early settler and realtor, suggested the name Englewood in 1868 for a new Chicago community along what now is 63rd Street, taking the name from the hometown of some early settlers, Englewood, New Jersey. Previously, the community had been called Junction Grove, but Lewis wanted a name with a bit more class.

Erie Street
658 N, from 456 E to 5968 W*

The street was named for Lake Erie, which in turn was named for the Erie Indians, a tribe living on the lake's south shore. The name meant "the cat people."

SOMETIMES I WISH WE WERE THE GOLDFISH PEOPLE OR SOMETHING

Ernst Court
64 E, from 862 N to 922 N

This street probably was named for Joseph H. Ernst, a brewer and alderman. From 1886 to 1890 and from 1892 to 1894, he represented a city ward centered near Fullerton and Western avenues.

Escanaba Avenue
2900 E, from 7810 S to 13247 S*

Named for the town of Escanaba, Michigan. It is an Algonquin word for "flat rock."

Esmond Street
10920 S at 1800 W to 11180 S at 1900 W

This street possibly was named for a black farmer named Esmond who lived in the area before it was developed as a residential community.

A second possibility is that Thomas Morgan, for whom Morgan Park was named, named this street for the British novel *The History of Henry Esmond*, written by William Makepeace Thackeray in 1852.

Essex Avenue
2500 E, from 7500 S to 9356 S*

Essex in the 1870s and 1880s was a community bounded by 71st Street, 75th Street, Stony Island Avenue, and the Illinois Central Railroad tracks. Apparently named for the county of Essex in southeast England, the Chicago community's early settlers were primarily British railway workers.

Estes Avenue
7100 N, from 1302 W to 7566 W*

George Estes, an early settler, was a member of the Rogers Park Building & Land Company in 1873, the major developer of the community of Rogers Park. He came to Chicago in 1869, died in 1887, and was buried in Rosehill Cemetery.

Euclid Avenue
1932 E, from 6700 S to 9656 S*

Euclid Parkway (Pvt.)
1908 E, from 7412 S to 7452 S

Named for Euclid, a Greek mathematician active in 300 B.C., who is called the father of geometry. He wrote the "Elements," a collection of geometrical theorems.

Eugenie Street
1700 N, from 138 W to 558 W

Frederick William Wolf, a mechanical engineer and architect, named this street for his daughter, Eugenie. Born in Germany in 1837, Wolf came to Chicago in 1867 and purchased a mechanical engineering firm at Canal and Randolph streets. He built breweries and several of Chicago's finest homes.

Evans Avenue
732 E, from 4300 S to 13434 S*

Evans Avenue (Pvt.)
732 E, from 13016 S to 13098 S

Dr. John Evans (1814-1897), for whom the suburb of Evanston was named, was a physician, a Chicago alderman, a founder of Northwestern University, and a territorial governor of Colorado. He was on the faculty of Rush Medical College from 1845 to 1856, and he served as a Chicago alderman from 1853 to 1855. He was Colorado's territorial governor from 1862 to 1865.

Evans Court
740 N, from 114 E to 120 E

Named for Evans Inc., a furrier and ladies' speciality store founded in about 1929 by A.L. Meltzer.

Evelyn Lane (Pvt.)
5350 N, from 8644 W to 8758 W

(source unknown)

Everell Avenue
6128 N, from 7200 W to 7643 W

George Everell Dutton (1866-1929) was president of the First Trust & Savings Bank of Chicago.

Everett Avenue
1738 E, from 5452 S to 5558 S

Everett Drive
1738 E in Jackson Park

Edward Everett (1794-1865), a Harvard president and U.S. secretary of state under President Millard Fillmore, was reknowned for his oratorical flare, although Abraham Lincoln upstaged him with his Gettysburg Address. Everett spoke before Lincoln at the dedication of the National Cemetery at Gettysburg on November 19, 1863. He spoke with enthusiasm and at length, and his audience was moved. But President Lincoln then stood and delivered his famous address. When Lincoln later complimented Everett on his speech, Everett wrote back, "I should be glad if I could flatter myself that I came as near the central idea of this occasion in two hours as you did in two minutes."

Evergreen Avenue
1332 N, from 200 W to 3554 W*

Named for the evergreen tree.

Ewing Avenue
3338 E at 9200 S to 3430 E
to 12040 S*

William Lee Davidson Ewing (1795-1846) was governor of Illinois for just fifteen days. In 1834, when U.S. Representative Charles Slade died of cholera, Gov. John Reynolds was chosen to serve out Slade's term. Ewing, as president of the Illinois Senate, succeeded Reynolds as governor. Fifteen days later the governor-elect, Joseph Duncan, was sworn into office.

Ewing, a lawyer born in Kentucky, was a colonel of the Spy Battalion during the Black Hawk War and, as an Indian Agent, directed the government-ordered removal of the Sacs and Foxes west of the Mississippi.

Exchange Avenue
2400 E at 7100 S to 2934 E
at 13258 S*

This is one of the busiest retail and business streets in South Chicago, hence its name.

Exchange Avenue
4136 S, from 800 W to 1200 W

Named for the Exchange Building, once the central business building in the old Union Stock Yards.

Exchange Court
124 W, from 1 N to 20 N

It is called a court, but it is more of a narrow alley alongside the American National Bank & Trust Company, between Clark and LaSalle streets. Motorcyclists use it as a parking lot.

Fairbanks Court
300 E, from 530 N to 754 N

N. K. Fairbanks (1829-1893), a meatpacker and banker, exemplified the life of the Chicago nouveau riche of his day, right down to the country digs in Lake Geneva and the cultural excursions to New York.

If the Algonquin Round Table once reflected the richness of the cultural life in New York, the Chicago Club's "Millionaires' Table," where Fairbanks presided, reflected the richness of business life in Chicago. As president of the Chicago Club, Fairbanks dined daily with such tycoons as sleeping car magnate George Pullman, railroad supplier John Crerar, State Street retailer Marshall Field, and banker Lyman J. Gage.

Fairbanks was born to a bricklayer and a bookkeeper in Sodus, New York. In 1855, as a representative of a New York grain commission business, he moved to Chicago and built a lard refinery. At various times he owned a meatpacking company, a Michigan mining company, and he ran a bank. He spent weekends with his wife and seven children on a 180-acre estate in Lake Geneva, and he traveled regularly to New York for the theater.

Fairfield Avenue
2732 W, from 7424 N to 11458 S

Fairfield Avenue (Pvt.)
2732 W, from 4900 N to 4946 N*

Asa C. Fairfield, for whom this street probably was named, was a Chicago landowner and developer in 1891.

A second possibility is that the street was named after Fort Fairfield, Maine, which in turn was named in honor of Col. John Fairfield (1797-1847).

The colonel was a two-term governor of Maine from 1838 to 1843.

Fairview Avenue
8300 W, from 5543 N to 5660 N

(source unknown)

Fargo Avenue
7432 N, from 1310 W to 7742 W*

In an age before supersonic jets and interstate highways, James Fargo was in the express-mail delivery business. It was, however, a business of chugging trains and huffing horses, and nobody could seriously expect delivery by the start of the next business day.

Fargo was born in Watervale, New York, in 1829, the seventh in a family of eleven children. At the age of fifteen, he moved to Buffalo and swept floors and ran errands in the main office of his brother William's express service, Wells & Company, which operated between Buffalo and Albany, and between Buffalo and Detroit.

Between 1848 and 1855, James ran the firm's Detroit office. Then he took over the Chicago office of the reorganized firm, which had merged with other express-mail firms and been renamed the American Express Company.

William Fargo and his partner, Henry Wells, went on in 1852 to found a

second company, Wells, Fargo & Company, which handled banking and express business created by the California Gold Rush.

Farragut Avenue
5232 N, from 1400 W to 8160 W*

David Glasgow Farragut (1801-1870), a hero of two of the most important Union naval victories of the Civil War, was the first admiral of the U.S. Navy.

Farrar Drive
3000 W in Douglas Park

Edwin T. Farrar was a commissioner of the West Park District from 1923 until he died on November 29, 1925.

Farrell Street
1200 W, from 2600 S to 3062 S

William V. Farrell was a subdivider in Bridgeport in 1872.

Farwell Avenue
6900 N, from 1122 W to 7360 W*

Farwell Avenue Circle Drive
6900 N in Loyola Park

John Villiers Farwell (1825-1908), a Chicago dry goods merchant who gave

John Villiers Farwell, 1825-1908

Marshall Field his start, was a man of such honesty that the city's aldermen once fired him.

At the age of twenty, he landed a job as recorder of the city's Common Council proceedings. Whatever the aldermen said, he dutifully wrote down. The aldermen were horrified. "He tried to be grave," according to an 1868 account in a volume called *Biographical Sketches of the Leading Men of Chicago*. "But he could not. His sense of the ludicrous got the better of his prudence. He could not refrain from making the City Fathers read in the paper as they sounded in the chamber. The town was entertained, but what was fun to the town was mortification to the Councilmen, and decapitation to the reporter." Farwell was fired.

John Farwell was born on a New York farm. When he was still a boy, his family moved to Ogle County, Illinois. There he was awarded a scholarship and attended Mount Morris Seminary, where the wealthy boys kept their distance. "He brought the odors of the field to the school room," one Chicago historian has noted. "The aristocracy of clothes

disdained association with the aristocracy of brains." But Farwell was not cowed. He walked among his fellow students thinking to himself how one day he would "buy them all without missing the money."

He eventually made his fortune running a series of highly successful dry goods stores, including one in 1861 with young Marshall Field as his junior partner.

In the Civil War, Farwell helped organize the Board of Trade Regiment for the Union Army. He also donated land and money to the YMCA, personally held religious services for prisoners in Bridewell Prison, and helped found the Illinois Street Mission, designed to assist wayward "saloon boys."

In 1891, Farwell retired from active business, wealthy enough, as he had once promised, "to buy them all."

Federal Street
60 W, from 300 S to 5458 S*

This street runs smack into a federal office tower that stands on the site of Chicago's old U.S. Courthouse, usually called the Federal Building. The old fourteen-story building, designed by Henry Ives Cobb, was constructed in 1905 and torn down in 1965. Its iron was sold to a South Side scrap dealer and some of its stone was sold for use in the North Shore suburbs as a bulwark against the waters of Lake Michigan.

Felton Court
362 W, from 1130 N to 1156 N

Charles E. Felton was superintendent of the Bridewell, the house of correction built in Chicago in 1871. Felton, who ran the prison in the 1870s and 1880s, introduced the idea of prison labor. Inmates manufactured bricks.

A second possibility for this street is Captain J.O. Felton, a real estate developer in 1857.

Horse sculpture by Ludivico di Luigi (1986) in the plaza facing Financial Place just outside the Midwest Stock Exchange.

G. Lane

Ferdinand Street
460 N, from 1600 W to 5470 W*

Ferdinand Fleetwood was the son of Stanley H. Fleetwood, a partner from 1856 to 1868 in one of the largest real estate firms in Chicago--Ogden, Fleetwood & Co. His partner was William B. Ogden, Chicago's first mayor.

Fern Court
418 W, from 1700 N to 1760 N

Named for the plant.

Field House Circle
1200 W in Sherman Park

This Chicago Park District street runs alongside the Sherman Park fieldhouse on the South Side.

Field Plaza Drive
1200 S in Grant Park

This street runs alongside the Field Museum of Natural History.

Fielding Avenue
518 W, from 7700 S to 7858 S

Named for William Fielding, a South Side realtor and subdivider in 1869.

Fifth Avenue
1 S at 2800 W to 912 S at 4948 W*

In order to attract business, this street, formerly named Colorado Avenue, was renamed Fifth Avenue—after the famous street in New York City.

Fillmore Street
1100 S, from 1300 W to 5958 W*

Fillmore Street (Pvt.)
1100 S, from 5600 W to 5758 W*

Named after Millard Fillmore (1800-1874), the thirteenth president of the United States, who served from 1850 to 1853.

Financial Place
156 W, from 300 S to 1000 S

This street begins alongside the Midwest Stock Exchange and continues for several blocks south from the financial district of downtown Chicago.

Fitch Avenue
7132 N, from 2400 W to 7342 W*

Joseph H. Fitch was an attorney who did work for A.S. Coyle, a real estate developer with the firm of National City Realty.

Fletcher Street
3132 N, from 820 W to 6974 W*

The Fletcher brothers—Isaac, Japhet, and Abraham—were immigrants from England and building contractors in the years immediately following the Chicago Fire of 1871. They specialized in cut-stone buildings.

Flournoy Street

700 S, from 1200 W to 5574 W*

Formerly known as Oregon Avenue, this street was named after Lafayette M. Flournoy, who was a real estate subdivider of the Near West Side in 1857.

Ford Avenue

658 W, from 2200 S to 2242 S

Thomas Ford (1800-1850), the Democratic governor of Illinois from 1842 to 1846, is best remembered for having saved the state's credit rating. At a time when tax revenues were too meager to meet the interest on the state's debt, Ford pressured foreign bond holders to advance money to complete the Illinois and Michigan Canal and then used the canal's shipping tolls to pay off the debt.

Ford added to his fame when he called out the state militia to preserve order in western Illinois after an anti-Mormon mob in Carthage murdered Mormon prophet Joseph Smith and his brother Hyrum.

Born in Fayette County, Pennsylvania, Ford was a Chicago municipal judge in the 1830s, and later served as a justice of the Illinois Supreme Court. But in his final years, he fell on hard times and was almost bankrupt when he died of tuberculosis.

Ford City Drive (Pvt.)

7700 S, from 4000 W to 4800 W

This street leads to the Ford City Shopping Center, which stands on the site of an aircraft engine plant operated by the Ford Motor Company in World War II.

Foreman Drive

9500 S in Calumet Park

Henry G. Foreman was a commissioner of the South Park District from 1902 to 1912.

Forest Avenue

300 E, from 9150 S to 13570 S*

Some historians say this street was named for Joseph K.C. Forest, who was Chicago's city clerk from 1873 to 1875 and who once wrote for the *Chicago Daily News.*

Forest Glen Avenue

5032 W at 5270 N to 4400 W at 6252 N

A village by the name of Forest Glen, centered at Peterson and Cicero avenues, was annexed to Chicago in 1889. Its forest was once the hunting grounds for the Potawatomie Indians. This street, which takes its name from the village, also marks the southern boundary of a Cook County forest preserve.

Forest Preserve Avenue

3200 N at 8900 W to 4400 N at 6800 W

This street runs along the southern edge of the Indian Boundary Golf Course, once a part of the Cook County forest preserve system.

Forestview Avenue

8750 W, from 4422 N to 4674 N

This street affords a view of the Cook County forest preserves that line the banks of the Des Plaines River.

Fork Drive

1000 N in Humboldt Park

This street creates a fork in Humboldt Drive in the park.

Notre Dame Church (1887-92) at 1336 W. Flournoy Street, built by French Catholics on the Near West Side.

G. Lane

Forrestville Avenue
532 E, from 4300 S to 13452 S*

Forrestville was a hamlet on the South Side in the 1850s near what is now Hyde Park. This street runs through the old village.

Foster Avenue
5200 N, from 853 W to 10000 W*

Foster Drive
5200 N in Lincoln Park

Foster Place
5200 N, from 7100 W to 7162 W

John H. Foster (1796-1874), a doctor and landowner, came to Chicago because his brother was killed by a drunken soldier. Bad luck for the brother; good luck for Chicago.

Foster was born in Hillsboro, New Hampshire, and became a surgeon in the Black Hawk War. In about 1835, his brother, an army officer stationed in Chicago, was shot and killed while trying to reprimand a drunken soldier. Foster came to town to take charge of his brother's extensive real estate holdings, and he never left.

Foster took a deep interest in public school education and for more than fifteen years was a member of the Chicago Board of Education and the Illinois State Board of Education. He donated $1,000 to the city to establish a fund for medals for exemplary grammar school students.

When he was 78, Foster was killed on Division Street when he was thrown from his carriage and landed on his head.

Francis Place
2156 N at 2600 W to 2022 N at 2790 W

John R. Francis (1866-1910) was the editor of a Chicago-based intellectual journal, *The Progressive Thinker,* which he founded in 1889. Francis was a great believer in spiritualism and predicted that one day a technological means would be invented for communicating with the dead.

Francisco Avenue
2900 W, from 7558 N to 10256 S*

Named after San Francisco, California.

Franklin Street
300 W, from 1156 N to 416 S*

Franklin Boulevard
500 N, from 3020 W to 3558 W

Benjamin Franklin (1706-1790) was a scientist, author, publisher, diplomat, and a leader of America's Revolutionary generation.

Fremont Street
900 W, from 1500 N to 3956 N*

Fremont Street (Pvt.)
900 W, from 2300 N to 2358 N

General John Charles Fremont (1813-1890) was an American explorer, politician, and soldier. He explored the frontier West and, in 1856, was the first presidential candidate of the Republican Party.

Front Avenue
438 E at 11300 S to 260 E at 12126 S*

This street fronts the Illinois Central Railroad tracks in the Pullman neighborhood.

Frontenac Avenue
550 W, from 6000 S to 6026 S

Louis de Buade (1620-1698), Comte de Frontenac et Palluau was a controversial governor of the New France colony in North America, a planner of French westward expansion, and a commander of French forces against the Iroquois and the English colonies in the 1690s. He encouraged the explorations of Jolliet, Marquette, and LaSalle.

Frontier Avenue
648 W, from 1500 N to 1558 N

This street name reflects Chicago's importance in the days of Fort Dearborn as a frontier post for westward expansion.

Fry Street
840 N, from 928 W to 1556 W*

Colonel Jacob Fry was a commissioner of the Illinois and Michigan Canal in 1843.

Fuller Street
2900 S, from 1300 W to 1516 W*

H.H. Fuller, a contractor in 1888, built many homes on the North and South Sides of Chicago.

A second possibility is Elam Fuller, a subdivider in about 1830.

Fullerton Avenue
2400 N, from 700 W to 6538 W*

Fullerton Drive
2400 N in Lincoln Park

Fullerton Parkway
2400 N, from 301 W to 658 W

Alexander N. Fullerton (1804-1880), a lawyer, real estate investor, and lumber merchant, lived the comfortable life of a man born to wealth. Fullerton's father was a bank president in Chester, Vermont, and the young Fullerton attended the exclusive Middlebury College in Connecticut. Graduating from Litchfield Law School in Litchfield, Connecticut, he came to Chicago in 1833 and began a law practice with Grant Goodrich. He invested in local real estate and, while the city boomed, stockpiled his riches. He also opened a lumber yard in 1838 on North Water Street.

Fullerton traveled a great deal to France, Italy, and Germany and was active in Whig and then Republican politics.

Fulton Street
300 N, from 500 W to 5968 W*

Fulton Market
300 N, from 640 W to 1248 W

Fulton Boulevard
300 N, from 3000 W to 3558 W

Alexander N. Fullerton, 1804-1880

Fulton Drive
300 N in Garfield Park

Robert Fulton (1765-1815), an American inventor, canal engineer, and painter developed the world's first commercially successful steamboat, the *Clermont*, on the Hudson River in 1807.

G

Gale Street
4926 N, from 5358 N . . . 5358 W to 5456 W

This street was probably named for Abram Gale, a real estate developer who built the first two brick stores on Randolph Street. He also developed the community of Galewood on 320 acres of land in what is now a part of the North Austin neighborhood. His wife opened the first millinery goods store in Chicago.

A second possibility is that this street was named for Stephen Francis Gale (1812-1905), who opened what may have been Chicago's first book and stationery store in 1835. He was also a real estate promoter and once headed the Chicago Fire Department.

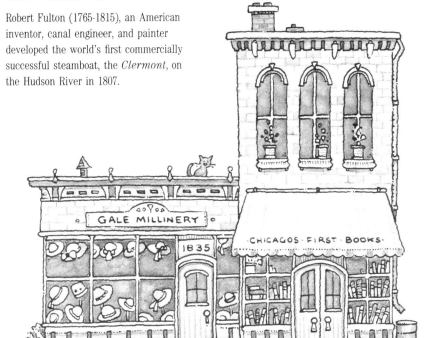

St. Basil Church (1925) on Garfield Boulevard at Honore reflected the faith and the economic rise of the Catholic community in Englewood.
A. Kezys

Garfield Boulevard
5500 S from 378 E to 2321 W

Garfield Drive
5900 S in Washington Park

Garfield Square Drive
512 N from 3600 W to 3624 W

President James A. Garfield (1831-1881) was nominated for the presidency of the United States in Chicago in 1881 and was assassinated that same year. He was shot by a disappointed office seeker who wanted to be made the U.S. consul to France. Garfield was the twentieth president of the United States.

Garland Court
70 E from 1 N to 322 N

The Michigan Stove Company named this street after their brand name: the Garland Stove. The Garland Building, built in 1915 with an addition in 1925, is on this street.

Garvey Court
69 W from 200 N to 234 N

The city council named this street after E. Garvey, president of E. Garvey and Company, 325 Wells Street.

Geneva Terrace
600 W from 2200 N to 2482 N

Named for Lake Geneva, Wisconsin, a popular nineteenth-century resort for Chicago's wealthy, which continues to be a summer and weekend haven for Chicagoans today.

Genoa Avenue
814 W from 8700 S to 9928 S*

Named for Genoa, Italy, the birthplace of Christopher Columbus.

George Street
2900 N from 800 W to 7158 W*

This street probably honors Sam George, said to have killed the last bear in downtown Chicago on October 6, 1834.

Two less likely possibilities are that the street was named by John Noble, an early Chicago settler, for King George III (1738-1820) or for St. George the dragon slayer. *See St. Georges Court.*

Germania Place
1536 N from 100 W to 118 W

German immigrants owned land in this part of town and named the street in honor of their homeland and the Germania Club, built in 1889 at Clark Street and Germania Place.

Gettysburg Street
5200 N from 5400 W to 5528 W

Civil War persons and places were a source of many street names in Chicago, and this street commemorates one of the war's most decisive and bloodiest battles. Union forces led by General George Meade defeated General Robert E. Lee's Confederate forces at Gettysburg, Pennsylvania, on July 1 to July 3, 1863. *See Meade Avenue.*

Giddings Street
4732 N from 2000 W to 6356 W*

L.R. Giddings was a prominent real estate investor in the mid-1880s. This street runs through one of his developments.

Gilbert Court
700 W from 8406 S to 8478 S

James K. Gilbert, a real estate developer and homebuilder, was particularly active after the Chicago Fire of 1871. Alone and with Robert C. Givins, of the firm Gilbert and Givins, he created several developments on the South Side. *See Givins Court.*

Giles Avenue
300 E from 3100 S to 3858 S

Lieutenant George L. Giles was a black officer of the 9th Infantry Regiment who was killed in World War I.

Givins Court
720 W from 8502 S to 8556 S

Robert C. Givins was a subdivider and home builder in the late 1800s. He dreamed of living in a castle, and in 1886 he built an "Irish Castle" overlooking Longwood Drive at 103rd Street in the Beverly neighborhood. It was modeled after a castle he had seen on the River Dee in Ireland. This street runs through a subdivision which Givens developed with James K. Gilbert.
See Gilbert Court.

Gladys Avenue
332 S from 700 W to 5574 W*

Gladys was a granddaughter of Sivert Tobias Gunderson, a Norwegian who immigrated to Chicago in 1848 and owned boats, traded in grain and lumber, and operated a sawmill. The family business, S.T. Gunderson & Sons, Homebuilders, developed large tracts of land in Chicago and named a number of streets for relatives. Haskins Avenue was named for one Gunderson granddaughter, while Langley Avenue was named for another relative.

Glenlake Avenue
6100 N from 932 W to 7818 W*

John L. Cochran, a real estate promoter who developed the community of Edgewater, named this street for Glen Lake, New York. Many Chicago land developers were from back East, and they named many streets for Eastern towns, resorts, lakes, and other points of interest.

Glenroy Avenue
1428 W from 10700 S to 10858 S*

This street is named for a narrow valley in the northwest of Scotland, famous for its "parallel roads," a geological formation running for about eight miles along what once was an ancient lake.

The Irish Castle, built by Robert C. Givins at 103rd and Longwood Drive in 1886, home of the Beverly Unitarian Church since 1942.

C.R. Childs, courtesy G. Schmalgemeier

Glenwood Avenue
1400 W from 4900 N to 7136 N

This street runs through a North Side area that once had many narrow, wooded valleys or glens, hence the name.

Goethe Street
1300 N from 86 E to 754 W*

Named for Johann Wolfgang von Goethe (1749-1832), perhaps the greatest of German poets. He was also a novelist, dramatist, and scientist. This part of the North Side was settled by German immigrants in the 1850s and 1860s.

The *Goethe Memorial* by Hermann Hahn, dedicated in 1914, in Lincoln Park at Diversey.

G. Lane

Goodman Street
5000 N from 5600 W to 5726 W

This street was most likely named for Charles Goodman of Ohio, a Union captain and quartermaster in the Civil War who was stationed at Camp Douglas, a prison camp for 18,000 Confederate soldiers on Cottage Grove Avenue between 31st and 33rd Streets. He kept the camp's books and improved conditions for the prisoners. After the war Captain Goodman settled in Chicago and worked in the real estate business.

A less likely possibility is that the street was named for James B. Goodman, another real estate man who flourished after the Civil War.

Gordon Terrace
4182 N from 632 W to 948 W*

G.H. Gordon was a real estate subdivider with the firm of Simon and Gordon, and this street is in one of the areas that he developed.

Governors' Parkway
400 N from 3400 W to 3564 W

The first capital of the Great Northwest Territory, which included Illinois, Indiana, Ohio, Michigan, and Wisconsin, was called Governors' Place and was located in Vincennes, Indiana. Vincennes, founded by a French Canadian explorer, Francois-Marie Bissot, Sieur de Vincennes, was founded around 1731 and served as the capital of the "new Indian Territory" from 1800 to 1813.

Grace Street
3800 N from 600 W to 8356 W*

This street was named for Grace Gurnee, daughter of land developer and Chicago Mayor Walter S. Gurnee. He served as mayor from 1851 to 1853.

Grady Court
1400 W from 2800 S to 2860 S

T.J. Grady, a subdivider, developed this area of Bridgeport.

Graham Court
48 E from 1334 N to 1350 N

Named for Ernest Robert Graham (1866-1936), a prominent Chicago architect and protégé of Daniel Burnham. Graham was Burnham's principal assistant in overseeing the World's Columbian Exposition of 1893, and he later helped D.H. Burnham & Company achieve national prominence. Following Burnham's death in 1912, Graham carried on Burnham's architectural practice first as Graham, Burnham & Company and, after 1917, as Graham, Anderson, Probst and White. Under Graham's leadership, this practice became one of the largest and most prominent in the United States, designing scores of major structures all over the country.

Grand Avenue
530 N at 558 E to 2420 N at 7194 W

This avenue was a muddy Indian trail called Whiskey Point Road in the 1860s. Its present name is said to have been inspired by Col. Thomas J.V. Owen, Chicago's first town president, elected in 1833, who said, "Chicago is a grand place to live." *See Owen Avenue.*

Grant Place
2232 N from 400 W to 558 W

Named for General Ulysses S. Grant (1822-1885), the eighteenth president of the United States, who served from 1869 to 1877. Oddly enough, Hiram Ulysses Grant was his given name, but he came to be called U.S. Grant in 1839 after his name was incorrectly transcribed on his application for West Point. He never corrected the error.

This short street runs along the north side of Grant Hospital in the Lincoln Park neighborhood.

Granville Avenue
6200 N from 940 W to 4358 W*

The land developer John L. Cochran (see Balmoral Avenue) probably named this street for Granville, New York. Some people claim, however, that the street was named for the North Side subdivider Granville Bates, or for one of the city's earliest school teachers, Granville Temple Sproat.

Navy Pier, formerly Municipal Pier, Grand Avenue at Lake Michigan; opened in 1916. This photo c. 1921.

Courtesy G. Schmalgemeier

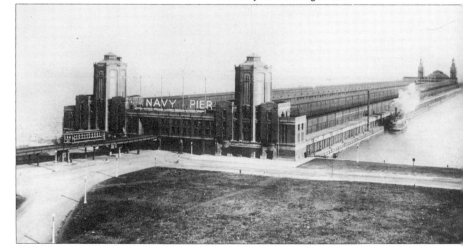

Gratten Avenue
1054 W from 3000 S to 3088 S

Despite the misspelling, Irish landowners in this area are believed to have named this street for Irish statesman Henry Grattan (1746-1820), who led the Irish parliamentary opposition to union with Britain.

Green Street
832 W from 830 N to 12930 S*

This street was named for Captain Russell Green, an Illinois militia officer from Chicago in the 1840s, or for land developer William Green, a partner in the firm of Sampson and Green in about 1881.

Green Bay Avenue
3400 E from 8300 S to 13558 S*

Named for Green Bay, Wisconsin.

Greenleaf Avenue
7034 N from 1222 W to 7358 W*

Luther Greenleaf, a North Side land developer, was a member of the Rogers Park Land and Loan Company in 1873, and the Ravenswood Land Company in 1868. *See also Touhy, Pratt, Lunt, Morse, Leland, and Kedzie streets.*

Greenview Avenue
1500 W from 800 N to 7656 N*

Named after Greenview, Illinois, a town located fifteen miles north of Springfield.

Greenwood Avenue
1100 E from 4212 S to 13300 S*

Greenwood Avenue (Pvt.)
1100 E from 13314 S to 13352 S

This avenue was named for Mississippi's Choctaw Indian Chief Greenwood LeFlore (1800-1865), or for William M. Greenwood, a lawyer and Chicago real estate developer in the 1840s.

Gregory Street
5530 N from 1400 W to 8758 W*

Named for St. Gregory's Church, which is located on this street at the northeast corner of Paulina Street.

Grenshaw Street
1132 S from 540 W to 4538 W*

(source unknown)

Gresham Avenue
3534 W from 2900 N to 3068 N

Walter Q. Gresham (1832-1895) was a Civil War general and a friend of President U.S. Grant. It was Grant who appointed him a federal judge in Chicago. Later, as postmaster general, Gresham reduced the postage for a letter from three cents to two cents in 1883. Although periodically considered presidential timber by the Republican Party, Gresham's highest position was that of U.S. secretary of state in 1893.

Walter Burley Griffin Place
10432 S from 1600 W to 1756 W

This short street celebrates a local architect who helped to plan the capital of Australia.

Walter Burley Griffin (1876-1937) was born in Maywood, studied and worked in Frank Lloyd Wright's studio in Oak Park, designed many Chicago area homes, and designed the landscape for Northern Illinois University in DeKalb. In 1912 he won a competition to plan Canberra, the new capital of Australia. This street has several houses that Griffin designed.

Grove Street
222 W from 1600 S to 2296 S

John P. Grove was a South Side land developer in about 1889.

Walter Burley Griffin, 1876-1937
Courtesy *Chicago Sun-Times*

Groveland Park (Pvt.)
3350 S from 600 E to 660 E

Groveland Park was a small, elegant South Side community developed after the Civil War in the Douglas neigborhood where Stephen A. Douglas, the U.S. senator from Illinois, had his home. The community, from which the street takes its name, featured a grove of trees. See also Oakenwald Avenue and Douglas Boulevard.

Grover Street
4900 N from 5620 W to 5749 W

Grover Cleveland (1837-1908) was the twenty-second and twenty-fourth president of the United States, serving from 1885 to 1889 and from 1893 to 1897.

Gullikson Road
7000 W from 6142 S to 6270 S*

Harry D. Gullikson developed the land through which this street runs.

Gunnison Street
4832 N from 754 W to 7152 W*

This street probably was named for Frederick A. Gunnison, a land developer with the firm of Wadsworth and Howland. The street runs through one of the firms's subdivisions.

A less likely possibility is that the street was named in honor of Captain John Williams Gunnison (1812-1853), a soldier and explorer who made a survey of Lake Michigan in 1841. Captain Gunnison surveyed Georgia and then the lake region of the North and Northwest. He was killed and his body mutilated by Indians in Utah.

H

Haddock Place
220 N from 76 E to 214 W

Haddock Place was named either for Alderman Edward Hadduck or for Charles G. Haddock, a lawyer and real estate promoter around 1871.

Charles G. Haddock saw opportunity when the Chicago Fire destroyed much of the city. He started a land title search company and did big business in the confusion after the fire. His company motto: "accuracy and dispatch."

Ald. Edward Hadduck, who served on the city council from 1838 to 1839, was a hotelier, a shrewd real estate investor, and a relative by marriage to Daniel Webster. His name was spelled with a "u," but given the kind of man he was, he probably never would have mentioned the error in the street name. When Hadduck died in 1881, he was eulogized as "reticent about his own affairs . . . .He took life easy and minded his own business strictly." So how might he have gotten a street named in his honor? He owned a part of the Loop before it was the Loop.

"I must say," one friend said upon Hadduck's death, "a man who lived a quieter or more unobtrusive life I never knew."

Hadduck had a premonition that he'd die at the age of 70. He did.

Haddon Avenue
1132 N from 1500 W to 5540 W*

Named for Haddon Hall, a medieval mansion in Derbyshire, England, the seat of the dukes of Rutland.

Haft Street
6300 N from 6344 W to 6374 W

John Haft was an early Chicago coal dealer in the firm of Habner and Haft.

Haines Street
1100 N from 800 W to 860 W

John C. Haines was the city's eighteenth mayor (1858-1860) and a Republican. Born in Deerfield, New York, Haines came to Chicago when he was seventeen years old and later became a partner in the first large flour mill in Chicago.

Before becoming mayor he was an alderman.

During Haines' term as mayor, the city council provided the first acreage for what would become Lincoln Park, the city's population pushed past 100,000, the first horse-drawn streetcars were run on State Street between Randolph and Twelfth, and from 1855 to 1860 Chicago public school enrollment almost tripled.

But history will best remember Haines for his connection to the nickname of "cops" being used to describe policemen. Under Haines, police wore a short blue coat, a blue navy cap with a gold band, and a brass star.

The police are said to have been nicknamed "coppers," after the mayor, who was familiarly referred to as "Copper Stock" Haines because of his speculations on the stock market. Others contend that the name "cops" is derived from "constables on patrol."

Hale Avenue
1900 W at 10301 S to 2100 W to 11858 S*

Revolutionary War patriot Nathan Hale (1755-1776) was hanged by the British as a spy. At the gallows he said, "I only regret that I have but one life to lose for my country."

Halsted Parkway
754 W from 6124 S to 6530 S

Halsted Street
800 W from 3766 N to 12960 S

William H. and Caleb O. Halsted were Philadelphia bankers who helped finance Mayor William B. Ogden's real estate ventures. The two brothers visited Chicago only once and eventually foreclosed on much of their Chicago property, but not before Ogden made a financial killing.

Halsted Street was originally called First Street, then Dyer Street, in honor of Charles Volney Dyer, an abolitionist who helped thousands of slaves along the underground railway.

In its very earliest days, it was known as "Egyptian Road" and wound its way south to the downstate territory known as "Little Egypt." Then, in the early 1900s, part of the street became known as "Migration Mile" because of the many immigrant groups settled along it. A tourist on Halsted might have seen men haggling in the open-air market of Maxwell Street, another person selling Mexican ice cream from a pushcart, and live lambs straining on tethers outside a Greek grocery.

Hamilton Avenue
2100 W from 7318 N to 10658 S*

Hamilton Avenue (Pvt.)

2130 W from 3900 S to 3950 S

This avenue is believed to honor Richard J. Hamilton, who was probably the first lawyer in Chicago in 1831. He was also the first circuit court clerk of Cook County and a Chicago real estate developer.

There is a possibility, however, that the avenue was named for Alexander Hamilton (1757-1804), the first U.S. secretary of the treasury.

Hamlet Avenue

1448 W from 11000 S to 11230 S

Named after a small village in Morgan Park on the city's far South Side, formerly known as Hamlet. The village may have taken its name from the play by William Shakespeare, but more likely it was called Hamlet because it was, indeed, a hamlet, a little village. Hamlet Avenue today runs alongside I-57.

Hamlin Avenue

3800 W from 6354 N to 11458 S*

Hamlin Boulevard

3800 W from 270 N to 424 S

This street was probably named for L.M. Hamlin and Family, early Chicago landowners, who sold their land to developer Edward J. Lewis.

It also might have been named in honor of Hannibal Hamlin (1809-1891), who was vice president of the United States during Lincoln's first term but dropped from the ticket on Lincoln's second time around.

Hampden Court

442 W from 2600 N to 2778 N

Named after Hampden, Massachusetts, by the real estate developer John S. Wright (1815-1874). Wright, who came to Chicago in 1832, spent his own money to build the city's first school building in 1837. *See Wrightwood Avenue.*

Harbor Avenue

3428 E from 9100 S to 9378 S

Named for and located near Calumet Harbor.

Harbor Drive

400 E from 151 N to 170 N

So named because of its proximity to the Monroe Street harbor on Chicago's lakefront.

Harding Avenue

3932 W from 6258 N to 11058 S*

This street may have been named for William Harding, a nineteenth-century Chicago real estate developer.

It may also have been named for Frederick Harding, a Civil War captain who developed land in Chicago in 1872. He organized the first company of Union soldiers in Chicago.

Harlem Avenue

7200 W from 7558 N to 6459 S*

Probably named for the community of Harlem, now Forest Park and River Forest. The little community also lent its name to the Chicago, Harlem and Batavia Railway, a steam railway line that ran from the West Side of Chicago through Oak Park and Harlem to Batavia in the 1880s.

Harper Avenue

1501 E from 5100 S to 9412 S*

William Rainey Harper (1856-1906) graduated from college at the age of fourteen and later, as the first president of the University of Chicago, helped to forge the future of this now-famous university. As an educator he held positions at various schools and colleges across the country, including the Baptist Union Theological Seminary in Morgan Park, then a separate village in what is now the Southwest Side of Chicago. Harper was invited to Chicago by John

William Rainey Harper, 1856-1906

D. Rockefeller, and he came on the condition that there would be complete freedom of teaching and a commitment to research.

Harper assembled a stellar faculty, quickly established a library, and was well known for his ability to get large donations from Chicago and New York businessmen.

A less likely possibility is that this avenue was named for William Harper, a nineteenth-century master carpenter and builder in Chicago.

Harrison Street

600 S from 85 E to 5574 W*

William H. Harrison (1773-1841) was the ninth president of the United States, serving only thirty-two days before he died.

Hart Street

1926 W from 400 N to 430 N

Hartland Court

1744 W from 500 N to 544 N

C. Hart was a land developer of this West Town area in 1888.

Hartwell Avenue

132 E from 6614 S to 6670 S

E.A. Hartwell was a land developer in the 1870s.

Harvard Avenue

326 W from 6300 S to 12658 S*

Harvard University, in Cambridge, Massachusetts, is the oldest university in the United States. Founded in 1636, it was named for John Harvard (1607-1638), who bequeathed the school his 400-volume library and half of his estate.

Haskins Avenue

1734 W from 7716 N to 7760 N

This street was named for Gladys Haskins, a granddaughter of S.T. Gunderson, an early Chicago subdivider. *See also Gladys Street.*

Hastings Street

1332 S from 1200 W to 2200 W*

Hiram Hastings was an early Chicago settler.

Haussen Court

3900 W from 3000 N to 3122 N

Frederick Haussen was a contractor, builder, subdivider, a member of the board of trustees of Jefferson Township, and a twenty-three year member of the Chicago public school board. Born in Prussia in 1830, he immigrated to the United States in 1850 and came to Chicago in 1852. He once owned most of the land through which this street runs.

Hawthorne Place

3442 N from 500 W to 598 W

Named for Nathaniel Hawthorne (1804-1864), the American author, who wrote *The Scarlet Letter* and other literary works.

Hayes Avenue

6532 N from 6644 W to 7058 W*

Samuel Snowden Hayes was a pre-Civil War Democrat who opposed slavery. Born on Christmas Day, 1820, in Nashville, Tennessee, Hayes was the son of a physician. A descendent of two old American families, his maternal grandfather was a founder of Princeton College. Other relatives included Samuel F.B. Morse, inventor of the telegraph, and Sidney Breese, a U.S. senator from Illinois.

Hayes' mother, Mary Snowden, died when Samuel was eight. His father died in 1837, poisoned with arsenic by a servant. Oddly enough, Hayes went to work in a drugstore in Louisville, Kentucky, learned the drug business, and then set out for the prairie lands. He sold drugs in Shawneetown, Illinois, for two years before he decided to practice law.

Admitted to the bar in 1842, Hayes lived for a while in downstate Mount Vernon, then in Carmi. In 1846 he was

Looking east on Hawthorne Place from Evanston Avenue (Broadway) c. 1910.

C.R. Childs, courtesy G. Schmalgemeier

elected to the Illinois legislature, a defiant White County Democrat among the ruling Whigs.

In 1851, Hayes moved to Chicago. He was a great friend of Senator Stephen Douglas, Illinois' leading Democrat, but he opposed Douglas's efforts to repeal the Missouri Compromise. A few years later Hayes spoke out forcefully against a move to bring Kansas into the Union as a slave state.

Although critical of the Lincoln administration, Hayes bucked many of his fellow Democrats by speaking out against slavery and backing the Union cause in the war. Despite this opposition within his own party, he felt the Democrats could exist without the institution of slavery.

Hayes Drive
6300 S in Jackson Park

Hayford Street
7544 S from 3700 W to 3936 W

John F. Hayford (1868-1925), a civil engineer, became director of the College of Engineering at Northwestern University in 1909.

Haynes Court
1316 W from 2810 S to 3052 S

William A. Haynes was a builder who once owned the land through which this street runs.

Hazel Street
842 W from 4200 N to 4554 N

Named for the shrub.

Heath Avenue
2322 W from 1300 S to 1338 S

Monroe Heath (1827-1894) was a California gold prospector who became Chicago's twenty-fourth mayor, serving from 1876 to 1879.

After a short and apparently unsuccessful stint as a forty-niner, Heath

came to Chicago and turned to painting buildings. In February, 1851, he began manufacturing dry colors and selling paint materials. His business burned down in 1870 and again in 1871, but Heath kept rebuilding. When he was elected alderman in 1871, he ran on the "fireproof ticket."

Heath was elected mayor in a rather strange way. In 1875 the City Council passed an order calling for an election of city officers under the new General Incorporation Act. Unfortunately, the order didn't mention the office of mayor. Nonetheless, city officials held an election, and a new mayor, Thomas Hoyne, was elected. But incumbent H.D. Colvin refused to give up his office. The dispute went to court and a special election was ordered. That's when Heath was elected to run the city.

In 1877, Heath's first full year as mayor, labor strikes prompted angry crowds onto the streets of Chicago. The man who restored order, however, was not Heath but Gen. Joseph T. Torrence, who commanded the Illinois National Guard. Torrence subdued the strikers and got the credit for it, along with a much longer street named in his honor.
See Torrence Avenue.

During Heath's term, the stockyards, an increasing nuisance, were pushed out of the city. An ordinance required new slaughterhouses to be built outside the city. They were. But the city later annexed those lands.

After serving as mayor, Heath left politics and moved to Arlington Heights.

Henderson Street
3334 N from 1212 W to 7040 W*

A.H. Henderson was a real estate developer who laid out a subdivision at the eastern end of this street in 1886.

Although this is less likely, it's also possible that the street was named for Charles Mather Henderson, an early Chicago merchant, or for Colonel Richard Henderson, an early Chicago settler.

Henry Court
2100 N from 2768 W to 2784 W

This street was probably named for Louis E. Henry, a developer of this community. But it could also have been named for General James D. Henry, who fought in the Black Hawk War, or for American statesman Henry Clay (1777-1852), a Kentucky congressman, senator, and secretary of state.

Hermione Street
6300 N from 6326 W to 6368 W

From Greek mythology, the daughter of Menelaus and the beautiful Helen of Troy.

Hermitage Avenue

1732 W from 7748 N to 9034 S*

Hermitage Avenue (Pvt.)

1732 W from 3900 S to 3950 S

"The Hermitage" was the Tennessee home of President Andrew Jackson. He was buried on the grounds of his estate, located east of Nashville.

Hermosa Avenue

1600 W at 10827 S to 1928 W at 11451 S

Named for Hermosa Beach, a city in southwestern California.

Hiawatha Avenue

4522 W at 6005 N to 6128 W at 7142 N

Hiawatha was the Indian hero of Longfellow's poem of the same name. The name means "he makes rivers." The historic Hiawatha of the 1500s helped form an organization of Indian tribes, the Iroquois.

Hickory Avenue

860 W from 1006 N to 1359 N

Hickory Creek was a meeting place for Chicago settlers in the early nineteenth century.

Higgins Avenue

4834 N at 5400 W to 5750 N at 7834 W

Van H. Higgins (1821-1893), who came to Chicago in 1837, was a lawyer, a land developer, and a judge of the Superior Court of Chicago. He was a charter member of the Chicago Historical Society.

Higgins Road

5800 N at 8401 W to 6100 N at 9200 W

This former Indian trail may have been named for F. Higgins, who, as early as 1834, owned the land through which this road runs.

All Saints Episcopal Church (1882-84) on Hermitage at Wilson Avenue in the Ravenswood neighborhood.

G. Lane

Van H. Higgins, 1821-1893

Highland Avenue

6330 N from 1400 W to 7286 W*

This street was probably named for the North Shore town of Highland Park. Or maybe it was so named because, viewed from its eastern end, it ran up to higher ground as it went west toward Ridge Avenue.

Hill Street
1100 N from 152 W to 350 W

Named for James Madison Hill, born in Maine in 1825, who became a land developer in Chicago.

Hillock Avenue
1100 W from 2500 S to 2947 S

Charles Hillock was a real estate developer and an alderman (1886-1888) of a South Side ward along the South Branch of the Chicago River.

Hirsch Street
1400 N from 2200 W to 5958 W*

Clemens Hirsch was an alderman (1881-1883) of a North Side ward along the North Branch of the Chicago River.

Hobart Avenue
5750 N from 6452 W to 6970 W

H.M. Hobart, born in 1851 in New York State, was a Chicago land developer. He subdivided the land through which this street runs in 1874.

Hobbie Street
1100 N from 600 W to 666 W

Albert G. Hobbie was a land developer in the 1840s.

Hobson Avenue
1700 W from 2048 N to 2064 N

In 1863 Union General Edward Henry Hobson (1825-1901) trailed notorious Confederate General John H. Morgan and his "Morgan's Raiders" for 900 miles before capturing 575 of Morgan's men in Ohio.

Hoey Street
964 W from 2702 S to 2712 S

This very short street was subdivided by the developer Thomas Hoey in 1854.

Holbrook Street
6100 N from 6200 W to 6368 W

Captain William B. Holbrook headed one of the Chicago Y.M.C.A. companies organized to fight in the Civil War.

Holden Court
25 E from 36 N to 2036 S*

This street honors an alderman who put Mrs. O'Leary in the history books.

Charles C.P. Holden (1827-1905) was a Chicago alderman from 1861 to 1872, during which time he worked to extend the city's water system and improve its streets and sewers. He also urged the use of lake tunnels to bring fresh water to the city.

Before joining Chicago's Common Council, Holden was an examiner of lands for the Illinois Central Railroad. He was a Cook County commissioner and one of the first commissioners of the West Park Board.

Perhaps most significantly, Charles Holden was president of the Common Council at the time of the Chicago Fire of 1871. It was his investigation that determined that the fire "began at O'Leary's barn at 8:45 p.m."

Holland Road
321 W at 8700 S to 46 W at 9074 S

This road ran through an area settled by Dutch immigrants.

Hollett Drive
6800 S in Marquette Park

R.P. Hollett was the attorney for the South Park District from 1899 to 1908.

Holly Avenue
1630 W from 2000 N to 2044 N

Named for the Christmas bush.

Hollywood Avenue
5700 N from 934 W to 4458 W*

Subdivider John L. Cochran, who was born in Sacramento, California, named this avenue for Hollywood, California. *See Balmoral Avenue for more on Cochran.*

Homan Avenue
3400 W from 1556 N to 11658 S*

Homan Boulevard
3400 W from 1 N to 160 N

Joseph Homan was a contractor and home builder with the firm of Homan & Brown & Company from 1873 to 1888.

Homer Street
1948 N from 1530 W to 5174 W*

Named for Homer, the Greek epic poet, author of the *Iliad* and the *Odyssey*, who probably lived in Asia Minor before 700 B.C.

Homewood Avenue
1800 W from 10930 S to 11506 S

Named for the south suburb of Homewood, Illinois.

Honore Street
1828 W from 7352 N to 11858 S*

Henry Hamilton Honore (1824-1916), a Chicago real estate developer, helped establish Chicago's parks and boulevard system.

Of French ancestry, Henry Honore was in the wholesale hardware business in Louisville, Kentucky, before coming to Chicago in 1855. This is why some historians credit him with naming Ashland Avenue, which ran through his subdivision, after Henry Clay's home in Kentucky.

Honore's daughter, Bertha, married Potter Palmer, of Palmer House fame, and she became Chicago's leading socialite in the late 1800s.

Henry Hamilton Honore tomb in Graceland Cemetery.

G. Lane

But it was Henry Honore's work in developing the city's parks that established his place in Chicago history. Referring to those accomplishments, Daniel Burnham said of Honore, "wherever his hand appeared, there has been big, broad development, . . . he has ever looked into the future."

Hood Avenue
6150 N from 1200 W to 7754 W*

This street was named for either David Hood, a Chicago landowner who lived on Ridge Avenue in 1847, or for Robert Hood, a land developer who lived in Cicero in about 1873.

Hooker Street
800 W from 932 N to 1258 N

Joseph Hooker (1814-1879) was a Union general in the Civil War.

Hopkins Place
8900 S from 2000 W to 2136 W

Named for J.W. Hopkins, a land developer in the 1880s, associated with the firm of Pryor and Hopkins.

Hortense Avenue
6334 N from 7408 W to 7762 W

Hortense de Beauharnais was the son of Josephine de Beauharnais, the wife of Napoleon Bonaparte. Josephine had two children, including Hortense, from a previous marriage before she married Napoleon.

Houston Avenue
3024 E from 8000 S to 13448 S*

Named for Sam Houston (1793-1863), frontier hero and president of the Republic of Texas before its annexation to the United States. He played a major role in the Mexican-American War and was instrumental in the annexation of Texas.

Howard Street
7600 N from 1306 W to 7761 W*

Howard Ure (1896-1984) was a director of the Howard Avenue Trust and Savings Bank in 1922. He was a director, and for a while a vice president, of the North Shore National Bank of Chicago from 1953 to 1973. Ure's family donated the right-of-way on Howard Street to the city.

Howe Street
634 W from 1144 N to 2058 N*

Edward G. Howe was a land developer with the firm of Hambleton & Howe. In 1888 the firm subdivided the Near North Side area through which this street runs.

Howland Avenue
8800 S from 2100 W to 2148 W

Named for George Howland (1824-1892), superintendent of Chicago's public schools from 1881 to 1885.

Hoxie Avenue
2600 E from 9600 S to 13700 S*

John R. Hoxie, who settled in Chicago in 1838, was a wealthy cattle man and a railroad builder. He was vice president of the Union Stock Yard National Bank from 1866 to 1867.

Hoyne Avenue
2100 W from 7546 N to 11160 S*

Hoyne Avenue (Pvt.)
2100 W from 3900 S to 3950 S

In the Land of Lincoln, Thomas Hoyne (1817-1883) is better remembered for besting old Abe in a trial than for the three months in 1876 when he served as the disputed mayor of Chicago.

Hoyne was the newly appointed United States attorney for the district of

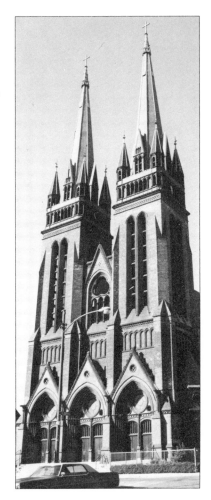

Illinois in 1853 when, in his first case, he prosecuted a mail robber. Abraham Lincoln defended the accused, but Hoyne won the case. The victory secured Hoyne's legal reputation.

A self-made man, Thomas Hoyne was born to a poor family in New York City and was orphaned at the age of thirteen. Going west to Chicago in 1837, he got his first public job, working for the clerk of the circuit court for $10 a week. In 1840 Hoyne was elected city clerk and drew up the city's first Thanksgiving Day proclamation. Later he was elected or appointed as a justice of the peace, U.S. attorney, U.S. marshal, and, finally, mayor of Chicago.

Hoyne was elected mayor in May, 1876, at a mass meeting of 40,000

St. Paul Catholic Church (1897-99) on Hoyne at 22nd Place in the Heart of Chicago neighborhood.

G. Lane

Chicago citizens. As mayor, he abolished the city's practice of borrowing money on certificates, a move credited with placing the city's credit rating on solid ground.

But on July 12, 1876, after Hoyne was in office for only three months, a special election was held and Monroe Heath was elected mayor. The circuit court had ordered the special election, ruling Hoyne had not been properly elected.

Although they were once adversaries in the courtroom, Hoyne and Lincoln were personal friends. When Lincoln was slain, Hoyne was part of the escort that brought the body to Chicago to lie in state. Hoyne himself died in a train crash while traveling to Niagara Falls.

Hoyt Avenue

2253 W from 3228 S to 3262 S

This avenue probably was named for Henry W. Hoyt, a developer of the land in this vicinity. It might, however, have been named for Dr. Homer Hoyt, a Chicago economist and real estate writer.

Hubbard Street

430 N from 122 E to 2458 W*

Gurdon S. Hubbard (1802-1886), an early fur trader and business tycoon, was called "Pa-pa-ma-ta-be" or "The swift walker" because of his distinctive and vigorous stride. Hubbard came to Fort Dearborn from Montreal for the first time in 1818. He was just sixteen years old and indentured with John Jacob Astor's American Fur Company. He wore a buckskin shirt and carried a knife and a tomahawk. He let his hair grow long and wore a blanket, Indian fashion.

On leaving Astor's employ after four years, Hubbard went into trade for himself, establishing inland posts from Chicago to the Ohio river. He became one of the most prosperous men in the country. In 1834 he closed out his fur-trading venture and made his permanent home in Chicago. He was a town trustee, a state legislator, and a founder of St. James Episcopal Church.

Hubbard was Chicago's largest meatpacker for a while, and he owned the city's largest warehouse.

Hudson Avenue

435 W from 658 N to 3178 N*

Named for the English navigator Henry Hudson, who explored America from about 1607 to 1611. He discovered the Hudson River in 1610.

Humboldt Boulevard

3000 W from 1600 N to 2168 N

Humboldt Drive

3000 W in Humboldt Park

Baron Friedrich Heinrich Alexander von Humboldt (1769-1859) was a German scientist. Humboldt Park was named for the baron, and the street was named for the park. The real estate development firm of Hansbrough & Hess apparently came up with the name for the park. Established in 1869, the park spurred the growth of the entire Humboldt Park community.

Hunt Avenue

8818 S from 2000 W to 2052 W

Leander Hunt was a Chicago police captain who lost his arm to a shotgun blast during the Beer Riots of 1855. The Beer Riots erupted during the administration of Mayor Levi D. Boone.

Boone was a member of the Know-Nothing Native American Party, which opposed the political and social rights of recent immigrants. He opposed the right of immigrants to vote, to hold public office, and to drink beer.

In line with that thinking, Boone raised license fees and enforced the Sunday closings of taverns. The problem was that the new rules applied to beer houses but not to saloons that sold only whiskey. Boone was trying to make running a tavern so expensive that only "reputable" tavern keepers would remain in business. This didn't sit well on the predominantly German "Nord Seite" (North Side), where beer gardens abounded. The Germans rioted and were later joined by the Irish. In a clash with the mob, Hunt was shot and later awarded a city medal.

Huntington Street

6200 N from 6100 W to 6378 W

This street was probably named for Alonzo V. Huntington, the state's

attorney in 1840 who prosecuted the first murderer in Chicago. The defendant, John Stone, was hanged for murdering Mrs. Lucretia Thompson, a Chicago woman. See Lowe Avenue.

However, it is also possible that this street was named for Samuel Huntington (1731-1796), a Connecticut signer of the Declaration of Independence.

Hurlbut Street

5800 N from 6500 W to 6948 W

Most likely, this street was named for Horatio N. Hurlbut, a physician and land developer who came to Chicago in 1851 at age 45. A more remote possibility is that the street was named for Henry H. Hurlbut, author of *Chicago Antiquities* in 1881.

Huron Street

700 N from 448 E to 5967 W*

Named for Lake Huron, one of the Great Lakes. The Huron Indians lived along this lake. The word *huron,* meaning "uncouth wretch," was coined by the French.

Hutchinson Street

4232 N from 642 W to 5558 W

Charles L. Hutchinson (1854-1924) has been called the "Father of the Art Institute of Chicago," which he helped to found when he was just six years out of high school. He was named president of the Art Institute in 1882, when it was still housed in rented rooms at the southwest corner of State and Monroe Streets.

Hutchinson, who was elected president of the Board of Trade when he was thirty-four, was also instrumental in the creation of the University of Chicago and the World's Columbian Exposition in 1893. He once said, "The movement to establish the University of Chicago must succeed." In the thirty-four years he

Charles L. Hutchinson, 1854-1924

served as treasurer of the university, its assets ballooned to $54 million.

As a commissioner of the South Park District, Hutchinson lobbied for the creation of small parks and playgrounds throughout the city for the neighborhood children.

Hyacinth Street

6134 N from 6232 W to 6372 W

Named for the garden plant.

Hyde Park Boulevard

5100 S from 800 E to 1656 E

Hyde Park Boulevard

1700 E from 5100 S to 5558 S

Hyde Park Drive

1700 E in Jackson Park

These streets were named by Paul Cornell, the developer who founded the community of Hyde Park in 1861. Cornell chose the name Hyde Park because he wanted to create a community that would be as elegant as the Hyde Park in New York and the Hyde Park in London. *See Cornell Avenue.*

I

Ibsen Street

6900 N from 7200 W to 7654 W

Named for Henrik Ibsen (1828-1906), the Norwegian playwright.

Illinois Street

500 N from 597 E to 392 W

The "Ininiwek," of which "Illinois" is a corruption, were once a powerful Indian confederacy. The first part of Ininiwek, *inini*, was an Indian word for man. But French settlers pronounced it as *illini*. And the Indian plural for *inini* was *ininiwek*. But the French settlers substituted their own plural ending, *ois*. Hence the word: Illinois.

Imlay Street

6500 N from 6500 W to 7062 W

Gilbert Imlay (1754-1828) was the author of *A Topographical Description of the Western Territory of North America,* published in 1792. He was also a shady Kentucky land speculator who had to flee the country to escape his financial and legal problems.

Imlay was a political adventurer who once worked with the French on a plan to wrestle Louisiana from Spain. While in France, he fathered an illegitimate daughter and treated the girl's mother so poorly that she twice tried to kill herself.

Nevertheless, Imlay's book on North America was well received in his day.

Independence Boulevard

3800 W from 500 S to 1414 S

Independence Square

1348 S from 3728 W to 3758 W

Named for the Declaration of Independence, adopted July 4, 1776, by the Second Continental Congress in Philadelphia, Pennsylvania.

Indian Road

5200 W from 5730 N to 6380 N*

This road runs along the edge of what once was Chief Billy Caldwell's reservation, now a part of the Cook County forest preserves and the Edgebrook and Sauganash neighborhoods. *See Caldwell and Sauganash Avenues.*

Pilgrim Baptist Church (1890-91), a Chicago landmark building designed by Adler and Sullivan, on Indiana Avenue at 33rd Boulevard.

A. Kezys

Indiana Avenue

200 E from 1200 S to 13765 S*

Indiana Avenue (Pvt.)

200 E from 13240 S to 13260 S

Named for the state of Indiana.

Indianapolis Avenue

From 3600 E at 10000 S to 4044 E at 10576 S

Named for the city of Indianapolis, Indiana.

Ingleside Avenue
930 E from 4700 S to 13520 S

Ingleside Avenue (Pvt.)
930 E from 13100 S to 13174 S

Named for Ingleside, Illinois, located north of Chicago near Fox Lake. Ingleside was a popular summer resort for Chicagoans in the nineteenth century.

Institute Place
828 N from 200 W to 360 W

The Moody Bible Institute, founded by Dwight L. Moody in 1889, is located on this street. *See Moody Avenue.*

Ionia Avenue
4400 W at 6000 N to 6000 W at 7168 N*

Named for Ionia, Michigan. Ancient Ionia was an area of western Asia Minor settled by Ionian Greeks in the sixth and seventh centuries before Christ.

Iowa Street
900 N from 1800 W to 5968 W*

Iowa Street (Pvt.)
884 N from 516 W to 532 W

Named for the Hawkeye state of Iowa. The state derives its name from the Iowa River. The river, in turn, takes its name from a Sioux Indian word for "sleepy ones." The nickname Hawkeye honors the Sauk Chief Black Hawk.
See Blackhawk Street.

Irene Avenue
3120 W from 3200 N to 3242 N

Irene Gross was the granddaughter of Charles E. Gross, a developer who subdivided this area around 1860.

Iron Street
1426 W from 3300 S to 3560 S

Iron Street (Pvt.)
1350 W from 3600 S to 3854 S

This street was named for the "Iron City" of Pittsburgh, Pennsylvania, or for the iron mills in Chicago, or for one of Abraham Lincoln's favorite horses, Iron Grey.

Irving Avenue (Pvt.)
2221 W from 3900 S to 3950 S

Irving Park Road
4000 N from 610 W to 12600 W*

Irving Park Drive
4000 N in Lincoln Park

This road was an Indian portage trail between the Great Lakes and the Des Plaines River, which drains into the Mississippi. The road was named in honor of Washington Irving (1783-1859), the American author who wrote such works as *The Legend of Sleepy Hollow.* A village called Irvington, later named Irving Park, was settled near the road after a railroad station was established in the area. By the middle 1870s Irving Park was considered a stylish suburb.

Isham Avenue
6458 N from 7402 W to 7632 W

Dr. Ralph Nelson Isham (1831-1904) was the doctor who signed the commitment papers that sent Abe Lincoln's wife to a sanatorium.

Isham, one of the driving forces that led to the establishment of Chicago's medical community, first arrived in Chicago in the 1850s. He soon impressed the populace by performing a successful tracheotomy, then an obscure procedure, on the son of a minister. From then on his reputation grew.

In 1859 Isham helped found what would later become Northwestern University Medical school, and his family helped support and develop Passavant Hospital, now a division of Northwestern Memorial Hospital.

Dr. Ralph N. Isham, 1831-1904

The Moody Bible Institute on LaSalle Street at Chicago Avenue.

G. Lane

One of Isham's relatives, Edward Isham, established one of Chicago's oldest law firms, Isham, Lincoln and Beale (1872 to 1988). The firm included Robert Todd Lincoln, Abe's son, as a partner. When Robert had his mother committed for eccentric behavior, Dr. Isham signed the papers.

Jackson Boulevard
300 S from 88 E to 6000W

Jackson Drive
300 S in Grant Park

Named for Andrew Jackson (1767-1845), the seventh president of the United States, who served from 1829 to 1837. *See also Hermitage Avenue.*

James Street
5150 S from 2000 W to 2108 W

There are two legitimate possibilities for the source of this street name: William James, a member of the Chicago Board of Trade and a land developer in the middle 1800s; or Colonel Josiah James, who settled in Chicago in 1848, owned a lumber yard, and invested in real estate.

Jane Court
1620 W from 10000 S to 10012 S

(source unknown)

Janssen Avenue
1434 W from 2200 N to 4924 N*

Bernard Janssen, a real estate investor, served as an alderman from 1877 to 1879. His ward was located southwest of North Avenue and the lake shore.

Jarlath Street
7232 N from 2600 W to 7728 W*

St. Jarlath, who died between 540 and 550, was an Irish monk and bishop who founded a monastery near Tuam, Ireland.

Jarvis Avenue
7400 N from 1212 W to 7726 W*

R.J. Jarvis was a friend of Patrick L. Touhy and Philip Rogers, and he worked with them in establishing the community of Rogers Park. *See Touhy Avenue.*

Jean Baptiste Point DuSable
Courtesy DuSable Museum of African-American History

Homes in the Jackson Boulevard Historic District, the north side of Jackson east of Ashland.

G. Lane

Jasper Place (Pvt.)
1444 W from 3600 S to 3656 S

Named for Jasper County in the southeastern part of Illinois. The county was named for Sgt. William Jasper (1750-1779), a Revolutionary War hero who was killed in an assault on Savannah, Georgia, while trying to plant the colors of the 2nd South Carolina Infantry. This seemed to be his kind of thing: three years earlier he had replaced the flag after it was shot down at Fort Sullivan.

Jean Avenue
6024 W from 6700 N to 6898 N

Named after Jean Baptiste Point DuSable (1745-1818), the founder and first settler of Chicago.

Around 1778, DuSable (or DeSaible) settled in a cabin on Sandy Point on the north bank of the Chicago River, just east of what is now Michigan Avenue. DuSable was a black man, probably a

native of Haiti, and was described as well-educated and handsome. Although much of his life remains a mystery, he traded with the Indians from his cabin on the river and lived there until 1796.

DuSable, who apparently had French blood, is believed to have sailed from Haiti to New Orleans to establish a fur trade or to get supplies for his father, who owned a warehouse. From there he traveled up the Mississippi and Illinois rivers, lived for a while in the Peoria area, and in the late 1770s or early 1780s he built a house/trading post at the mouth of the Chicago River.

Information on DuSable is sketchy. One recollection written by August Grignon of Butte des Morts, Wisconsin, and later published by the Wisconsin Historical Society, reads: "My brother, Perish Grignon, visited Chicago about 1794 and told me that Point DeSaible was a large man, that he had a commission for some office, but for what particular office or from what government, I cannot now recollect. He was a trader, pretty wealthy, and drank freely. I know not what became of him."

DuSable and his wife and children were believed to have left Chicago for Peoria, later moving to St. Charles, Missouri, where he died at the home of a daughter in 1818. *See DuSable Street.*

Jefferson Street
600 W from 470 N to 1938 S

Named for Thomas Jefferson (1743-1826), the third president of the United States, who served from 1801 to 1809. When the settlement of Chicago was first platted in 1830, this street was the town's western border. *See Canal Street.*

Jeffery Avenue
2000 E from 9100 S to 13758 S*

Jeffery Boulevard
2000 E from 6700 S to 9058 S

Jeffery Drive
2200 E in Jackson Park

In all probability, this street was named for Edward T. Jeffery, general superintendent and chief engineer of the Illinois Central Railroad in 1877, and general manager of the railroad in the 1880s.

A remote possibility is that this street was named for the journalist John B. Jeffery, who came to Chicago in 1863 and joined the staff of the *Chicago Morning Post.*

Jensen Boulevard
5600 W in Columbus Park

Jens Jensen (1860-1951) was a Danish-born landscape architect who came to Chicago in 1886 and worked as a laborer with the West Park Commission. He eventually became superintendent of Humboldt Park, only to be fired in 1900 when he exposed the graft of a contractor. On a wave of municipal reform in 1907, Jensen was hired as the West Park superintendent and landscape architect. He helped redesign Humboldt, Garfield, and Douglas parks, and he created Columbus Park, through which his street runs. Jensen also designed the Lincoln Memorial Gardens in Springfield, Illinois.

Jerome Street
7534 N from 2518 W to 7742 W*

Benjamin M. Jerome was a cashier of the United States Express Company in Chicago in 1885. The street was named for him by the developers of Rogers Park.

Jersey Avenue
3200 W from 5600 N to 6126 N

This street takes its name from Jersey City, New Jersey, or from Jersey, one of the islands in the English Channel. In 1957 the people living on this stretch of what was then Kedzie Avenue felt their street needed a name that didn't make people think of factories, noise, and dirt. So they named it Jersey.

Jessie Court
2050 W from 400 N to 420 N

Despite the misspelling, this street may have been named for Jesse Whitehead, a Chicago landowner who sold his land to the development firm of Cochran & Baker in 1858. The street may, however, have been named for Jessie Fletcher, the daughter of Isaac Fletcher, another land developer.

Pope John Paul II Dr.
4300 S from 2400 W to 3158 W

See listing under "P."

Jones Street
2318 W from 2600 N to 2661 N

In all likelihood, this street was named for J.W.M. Jones, a developer of the land around this street. But there is an outside chance it was named for William Jones (1831-1886), originator of the "co-ed plan" for students at Northwestern University. William Jones taught at the Northwestern Female College from 1856 to 1869.

Jonquil Terrace
7700 N from 1402 W to 1742 W

Named for the jonquil, a Mediterranean bulbous herb with yellow or white clustered flowers.

Jourdan Court
812 W from 1900 S to 1942 S

(source unknown)

Julia Court
2142 N from 2700 W to 2718 W

(source unknown)

Julian Street
1450 N from 1600 W to 1758 W

Named for Julian S. Rumsey, Chicago's nineteenth mayor, who served from 1861 to 1862. He came to Chicago in 1835 to work in the grain business of his uncle, George Dole. In that job he was said to have helped load, by wheelbarrow, the first cargo of grain shipped from Chicago. Rumsey later became a charter member of the Board of Trade.
See Rumsey Avenue.

Juneway Terrace
7736 N from 1400 W to 1832 W

S.T. Gunderson began to subdivide this area in the month of June, and since it was located along the wayside of Evanston's Calvary Cemetery, he called it Juneway.

Junior Terrace
4323 N from 644 W to 854 W

The "junior" comes from Stockton Junior High School, which was first located on this street.

Justine Street
1532 W from 356 N to 12258 S*

This street honors either Justin Butterfield, an attorney for the Illinois Central Railroad; or Justine Coch, daughter of a real estate dealer; or Henry Wentworth Justine (1838-1927), a Civil War veteran and real estate dealer.

K

Kamerling Avenue
1332 N from 4000 W to 5540 W*

From 1893 to 1895, William L. Kamerling was the alderman of a ward southwest of North Avenue and the Chicago River.

Kanst Drive
(in Marquette Park)

Named for Frederick Kanst, who was superintendent of the floral and nursery departments for the South Park District greenhouses from 1873 to 1884. He was born in Magdeburg, Prussia, in 1847 and immigrated with his family to the United States in 1868, settling near Momence, Illinois.

Karlov Avenue
4100 W from 6360 N to 8656 S*

Karlov Avenue (Pvt.)
4100 W from 3924 S to 4164 S

Named for the town of Karlov, Hungary.

Kasson Avenue
4032 W from 4424 N to 4732 N

This avenue was named for either Mary Kasson, sister-in-law of Chicago's first mayor, William B. Ogden (*see Ogden Avenue*), or for the Kasson Indians in Minnesota.

Kearsarge Avenue
4152 W from 2900 N to 3018 N

The Union warship, the USS *Kearsarge*, which weighed 1,031 tons and carried eight guns and 162 men, sank the Confederate warship *Alabama* on June 19, 1864, off the coast of Cherbourg, France. Crowds watched the sea battle from the Normandy cliffs. The ship was named after New Hampshire's Mount Kearsarge. It is an Indian word that means "highest place."

Keating Avenue

4732 W from 6340 N to 8656 S*

William H. Keating (1799-1840) was a geologist and historiographer of Stephen H. Long's 1823 exploration of the headwaters of the Mississippi River. *See Long Avenue.*

Kedvale Avenue

4132 W from 6360 N to 8656 S*

(source unknown)

Kedzie Avenue

3200 W from 7559 N to 11476 S*

Kedzie Boulevard

3200 W from 2156 N to 2614 N

Many Chicago streets are named for the people, or for the relatives of the people who owned the land over which the streets run. Kedzie Avenue is one such street. Both Chicago and Evanston have Kedzie streets, both named for John Hume Kedzie (1815-1903).

Born in Stamford, Connecticut, Kedzie was the son of Scottish immigrants. According to family records, as quoted in *Chicago: Its History and Its Builders*, "No Kedzie is known to have been arrested as a violator of the civil law, to have been intemperate, or dependent on charity, or paid less than one hundred cents on the dollar, and none have reached the early years of adult life without having become a member of the church."

John Kedzie came to Chicago in 1847 as an attorney. Although licensed to practice law in New York, he thought there might be more opportunity for a lawyer in the growing city of Chicago. But as soon as he saw the real estate opportunities in town, he turned from his case files to building a real estate empire.

Kedzie developed parts of the North and West Sides and several suburbs, including Evanston, where he lived. In 1868, he and his partners formed the Ravenswood Land Company, and in 1869 they purchased and developed 194 acres near the Chicago and North Western Railroad tracks in the town of Lake

The *Illinois Centennial Monument* (1918) at Logan Square, where Kedzie meets Logan Boulevard. Column by Henry Bacon, reliefs by Evelyn Longman.

View. The land company's board of directors included Kedzie, Cyrus P. Leland, John P. Wilson, and Luther L. Greenleaf. By no coincidence, Kedzie, Leland, Wilson, and Greenleaf are all Chicago street names.

An outspoken critic of slavery, Kedzie helped organize the Republican Party in Illinois and served in the state legislature. He built a magnificent home in Evanston, which burned down in 1873. He built another magnificent home in Evanston, which burned in 1880. A diehard Evanston booster, he built yet another home there.

Keefe Avenue

524 E from 6830 S to 6876 S

Although Thomas P. Keefe owned the land over which this street runs, it was developed by another subdivider, who named the street for Keefe.

The Chicago Academy of Sciences building in Lincoln Park at Armitage, donated by Matthew Laflin in 1893.

Courtesy the Chicago Academy of Sciences

Keeler Avenue
4200 W from 6360 N to 8656 S*

Keeler Street (Pvt.)
4200 W from 3954 S to 4164 S

Named for Cyrus Keeler, one of Chicago's first constables. The city gave him a medal for bravery during the Beer Riots of 1855. *See Hunt Avenue.*

Keeley Street
1200 W from 2800 S to 3064 S

Named for Alderman Michael Keeley, who represented a South Side ward along the South Branch of the Chicago River from 1868 to 1870. He was president of the Irish American Club in 1884.

Keene Avenue
4700 W from 6200 N to 6258 N

Named for J. Keene, who was active in Chicago politics and was the recording secretary of the Irish-American Club in 1884.

Kelso Avenue
4134 W from 4600 N to 4756 N

This avenue was named for either John Kelso, a soldier at Fort Dearborn, or for Kelso, Washington.

Kemper Place
2332 N from 600 W to 658 W

This street runs through a subdivision laid out by William Kemper, a land developer in the 1870s.

Kenmore Avenue
1038 W from 1838 N to 6358 N*

Kenmore was the elegant colonial home in Fredericksburg, Virginia, of Colonel Fielding Lewis (1725-c.1782). Lewis' wife, Betty, was General George Washington's sister.

John F. Kennedy, 1917-1963

Kennedy, John F., Expressway
700 W at 400 S to 9200 W at 5800 N

Named for John Fitzgerald Kennedy (1917-1963), the thirty-fifth president of the United States, who served from 1961 until his assassination on November 22, 1963.

Kenneth Avenue
4432 W from 5958 N to 8656 S*

Named for Kenneth I and Kenneth II, kings of Scotland.

Kennicott Avenue
4240 W from 4500 N to 4728 N

This avenue was probably named for Robert Kennicott (1835-1866), a nationally renowned naturalist, traveler, and founder of the Chicago Academy of Sciences. He died on the banks of the Yukon River while on an expedition.

A less likely possibility is that this avenue was named for Dr. John A. Kennicott, the first settler of the Kenwood community on Chicago's South Side. *See Kenwood Avenue.*

Kennison Avenue
4500 W from 5000 N to 5046 N

David Kennison (1736-1852)—that's right, he died when he was 115 years old—was "Chicago's Revolutionary Hero" and the last survivor of the 1773 Boston Tea Party. Kennison fought at

Brandywine and Bunker Hill, and for nineteen months he was a prisoner of the Mohawk Indians. He narrowly escaped the Fort Dearborn Massacre, where he was serving as a private, when he was dispatched to Detroit for special duty.

At the age of seventy-five Kennison received his only war injury. He was wounded in the hand by grape shot in the battle of Sackett's Harbor and Williamsburg in the War of 1812. He outlived four wives, managed and lectured at a Chicago museum—where he was something of a celebrity—and was living on a meager $96-a-year pension at the time of his death. One newspaper dubbed Kennison "Chicago's Revolutionary Hero." He was buried with military honors in the city cemetery which is now a part of Lincoln Park.

Kenosha Avenue
4238 W from 2900 N to 3156 N*

Kenosha is a Chippewa Indian word for "pickerel." The street was named for the city of Kenosha, Wisconsin.

Kensington Avenue
11552 S from 100 E to 628 E

Kensington, possibly named for a section of London, was once a village in what is now the community of West Pullman. Kensington was founded in the 1850s. It had a population of 1,278 by 1883 and was annexed to Chicago in 1889.

Kenton Avenue
4600 W from 5858 N to 8656 S*

Simon Kenton (1755-1836) was a pioneer, hunter, Indian fighter, and friend of Daniel Boone. Kenton was said to have saved Boone's life in a fight with Indians.

Kentucky Avenue
4624 W from 4800 N to 4970 N

Named for the state. Although there is confusion over the exact meaning of this Indian word, it means something like "meadow land" or "prairies."

Kenwood Avenue
1332 E from 4700 S to 9364 S*

Dr. John A. Kennicott was the first settler of the community that came to be called Kenwood. He named his own estate "Kenwood" in honor of his mother's birthplace in Scotland, building his then-suburban retreat south of 43rd Street in 1856. In time, Kenwood had so many large homes that it was called the "Lake Forest of the South Side." Kenwood was annexed to Chicago in 1889.

Keokuk Avenue
4144 W from 4400 N to 4540 N

Keokuk (1790-1848) was a blue-eyed, part white, chief of the Sauk Tribe. He opposed Black Hawk's War in 1832. *See Blackhawk Street.*

Keota Avenue
5800 W from 6600 N to 6796 N

Keota is an Indian word. It possibly meant "the fire has gone out."

Kerbs Avenue
4724 W from 5626 N to 5767 N

Named for J. Kerbs, a Chicago pioneer and landowner in about 1858.

Kercheval Avenue
4600 W from 5700 N to 5798 N

Captain Gholson Kercheval was a sub-agent to Thomas J.V. Owen, the federal Indian Agent in Chicago in 1831. In a foreshadowing of later Chicago politics, Kercheval got his job through clout. He was Owen's brother-in-law. See Owen Avenue. Kercheval was captain of the Chicago militia, which was organized to protect the settlers from Indians, and he had a small trading post at Wolf Point, at the fork of the Chicago River. Wolf Point, by the way, was named for an Indian called "Moa-Way"--meaning "the wolf"—who lived there. In 1831 Kercheval was a charter member of the Cook County Board of Commissioners.

William D. Kerfoot, 1837-1919

Kerfoot Avenue
700 W from 8300 S to 8444 S

On the Wednesday after the Chicago Fire of 1871, pointy-bearded realtor William D. Kerfoot (1837-1919) hammered together a shack at Washington and Randolph streets, hung a sign that read, "All gone but wife, children and energy," and reopened for business.

That Bill Kerfoot, folks said, sure is some kind of optimist. But in the tradition of Chicago business tycoons, Kerfoot proved more savvy than optimistic. He obtained a map and set of plats of the city, and when Eastern speculators came looking for fire-sale bargains, he was there to greet them.

Kerfoot made millions of dollars from the fire. Chicago, in turn, rebuilt rapidly, partially because of Kerfoot's business contacts back East and abroad. Millions of dollars were invested in Chicago real estate by people who had never even seen the town. But they trusted Kerfoot.

He was born in Lancaster, Pennsylvania, the son of a socially prominent physician. He married a Kentucky woman, Susan B. Mooklar, and they had eight children, three of whom died in youth.

Kewanee Avenue

4200 W from 4700 N to 4756 N

Kewanee is a Chippewa Indian word for "prairie hen." There is also a Kewanee, Illinois.

Keystone Avenue

4032 W from 120 N to 6360 N*

Named for the Keystone state of Pennsylvania. It was called Keystone because of its central location among the original thirteen states. There were six states to the north of Pennsylvania and six states to the south.

Kilbourn Avenue

4500 W from 6156 N to 8656 S*

This avenue was named for Kilbourn, Wisconsin, located near the Wisconsin Dells.

Kildare Avenue

4300 W from 6360 N to 8656 S*

Kildare Boulevard (Pvt.)

4300 W from 4000 S to 4658 S

Named for County Kildare, Ireland.

Kilpatrick Avenue

4700 W from 6352 N to 8656 S

Kilpatrick Avenue (Pvt.)

4700 W from 7200 S to 7658 S

Union General Hugh Judson Kilpatrick (1836-1881), who led several cavalry assaults on Confederate troops at Gettysburg, originated the curious saying, "The cavalry can fight anywhere except at sea." *See Gettysburg Street.*

Kimball Avenue

3400 W from 1600 N to 6220 N

This street was probably named for Walter Kimbell, a landowner and subdivider who was said to have donated the ground for Kimball Avenue to the city.

A second possibility is that the street was named for Walter Kimball—the name spelled with an "a" as in the the street name—who was a charter officer in 1835 of Chicago's first bank, a branch of the Illinois State Bank.

Kimbark Avenue

1300 E from 4700 S to 9358 S*

Seneca D. Kimbark, who moved to Chicago from New York in the 1850s, was in the manufacturing and iron businesses. He was a charter member of the South Park District board of commissioners. While he was a commissioner, the board established Washington and Jackson parks and the grand boulevard known as the Midway. *See Midway Drive and Midway Plaisance.*

Kimberly Avenue

4700 W from 5000 N to 5094 N

Edmund S. Kimberly was elected one of the village's first trustees in 1833. He was also the clerk of the town meeting at which it was resolved that Chicago should incorporate. He voted for it.

Kingsbury Street

400 W from 400 N to 2082 N*

This street was probably named for E.S. Kingsbury or Col. Henry W. Kingsbury, real estate developers around 1833.

Kingsdale Avenue

4744 W from 5728 N to 5867 N

Richard J. Hamilton, a land developer, named this area for his parents' hometown, Kingsdale, Pennsylvania. The street takes its name from the real estate subdivision. *See Hamilton Avenue.*

Kingston Avenue

2524 E from 7300 S to 9356 S*

Paul Cornell, the founder of Hyde Park and other Chicago communities, was born in the state of New York and named this avenue for Kingston, New York. *See Cornell Avenue.*

Kinzie Street

400 N from 30 E to 5470 W*

Named for John Kinzie (1763-1828), one of Chicago's earliest settlers and probably the first Chicagoan to be pursued by the law.

Kinzie came to Chicago as a silversmith and fur trader and moved into Jean Baptiste Point DuSable's former house on the north bank of the Chicago River in 1804. That house was located just east of where Michigan Avenue is today.

In 1812, Kinzie was the subject of what was probably the first murder investigation in Chicago. While heading home from Fort Dearborn one day, he was followed by the fort's Indian interpreter, Jean Lalime, with whom he had a long-standing quarrel. When Lalime attacked him, Kinzie killed LaLime and then hid until officers at the fort determined it was "justifiable homicide."

Later that year, in August, Indians who respected and trusted Kinzie saved him and his family from the Fort Dearborn massacre.

A Chicago street is named for his wife Eleanor, and two streets are named for his daughter Ellen Marion Kinzie. *See Ellen Street and Marion Court.* Ellen was the first white child born in Chicago

(December, 1804), and she was the bride in the first Chicago wedding (July 20, 1823). Wolcott Avenue might have been named for Ellen's first husband, Dr. Alexander Wolcott.

Kinzua Avenue
5432 W from 6401 N to 6757 N

Kinzua Creek is in central Pennsylvania. Kinzua is an Algonquin Indian word for "the wild turkeys gobble."

Kiona Avenue
4250 W from 4600 N to 4738 N

Kiona is an Indian word; the meaning of which is uncertain. It may have been the name of a tribe.

Kirby Avenue
4660 W from 5800 N to 5867 N

Abner Kirby was a Chicago hotel owner and a partner in the Kirby & Carpenter Lumber Company, which was in business in about 1863.

Kirkland Avenue
4338 W from 2200 S to 8060 S*

This street probably was named for Scottish-born Alexander Kirkland, a commissioner of the city's Department of Public Buildings in 1879. It may have been named, however, for E.S. Kirkland, a real estate developer in the 1880s.

Kirkwood Avenue
4600 W from 6032 N to 6350 N

Arthur J. Kirkwood owned an early machinery dealership, A. J. Kirkwood & Co. He and his brother Thomas moved to Chicago from Oshkosh, Wisconsin, and bought the 13-year-old machinery company in 1872.

Knox Avenue
4632 W from 6350 N to 8656 S*

Revolutionary War General Henry Knox (1750-1806), a close adviser of General George Washington and a congressman, served as America's first secretary of war from 1789 to 1794.

Kolin Avenue
4332 W from 1564 N to 8656 S*

Kolin Avenue (Pvt.)
4332 W from 4500 S to 4658 S

Named for Kolin, Czechoslovakia.

Kolmar Avenue
4532 W from 6350 N to 8656 S*

Named for city of Kolmar (German) or Colmar (French), on the French-German border. The city has changed hands over the decades and is now a part of France.

Komensky Avenue
4032 W from 1200 S to 8656 S*

Komensky Avenue (Pvt.)
4032 W from 11301 S to 11459 S

John Amos Komensky—also Comenius—(1592-1670) was a Czechoslovakian educational reformer and religious leader.

Kostner Avenue
4400 W from 6361 N to 8656 S*

Kostner Avenue (Pvt.)
4400 W from 7200 S to 7658 S

Joseph Otto Kostner was a West Side alderman from 1917 to 1925.

Kreiter Avenue
3526 E from 9350 S to 9478 S

J.H. Krieter—the street name was misspelled—was a commissioner of public highways in Chicago from 1854 to 1859.

Kruger Avenue
4800 W from 4840 N to 4942 N

This street was named for either Herman F. Kruger, a North Side alderman from 1907 to 1909, or Ludwig Kruger, a real estate promoter in 1858.

L

Lacey Avenue
4700 W from 5762 N to 5772 N

In 1778 John Lacey (1755-1814), though only twenty-three years old, was made an American brigadier general in the Revolutionary War. After the war he became a justice of the peace and a member of the New Jersey state legislature.

La Crosse Avenue
4832 W from 6348 N to 6458 S*

Lacrosse is the French name for an Indian ball game. There is also a city of La Crosse, Wisconsin.

Lafayette Avenue
30 W from 5500 S to 12358 S*

This avenue was named for a man who Thomas Jefferson said had "a canine appetite for popularity and fame." Marie Joseph Paul Yves Roch Gilbert du Motier (1757-1834), Marquis de Lafayette, was a Frenchman who fought in the American Army during the Revolutionary War. He was a member of General George Washington's staff.

Laflin Place (Pvt.)
1500 W from 3612 S to 3656 S

Laflin Street
1500 W from 356 N to 12258 S*

Matthew Laflin (1803-1897), one of Chicago's first real estate tycoons, founded one of Chicago's earliest stockyards, its first bus service, and its first waterworks.

Born in Southwich, Massachusetts, Laflin came to Chicago in 1837 and began spending money with abandon. His dicey investments reaped a fortune. During the 1840s and 1850s, he paid $300 for 140 acres of land within the city. That property grew to be worth millions in his own lifetime.

When, in 1849, Laflin bought about 100 acres of prairie on the West Side near Madison and Ogden, many Chicagoans thought he had finally lost his mind. But Laflin just laughed. With a gambler's haste, he built barns, sheds, and cattle pens for a stockyard and a large three-story wooden hotel, the Bull's Head.

Two years later he started the city's first bus line along a plank road, which he also built, to transport people between his West Side hotel and the State Street markets. He erected a tollgate on the plank road where it intersected with Blue Island Avenue. He made money coming and going.

Laflin also helped to set up one of the first waterworks in Chicago by building a pine-log reservoir at Lake Street and the lake shore. Lake water was funneled into the reservoir and distributed via wooden pipes throughout the city.

The Chicago Academy of Sciences in Lincoln Park is housed today in a building donated by Laflin to the academy, the Matthew Laflin Memorial Building.

Lake Street
200 N from 234 E to 5968 W

This street was so named because it ran east all the way to Lake Michigan.

Lake Park Avenue
428 E at 2400 S to 1517 E at 5658 S*

This street runs just west of the shore-front Burnham Park, hence its name. It is also just west of the Illinois Central railroad tracks.

Lake Shore Drive
934 W at 5658 N to 2024 E at 6700 S

Lake Shore Drive
1000 N from 140 E to 250 E

Lake Shore Drive was named by Potter Palmer (see Palmer Boulevard), whose mansion at Schiller Street overlooked the Drive and Lake Michigan. It wasn't until 1946 that the entire length of this shoreline road was called Lake Shore Drive. Prior to that, the South Side stretch was called Leif Erickson Drive and the downtown stretch was called Field Drive.

Lakeside Place
4732 N from 748 W to 954 W

So named because of its close proximity to Lake Michigan. At one time, before the landfill for the the northern extension of Lincoln Park, this street ran all the way to the lake.

Lake Shore Drive
David A. Miller

Lakeview Avenue
400 W from 2400 N to 2750 N

This street takes its name from the community of Lake View, which grew up around the Lake View House, a three-story wooden hotel built in 1854. The hotel stood on the lake shore just south of Irving Park Road, and around it were the summer homes of wealthy Chicagoans. The town of Lake View was annexed to Chicago in 1889.

Lakewood Avenue
1300 W from 2036 N to 6934 N*

This avenue was named by the developer of Chicago's Edgewater community, John L. Cochran, after the town of Lakewood, New Jersey.

Lambert Avenue
4824 W from 5700 N to 5718 N

Named for the Englishman John Lambert, who wrote an account of his travels in Canada and the United States in about 1806.

Lamon Avenue
4900 W from 5480 N to 6458 S*

Lamon Avenue (Pvt.)
4900 W from 4300 S to 4374 S

Ward Hill Lamon (1828-1893) was Abraham Lincoln's law partner in Danville, Illinois, in 1852.

Landers Avenue
5000 W from 5900 N to 6246 N

This street was probably named for Paul Landers, a member of Father Damen's Holy Family Church. See Damen Avenue. Landers was a Chicago landowner in the 1850s.

Although less likely, the street might have been named for General Frederick West Lander (with no "s" on the end) (1821-1862), an explorer who trekked the West for railroad companies, wrote patriotic poems, and died in the Civil War.

Langley Avenue
700 E from 3900 S to 13399 S*

Langley Avenue (Pvt.)
700 E from 13101 S to 13383 S

This street was probably named for Esther Langley, a relative of real estate subdivider and landowner S.T. Gunderson. *See Gladys Avenue.*

Lansing Avenue
4900 W from 5700 N to 5890 N

Named for Lansing, Michigan, the state's capital.

Laporte Avenue
4932 W from 5459 N to 6458 S*

Laporte Avenue (Pvt.)
4932 W from 4300 S to 4332 S

These streets were named for either LaPorte, Indiana, or for the LaPorte family, early landowners in the area of the future West Side.

Laramie Avenue
5200 W from 5360 N to 6310 S*

This avenue may have been named for Peter Laramie, a French Canadian trader.

Larchmont Avenue
3932 N from 1800 W to 1942 W

Named after Larchmont, New York.

Larned Avenue
5232 W from 5200 N to 5358 N

Edwin C. Larned (1820-1884) was a Chicago lawyer, a pal of Abe Lincoln, and an orator renowned in his day for opposing slavery at every turn. "The right of a master to a slave is the right of power," Larned once said in a speech that was widely reprinted throughout the Northwest. "It is the right of the strong over the weak. It is might, not right." Larned was born in Providence, Rhode Island, and came to Chicago in 1847. He was tall, slender, and loquacious. He defended abolitionists in the courtroom and raised troops and provisions in Chicago for the Union cause. In 1861 President Abraham Lincoln named him U.S. district attorney for the Chicago region.

Although Larned was in Europe during the Chicago Fire of 1871, he returned to work with the Relief and Aid Society to help fire victims.

Larrabee Street
600 W from 658 N to 2158 N

This street was most likely named for the Larrabee family, which included Charles H. Larrabee, a Chicago city attorney in the 1840s; William M. Larrabee, secretary of the Galena and Chicago Union Railroad; and C.R. Larrabee, secretary of St. James Hospital in 1854.

LaSalle Drive
150 W to 60 E in Lincoln Park

LaSalle Drive
140 W from 316 N to 1724 N

LaSalle Street
140 W from 230 N to 12528 S*

Robert Cavalier (1643-1687), Sieur de La Salle, was a French explorer who passed through the Chicago area in 1682 and immediately saw its potential. While at the Chicago portage, which is inland from Lake Michigan, LaSalle said, "This will be the gate of the empire. The typical man who will grow up here must be enterprising. Each day as he rises, he will exclaim, 'I act, I move, I push.'"

LaSalle might have pushed too hard. Although he is credited with leading the first expedition to trace the Mississippi River, he was extremely difficult to get along with. While he was heading for Canada from Texas, his followers mutinied and killed him.

Las Casas Avenue
4924 W from 5658 N to 5698 N

Bartolome de las Casas (1474-1566) was a Spanish Dominican priest who was known as the Apostle of the Indies and the Protector of the Indians. He led a movement on behalf of the Indians in the West Indies, Peru, and Central America. He sought to ban Indian slavery and forced labor.

Latham Avenue
5000 W from 5434 N to 5464 N

Andrew J. Latham was a director of the Chicago Board of Trade in 1870.

Latrobe Avenue
5232 W from 5386 N to 6440 S*

Charles Joseph Latrobe (1801-1875) was a famous English traveler to America, a traveling companion to Washington Irving, and a best-selling author. In his book, *The Rambler in North America, 1832-1833*, Latrobe wrote of his 1833 visit to Chicago. Apart from Potawatomies and "land speculators as numerous as the sand," he wrote, "You will find horse-dealers, and horse stealers, rogues of every description, white, black, brown, and red, half-breeds, quarter-breeds, and men of no breed at all . . ."

Latrobe visited Chicago at a time when large numbers of Indians were gathered near town while a treaty was being negotiated to relocate them west of the Mississippi.

"The little village was in an uproar from morning to night, and from night to morning," he wrote. "During the hours of darkness, when the housed portion of the population of Chicago strove to obtain repose in the crowded plank edifices of the village, the Indians howled, sang, wept, yelled and whooped in their various encampments. With all this, the whites seemed to me to be the more pagan than the red men."

". . . The interior of the village was one chaos of mud, rubbish, and confusion," he wrote. "Frame and clapboard houses were springing up daily under the active axes and hammers of the speculators, and piles of lumber announced the preparation for yet other edifices of an equally light character."

What did Latrobe do for fun while in Chicago? " . . . we spent much of our time in the open air. A visit to the gentlemen at the fort, a morning's grouse-shooting, or a gallop on the broad surface of the prairie, filled up the intervals in our perturbed attempts at reading or writing indoors, while awaiting the progress of the treaty."

"I loved to stroll out towards sun-set across the river, and gaze upon the level horizon, stretching to the north-west over the surface of the Prairie, with innumberable objects far and near."

The treaty was forged after delays caused by cloudy skies, which the Indians felt were bad conditions for working on a treaty. But after the signing, Latrobe left town to continue his travels across America.

Lavergne Avenue
5000 W from 5158 N to 6458 S*

This street was named after the settlement of LaVergne, now a part of the suburb of Berwyn, Illinois.

Lawler Avenue
5032 W from 5490 N to 6443 S*

Named for Michael K. Lawler, a Union general in the Civil War.

Lawndale Avenue
3700 W from 6354 N to 11424 S*

Named for the West Side community of Lawndale.

Lawrence Avenue
4800 N from 748 W to 9100 W*

Lawrence Avenue
4800 N in Lincoln Park

Bradford A. Lawrence was a friend of Lazarus Silverman (1830-1909), a banker and subdivider. While the two were walking along together in Silverman's new Montrose subdivision, Silverman apparently said, "Let's call this Lawrence Avenue."

Lawrence-Wilson Drive
In Lincoln Park

This street in Lincoln Park joins Lawrence and Wilson Avenues.

Leader Avenue
5124 W from 5900 N to 6340 N

This street honors Billy "Sauganash" Caldwell, leader of the Potawatomie Indians in the early 1830s. *See Caldwell and Sauganash Avenues.*

Leamington Avenue
5132 W from 5332N to 6322 S*

Named for Leamington, England, a health resort on the Leam River. It is known for its mineral waters.

Leavenworth Avenue
5300 W from 5534 N to 5552 N

General Henry Leavenworth, who established an army post at Fort Leavenworth, Kansas, in 1827, was once stationed at Fort Dearborn.

At the southeast corner of Lawrence and Broadway, the Uptown National Bank building (1924), recently restored to its full beauty.

G. Lane

Looking south across the lagoon in Lincoln Park, 1988.

G. Lane

Leavitt Street

2200 W from 6510 N to 10658 S*

Leavitt Street (Pvt.)

2200 W from 3900 S to 3950 S

Named for David Leavitt, a New York banker, who was appointed a trustee of the Illinois and Michigan Canal in 1844. *See Canal Street.*

Leclaire Avenue

5100 W from 5368 N to 6450 S*

Antoine LeClaire was an Indian interpreter for the army at Fort Armstrong at Rock Island, Illinois. After a treaty with Black Hawk was signed in 1832, LeClaire bought land in Iowa for $150. He later sold it to a development group headed by Colonel George Davenport. Davenport, Iowa, now stands on LeClaire's land.

Lee Place

740 N from 2000 W to 2058 W

Charles Lee was among the first settlers in the Chicago area after the building of Fort Dearborn in 1803. His farm, known as "Lee's place," was located on both sides of the South Branch of the Chicago River and included parts of what is now Bridgeport. But his home was on the lakefront near the fort.

Legett Avenue

5145 W from 5972 N to 6388 N

The best bet is that this street was named for the journalist and abolitionist William Leggett (1801-1839), although the name is spelled differently. He lived in Illinois in his late teens.

Lehigh Avenue

5400 W from 6336 N to 7158 N

Named for Lehigh, Illinois. The name is derived from the Delaware Indian word *lechua*, meaning "fork in the river."

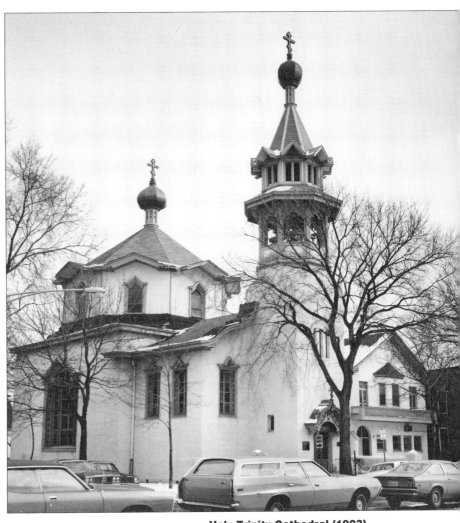

Holy Trinity Cathedral (1903), 1121 N. Leavitt Street, a Chicago landmark church designed by Louis Sullivan.

A. Kezys

Lehmann Court

600 W from 2700 N to 2736 N

Ernest J. Lehmann was born in the duchy of Mecklenburg, Germany, in 1849 and moved to Chicago sixteen years later. He worked as a bellboy, a bootblack, and a peddler, and in 1875 he founded the "The Fair" department store. It stood on the northwest corner of Adams and State Streets and became a part of the Wieboldt chain of stores in the 1960s. *See Marble Place.*

Leland Avenue

4700 N from 742 W to 8768 W*

Cyrus P. Leland was a member of the Ravenswood Land Company, founded in 1868, which developed parts of the Lake View and Ravenswood communities. He was also a member of the Rogers Park Building and Land Company. *See Touhy and Kedzie Avenues.*

Le Mai Avenue
5232 W from 6200 N to 6442 N

Joseph Le Mai's claim to fame in Chicago was that he bought the cabin of Chicago's first settler, Jean Baptiste Point DuSable, in 1796. He lived there with his Indian wife for eight years and then sold the cabin to John Kinzie, another early settler. *See Jean and Kinzie Streets.*

Lemont Avenue
5000 W from 5800 N to 6350 N*

This avenue was named for Lemont, Illinois. The word is French for "the mount."

Le Moyne Drive
1500 N in Humboldt Park

Le Moyne Street
1500 N from 1200 W to 5958 W*

John Le Moyne was a lawyer and congressman from Chicago in the late 1800s. Born in Pennsylvania in 1828, he moved to Chicago in about 1852. He served in Congress in the 1870s and was a founder of Chicago's Philharmonic Society and other organizations devoted to music.

Lenox Avenue
5124 W from 6100 N to 6358 N

This avenue may have been named for John Powell Lenox, a Chicago art collector who was born in New York in 1851. Most of his art works had Christ as their subject.

Leona Avenue
5150 W from 6200 N to 6404 N*

Named for Leona, Pennsylvania.

Leonard Avenue
5248 W from 5558 N to 5942 N*

The Rev. J.H. Leonard ministered to the sailors who lived or passed through Chicago in the 1850s. He was associated with Chicago's Bethel Chapel, then located near the lake and north of the Chicago River. From the chapel it was an easy walk to the vessels and boarding houses of the boatmen and sailors. Leonard was assigned to Chicago in 1854 by the Seamen's Friend Society of Cleveland, Ohio.

Leoti Avenue
4924 W from 6152 N to 7046 N

The origin of this street's name is something of a mystery. According to the files maintained by Chicago's Bureau of Maps and Plats, Leoti may have been the name of a white girl who was captured by Indians. Or, it may be an Indian word for "prairie flower."

Leroy Avenue
5200 W from 6200 N to 6424 N

Named for the city of LeRoy, New York.

Lessing Street
928 W from 800 N to 868 N

Named for Gotthold Ephraim Lessing (1729-1781), a German dramatist, critic, and philosopher.

Lester Avenue
5500 W from 4900 N to 4946 N

This avenue probably was named for Thomas Lester, an Englishman who served as a Union officer in a Chicago regiment in the Civil War and was killed in battle on May 15, 1864. He had settled in Chicago in 1833.

A second possibility is that the street was named for Thomas Lester, an early Chicago manufacturer.

Levee Street
2724 S from 1532 W to 1566 W

A levee, which is an embankment designed to restrain water and prevent flooding, once was located at one end of this street.

Lexington Street
728 S from 540 W to 5344 W*

The Battle of Lexington was fought April 19, 1775. It signaled the beginning of the American Revolution.

Leyden Avenue
200 E from 13700 S to 13796 S

Named for the city of Leyden in The Netherlands.

Liano Avenue
5256 W from 5200 N to 5276 N

Liano was an Indian word and perhaps meant "little."

Liberty Street
1344 S from 700 W to 742 W

The Liberty Bell, a symbol of American independence, was cast in London in 1752. In 1915, the Liberty Bell was exhibited in Chicago. It is now on display in the Independence National Historical Park in Philadelphia.

Lieb Avenue
5444 W from 5200 N to 5466 N

General H. Lieb, a Swiss immigrant in 1851, enlisted in Company B of the 8th Illinois Infantry during the Civil War. In 1865, he was promoted to brigadier general. In 1873, when he was forty-seven, Lieb was elected city clerk in Chicago. In 1880 he was appointed superintendent of the water office of the Chicago Board of Public Works.

***Lincoln, the Man* (popularly known as the *Standing Lincoln*) by Augustus Saint-Gaudens in Lincoln Park near North Avenue, dedicated May 31, 1926.**

G. Lane

Lightfoot Avenue
5924 W from 6600 N to 6758 N

This street was named for Lightfoot, Virginia. The city was named for an Indian chief.

Lill Avenue
2534 N from 800 W to 1456 W*

William Lill, an Englishman who walked to Chicago from Louisville, Kentucky in 1835, built what may have been Chicago's first brewery. In September of 1839, Lill and William Haas, financed by Chicago's first mayor, William B. Ogden, started their brewery. It produced about nine barrels of beer a week. In 1857, Lill, then in partnership with Michael Diversey, built a brewery that covered a whole city block. *See Diversey and Ogden avenues.*

Lincoln Avenue
164 W at 1800 N to 3551 W at 6374 N

Lincoln Street (Pvt.)
1900 W from 3900 S to 3950 S

Lincoln Park West
300 W from 1800 N to 2358 N*

Named for Abraham Lincoln (1809-1865), the sixteenth president of the United States, who served from 1861 to 1865. He was nominated for the presidency at a Republican Party convention in the Wigwam, a building located on the southeast corner of what is now Lake Street and Wacker Drive. Lincoln was a resident of Illinois and the first president not to come from one of the thirteen original colonies.

Lind Avenue
5300 W from 5200 N to 5324 N

Named after Sylvester Lind, a Scottish carpenter who settled in Chicago in 1837. He soon turned to real estate development and subdivided land in the area of Wacker Drive and Randolph Street. In the 1850s, Lind was a founder of the North Shore suburb of Lake Forest, home to many of Chicago's wealthiest businessmen. With some interruptions, he was the mayor of Lake Forest from 1868 to 1884.

Linden Place
3000 W from 2400 N to 2558 N

The linden is a medium-to-large tree requiring rich, damp soil.

Linder Avenue
5500 W from 5864 N to 6458 S*

This avenue most likely was named for Usher F. Linder (1809-1876), the attorney general of Illinois from 1837 to 1839. He was a Chicago lawyer from 1860 until his death.

Lipps Avenue
5300 W from 4804 N to 4892 N

William F. Lipps was a West Rogers Park alderman from 1905 to 1921.

Lister Avenue
1830 W from 2200 N to 2364 N

Walter Lister was born in England in 1832, and his family immigrated to America in 1840. He moved to Chicago to manufacture glue in 1855 and turned to real estate development in 1873. Lister married Margaret Bickerdike, the daughter of one of Chicago's biggest real estate subdividers, George F. Bickerdike. This street runs through a Bickerdike subdivision.

Nativity of the Blessed Virgin Mary Church (1957) on Lithuanian Plaza Court in the Marquette Park neighborhood.

G. Lane

Lithuanian Plaza Court
6900 S from 2400 W to 2758 W

Named in honor of the many Lithuanians who live in the Marquette Park neighborhood.

Lituanica Avenue
900 W from 3100 S to 3830 S

This street, which runs through the heart of Bridgeport's early Lithuanian community, commemorates a monoplane. Two Lithuanian-born Chicago aviators died when their monoplane, *Lituanica,* crashed on July 13, 1933, in a forest in Germany.

Stephen Darius and Stanley Girenas took off from New York City to race with fabled flier Wiley Post across the Atlantic. Without parachutes or a radio, the pair planned to fly on to Kaunas, Lithuania. Their only technological aid was an ice indicator strapped to the wing.

The plane, which Darius flew for the *Chicago Daily News* from 1929 to 1931, was purchased with donations from Lithuanian Americans. The fliers, both of whom lived on the South Side, apparently searched for hours for a safe landing place, which they never found.

Livermore Avenue
5520 W from 6200 N to 6260 N

Mary Livermore was a Civil War nurse in charge of military nurses in the West. A suffragist, she organized the Ladies' Northwestern Fair in 1863 for the aid of Union soldiers. It ran for two weeks and included exhibits, various goods for sale, and hot dinners.

Lloyd Avenue
1300 W from 2930 S to 3038 S

This street was named for either Henry Demarest Lloyd (1847-1903), chief editorial writer in 1880 for the *Chicago Tribune,* then owned by Joseph Medill; or for Alexander Lloyd (1805-1871), a lumberman and builder who served as mayor of Chicago in 1840 and 1841.

Lock Street
1500 W from 2800 S to 3084 S

So named because it runs by the Bridgeport Lock on the Illinois and Michigan Canal. *See Canal Street.*

Lockwood Avenue
5300 W from 5740 N to 6458 S*

Named for Samuel Drake Lockwood (1789-1874), a one-time Illinois secretary of state and Illinois supreme court justice (1825-1848).

Lockwood, described by his biographer, William Coffin, as "quiet and unobtrusive," was a teetotaler and forbade dancing and card playing in his house. Newton Bateman, then president of Knox College, said Lockwood's name was synonomous with "integrity and purity." Nonetheless, this respected Justice, who held strong anti-slavery sentiments and played an active role in organizing the Republican Party, was once mistakenly arrested for counterfeiting.

When Lockwood was a young man traveling on the Allegheny and Ohio Rivers, a banker had apparently convinced him and his traveling companions to exchange their dollars for freshly printed bills—which turned out to be phonies. Coincidentally, the sheriff who arrested Lockwood later appeared before the judge in Edwards County, Illinois.

Locust Street
900 N from 140 W to 424 W

Locust Street (Pvt.)
914 N from 436 W to 532 W*

These streets were named for the locust tree, native only to the United States and Mexico. The timber was valued for its use in log cabins, fenceposts, and ships' masts because of its durability and strength.

Logan Boulevard
2800 N at 2217 W from 2600 N to 3116 W*

Logan Square
2608 N from 3118 W to 3214 W

Union General John "Black Jack" Alexander Logan (1826-1886), three times an Illinois congressman and twice a senator, was the man credited with originating Memorial Day.

General Logan was twice wounded in battle and had a horse shot out from under him in the Battle of Belmont (as in Belmont Avenue). He believed passionately in the sanctity of the Union and was considered one of the most distinguished "volunteer soldiers" of his time.

It was General Logan who came up with the idea of Memorial Day to honor the dead of the Civil War. His idea became a reality on May 30, 1868.

Loleta Avenue
5826 W from 6600 N to 6860 N

This street was named for either Loleta, Pennsylvania, or Lolita Armour, the wife of meatpacker J. Ogden Armour.

London Avenue
5348 W from 4732 N to 4766 N

Named for London, England.

Long Avenue
5400 W from 5540 N to 6458 S

An early visitor to Chicago, Stephen H. Long (1784-1864), once observed, "the village presents no cheering prospects, as, not withstanding its antiquity, it contains but few huts, inhabited by a miserable race of men, scarcely equal to the Indians, from whom they are descended."

Long was an Ivy League man, educated at Dartmouth College. An engineer by profession, in 1816 he explored the country between the Missouri River and the Rocky Mountains. One of the highest peaks in the Rockies was named in his honor.

It was on an 1823 journey through Chicago that Long expressed his negative opinions about the city. "As a place of business it offers no inducement to the settler, for the whole amount of the trade of the lake did not exceed the cargoes of five or six schooners, even at the time when the garrison received its supplies from Mackinac."

Perhaps it was Long's other achievements that compelled Chicagoans to name a street in his honor. In 1817 he called attention to a 70-yard sandbar that obstructed the Chicago River's entrance to the lake. While employed as a civil engineer on the Baltimore & Ohio Railroad, he wrote the first treatise on railroad building ever published in this country. From 1837 to 1840 he was engineer-in-chief of the Western & Atlantic Railroad in Georgia, where he invented a new type of truss bridge which was widely used elsewhere. Near the end of his life he lived in Alton, Illinois. He died there on September 4, 1864.

Longmeadow Avenue
4930 W at 6384 N

The shortest street in Chicago, it runs a mere 31.6 feet.

Longwood Drive
2100 W at 8700 S to 2200 W at 11864 S*

This beautiful tree-lined drive runs alongside a wooded ridge that rises about 100 feet above current lake levels. Folklore has it that the wooded ravines here once served as a hideaway for horse thieves. Longwood Drive boasts the longest block in the city. Between 111th Street and 114th Place, a single uninterrupted block runs almost a half mile.

Loomis Boulevard
1400 W from 4700 S to 8656 S

Loomis Place (Pvt.)
1416 W from 3600 S to 3758 S*

Loomis Street
1400 W from 356 N to 12258 S*

Named for Horatio G. Loomis, an early Chicago settler, who was a charter director of the Chicago Board of Trade in 1848.

Loop Drive
500 E in Washington Park

This street forms a small loop in Washington Park.

Lorel Avenue
5332 W from 2458 N to 6458 S*

Although misspelled, this street's name may have been intended to honor the laurel tree.

Loring Avenue
5450 W from 5202 N to 5324 N

Malek A. Loring (1842-1907), who served in the Navy in the Civil War, settled in Chicago in 1868 to work as a day clerk at the Matteson House Hotel. By 1875 he was a part owner of the hotel. It was a six-story building and had 175 rooms in 1882, the year Loring and his partners sold it.

Longwood Drive, looking north from 95th Street, June 1926.

C.H. Childs, courtesy G. Schmalgemeier

Loron Avenue
5900 W from 6600 N to 6892 N

Lorin Graves—the street name is a misspelling—was an early Chicago settler who owned a cottage at what is now 31st and Cottage Grove. *See Cottage Grove Avenue.*

Lothair Avenue
2000 W from 11144 S to 11472 S

Named after Lothair I (795-855), a Frankish emperor and King of Italy.

Lotus Avenue
5432 W from 5558 N to 5458 S*

The lotus tree or bush is native to southern Europe and linked to the legends of Greek history. The lotus fruit was eaten by "lotus-eaters" and produced a dreamy laziness.

Louise Avenue
4900 W from 5814 N to 6324 N*

Named after Lake Louise in the Canadian Rockies of Alberta.

Lovejoy Avenue
5444 W from 5102 N to 5468 N*

This avenue was probably named for Elijah Parish Lovejoy (1802-1837), a martyr to the causes of free speech and abolition. Lovejoy, publisher of the anti-slavery *Alton Observer*, was killed by a mob in Alton, Illinois, in 1837 while trying to protect his printing press.

A less likely possibility is that this street was named for Owen Lovejoy, a Chicago settler in about 1851.

Lowe Avenue
632 W from 2400 S to 12943 S*

Samuel J. Lowe was an early Chicago constable and sheriff. Although born in England, Lowe was no Anglophile. And if somebody proposed the possibility of English superiority in Lowe's house, he might be shown the door. And yet, Lowe was said to have been a hospitable man.

A justice of the peace and two-term sheriff (1842 and 1844), Lowe was firm and cool-headed. He never backed down, but he never resorted to weapons. He was sheriff at a time when the Chicago jail was a log building and the state prison was at Alton.

Lowe was an easy-going and friendly man, but his job required that he witness the 1840 execution of John Stone, convicted of murdering a Chicago woman. In one early Chicago history book, it was noted, "The inner heart of Mr. Lowe would gladly have turned him aside from seeing the death agony, even while his high sense of duty led (him) to unflinchingly stand upon the scaffold."

Lowell Avenue
4332 W from 1600 N to 6360 N*

F.W. Lowell was the first teacher in the Andersonville School at Foster and Ashland Avenues in about 1861.

Loyola Avenue
6550 N from 1000 W to 1954 W*

Named for St. Ignatius Loyola (1496-1556), the founder of the Society of Jesus, known as the Jesuits. Both Loyola University and St. Ignatius Church are located close to this street in the Rogers Park neighborhood.

Lucerne Avenue
5100 W from 6054 N to 6066 N

Named for Lake Lucerne and the city of Lucerne in central Switzerland.

Ludlam Avenue
5470 W from 5200 N to 5464 N

Dr. Reuben Ludlam (1831-1899), a Chicago doctor who taught at Hahnemann Medical College, advanced theories on such matters as the peculiar odor of the breath. He also published essays entitled, "The Pulse" and "Capillary Bronchitis." Ludlam was a proponent of the principles of homeopathy and dean of the Hahnemann Medical College, where he had been a member of the faculty since 1859. He was also a member of the Chicago Relief and Aid Society, which came to the aid of fire victims after the fire of 1871.

Luella Avenue
2232 E from 7100 S to 13758 S*

George A. Springer (1815-1899), a Chicago real estate investor, at one time operated a boat line on the Mississippi River. His boat, the *Luella,* was the first successful passenger steamer to run between St.

Loyola University of Chicago, Lake Shore Campus in 1974. Mundelein College is at the upper right of the photo.
Loyola University of Chicago Archives

Louis, Missouri, and Cairo, Illinois. During the Great Flood of 1844, the *Luella* was the only ferry in operation between St. Louis and the Illinois side of the river, and Springer made a bundle. Four years later he moved to Chicago and began investing in real estate. *See Mendota Avenue.*

Lumber Street
401 W from 1800 S to 2374 S*

This street runs through what was once the lumber district in Chicago.

Luna Avenue
5532 W from 5880 N to 5458 S*

5600 W from 6200 N to 6316 N

Benjamin Lundy (1789-1839) was editor of an abolitionist newspaper, *The Genius*, in Lowell, Illinois.

Lunt Avenue
7000 N from 1110 W to 7760 W*

Lunt Avenue Circle Drive
7000 N in Loyola Park

Stephen P. Lunt was a member of the Rogers Park Building and Land Company, founded in 1873, which developed the community of Rogers Park. *See also Touhy, Pratt, Morse, and Greenleaf Avenues.*

Luther Street
2442 S from 2600 W to 2658 W

Martin Luther (1483-1546), the German cleric and religious philosopher, broke from the Roman Catholic Church and laid the intellectual groundwork for Protestantism.

Lyman Street
1028 W from 2900 S to 3098 S

This street was probably named for David B. Lyman, a Chicago lawyer and businessman, whose father was a minister in the Sandwich Islands. Born in 1840, Lyman eventually moved to Chicago, where he was a respected real estate lawyer and president of the Chicago Title & Trust Company in 1891.

A less likely possibility is that this street was named for Lyman Trumbull (1813-1896), a United States senator from Illinois. *See Trumbull Avenue.*

Lynch Avenue
5500 W from 5301 N to 5590 N

This avenue was probably named for Thomas Lynch (1749-1779), a signer of the Declaration of Independence. It could have been named, however, for a Chicago whiskey distiller, Thomas Lynch, who died in 1893.

Lyndale Street
2232 N from 2100 W to 4560 W*

Named after the community of Lyndale, located in this area in about 1867.

Lyon Avenue
628 E from 9300 S to 9434 S

John B. Lyon (1829-1904) came to Chicago in 1857, purchased a membership on the Chicago Board of Trade for $15, and got rich. He remained with the board for forty-six years, but he also invested in real estate.

Lytle Street
1242 W from 612 S to 1140 S

Union Brigadier General William H. Lytle (1826-1863) was a soldier and poet from Cincinnati. Lytle, whose poem "Anthony and Cleopatra" glorified love and war, was fatally wounded while leading a charge at the Battle of Chickamauga, Georgia.

M

MacChesney Court
72 E from 300 N to 340 N

(source unknown)

Mackinaw Avenue
3332 E from 8232 S to 13558 S

Mackinaw is the Chippewa Indian word for turtle.

Madison Avenue Park (Pvt.)
5046 S from 1200 E to 1380 E

Madison Street
Baseline N&S, from 100 E to 5968 W

Named for James Madison (1751-1836), the fourth president of the United States, who served from 1809 to 1817.

Magnet Avenue
5642 W from 5300 N to 5449 N

Named after magnetite, which attracts iron or steel.

Magnolia Avenue
1232 W from 1400 N to 6474 N*

Unlike local streets that are named after flowers and trees, Magnolia Avenue memorializes a Chicago tugboat captained by Joseph Gilson.

Gilson's bravery stood out among the tugboat captains in Chicago, "who were known and noted for their skill and courage all over the U.S." He was the "bravest of the brave," and was so in love with danger that he found it difficult to get men to work with him.

Gilson's story and that of the *Magnolia* are told in a pamphlet entitled "The Hero of the Chicago Fire." When the fire began on October 8, 1871, Gilson readied his tug to save his household belongings. But when he saw burning ships on the river and people stranded

along the lakefront, he hurried to save their lives.

"Indifferent to the danger," he lassoed a burning vessel that was headed toward a pier crowded with people and tugged it out of harm's way. He hauled boats full of people out to the safety of the lake. And he refused all offers of money for his service. As flaming warehouses and burning ships collapsed into the water, the *Magnolia* was the last to leave the mouth of the river.

The pamphlet goes on to say Gilson "belongs to that class of men who know of no fright, those men who only look upon danger when it ceases to be such." His only vice, the pamphlet says, was a love of publicity. On the first page of the pamphlet at the Chicago Historical Society is a handwritten inscription which reads: "Compliments of Capt. Jos. Gilson to Union Catholic Library."

Major Avenue
5700 W from 5858 N to 6458 S*

Dr. Laban Major was a founder of an early Chicago medical school, Bennett College of Eclectic Medicine and Surgery, established in 1868. He was also a trustee of the school and its president.

Malden Street
1300 W from 4400 N to 4758 N

The British Fort Malden, established in 1796 at the mouth of the Detroit River, was captured by the Americans in 1813.

Malta Street
1506 W from 9900 S to 10258 S

Named for the island of Malta in the Mediterranean Sea.

Mandell Avenue
5624 W from 6200 N to 6255 N

This street probably was named for E.B. Mandell, an early real estate developer of this far Northwest Side area.

Mango Avenue
5732 W from 1600 N to 5768 N*

Named for the tropical mango tree.

Manila Avenue
5800 W from 5300 N to 5360 N

This street name celebrates Admiral George Dewey's destruction of the Spanish fleet in Manila Bay in 1898 in the Spanish American War. There were no American losses. Manila is the capital of the Philippines.

Manistee Avenue
2734 E from 7900 S to 13143 S*

Manistee, Michigan, takes its name from an Algonquin Indian word for "the island in the river." The street was named after the town.

Mankato Avenue
6300 W from 7000 N to 7198 N*

The city of Mankato, Minnesota, and the Mankato River, from which this street took its name, were named for an Indian tribe. The word literally means "the blue earth." Mankato was also the name of a chief of that tribe who was killed in 1862.

Mannheim Road
10400 W from 4400 N to 6400 N

In the 1840s immigrants from Mannheim, Germany, created a new community called Mannheim in an area that now is a part of Franklin Park. The road takes its name from the German settlement.

Mann Drive
6800 S in Marquette Park

In 1895 and 1896, James R. Mann, a congressman from Chicago's Hegewisch community, was also the attorney for the South Park District, which included Marquette Park.

Manor Drive
2734 W at 4400 N to 2949 W at 4772 N

Named for Manor, Pennsylvania.

Manton Avenue
5600 W from 5700 N to 5998 N

Named for Manton, Michigan.

Maple Street
1100 N from 1 W to 150 W

Named for the maple trees once found in large numbers in this area.

Maplewood Avenue
2532 W from 7556 N to 11856 S*

Maplewood, so called because of the many maple trees planted here, was once a village on what is now the Near Northwest Side of Chicago.

Marble Place
120 S from 1 W to 778 W*

In 1877 a building on this street was faced with marble. It was on Marble Place that Ernest J. Lehmann, owner of The Fair store, broke with the usual business practice of pricing goods in round numbers by offering goods at the strange and precise price of $1.99. *See Lehmann Court.*

Marcey Street
1000 W from 1634 N to 1942 N

Pierre Marcey was a French historian of the Northwest.

Margate Terrace
4930 N from 814 W to 940 W

This street was named after Margate, England, a popular seaside resort on the southeastern coast of England.

Maria Court
8500 W from 4520 N to 4738 N

Maria was the mother of Albert J. Schorsch, Sr., a real estate developer. *See Schorsch Street.*

Marin Drive
(in Humboldt Park)

Luis Munoz Marin (1898-1980), governor of Puerto Rico for sixteen years, was more responsible than anyone else for Puerto Rico's transition in the late 1940s from an exploited U.S. possession to a self-governing, self-respecting commonwealth. He became Puerto Rico's first elected governor in 1948 and served until he stepped down in 1964.

An economic visionary, Marin converted the island, once heavily dependent on its sugar crop, to a manufacturing state with plants for chemical products, electronic parts, television sets, cement, clothing, and tuna packing. He distributed government land, puchased from the sugar companies, to the peasants, and he brought electric power to hundreds of rural villages.

Marine Drive
610 W from 4000 N to 5132 N

This street, in close proximity to Lake Michigan, once passed in front of the U.S. Marine Hospital, "the harbor and refuge for those following a seafaring life" which opened in 1873. Its buildings and beautiful gardens stood on the site where the Disney Magnet School stands today at 4140 N. Marine Drive.

Marion Court
1838 W from 1200 N to 1272 N

Ellen Marion Kinzie was the first white child born in Chicago. She was born in December of 1804. Ellen's father was an early settler who housed his family in a cabin orginally owned by Chicago's first settler, Jean Baptiste Point DuSable. *See Kinzie and Jean Streets.*

Markham Avenue
5900 W from 5700 N to 5981 N

Named for Charles Henry Markham (1861-1930), who went from being a baggage master on the Southern Pacific Railroad in 1887 to president of the Illinois Central Railroad in 1911. As president he took the first steps toward selling the valuable air rights over Illinois Central property in downtown Chicago.

Marmora Avenue
5900 W from 2100 N to 6068 N*

On the Island of Marmora (or Marmara), Turkey, marble has been quarried since antiquity. Marmor means wrought marble.

Marquette Avenue
2700 E from 7600 S to 13105 S*

Marquette Drive
6600 S in Jackson Park

Marquette Road
500 E from 6600 S to 6658 S

Marquette Road
6700 S from 456 E to 4758 W

Father Jacques Marquette (1637-1675) was a French Jesuit missionary priest. He and Quebec-born explorer Louis Jolliet were the first Europeans to visit the Chicago portage. When the two men passed through the area in 1673, Jolliet was said to have told Marquette, "Here some day will be found one of the world's great cities."

Marquette was seeking to save souls; Jolliet was searching for gold. But they wanted to find a great river that was said to be running through the West. Together they were the first white men to explore the upper Mississippi River.

Marshall Boulevard
2900 W from 1900 S to 2358 S

James A. Marshall came to Chicago in 1832 and became a real estate agent. He was a member of the firm of Knight and Marshall. He was also secretary of the Chicago Real Estate Board.

Marshfield Avenue
1632 W from 7742 N to 11858 S*

This street was named for either the marshy ground over which part of the road once ran, or for Marshfield, Massachusetts.

**Rev. Martin Luther King, Jr.,
singing "We Shall Overcome" at
State and Madison streets in
July 1965.**

Courtesy *Chicago Sun-Times*

Dr. Martin Luther King, Jr. Drive (Pvt.)
348 E from 13022 S to 13274 S

Dr. Martin Luther King, Jr. Drive
344 E at 2201 S to 400 E at 13456 S*

Dr. Martin Luther King, Jr. (1929-1968), the black civil rights leader and Nobel Peace Prize winner, adhered to a philosophy of non-violent civil disobedience in fighting racial discrimination. To protest segregated housing in Chicago, King led 600 demonstrators through crowds of angry whites in Gage Park in the summer of 1966. During the march, Rev. King was struck on the head by a rock and stumbled, but he continued marching.

Mary Street
1100 W from 2500 S to 2510 S

Mary J. Dennis, a real estate subdivider in 1868, developed the land in this community.

Maryland Avenue
832 E from 4900 S to 13458 S*

Maryland Avenue (Pvt.)
832 E from 10300 S to 10358 S

Named for the state of Maryland.

Mason Avenue
5932 W from 7158 N to 6258 S*

Roswell B. Mason (1805-1892), the city's thirteenth mayor, was known as the "Fire Mayor," and was credited with saving Chicago from disgrace in the aftermath of the Great Fire of 1871. Elected as part of a large movement to fight corruption, Mason kept donated money out of the hands of the city council. Mason believed, as others did too, that if the council controlled these funds, they would end up in aldermanic pockets. Mason decided instead that the money should be disbursed by the Relief and Aid Society. This proved to be a wise decision, since the mayor had earlier sent a message back East that read, "Before morning one hundred thousand people will be without food and shelter. Can you help us?"

While the fire spread, Mason continued to work in the Courthouse until the bell tower crashed through the flaming roof. He helped set the County Jail prisoners free, personally directed the razing of buildings on Wabash Avenue and Harrison Street, and called upon Civil War General Philip H. Sheridan (Sheridan Road) to declare martial law and keep order.

His obituary in the *Chicago Evening Post* referred to his term in office as a "wise, cool-headed administration which did much to restore the people to their normal frame of mind."

Roswell B. Mason, 1805-1892

Mason's remarkable decisiveness, however, had it's drawbacks. Before he was mayor he helped create the Great Grand Crossing community and indirectly caused a train crash that killed eighteen people and injured forty.

While Mason was construction head for the Illinois Central Railroad in the early 1850s, both the IC and the Michigan Southern Railroad claimed a right-of-way at what is now 75th Street and South Chicago Avenue. The management of the Michigan Southern blocked the IC from crossing their tracks, so Mason arranged one night to kidnap a Michigan Southern guard and build a crossing.

The fatal train crash that followed in 1853 prompted the city council to insist that all trains make a full stop at the junction. A settlement grew up around the junction and it came to be called the Greater Grand Crossing community.

Massasoit Avenue
5732 W from 1556 N to 6258 S*

Massasoit, an Algonquin Indian word for "Great Chief," was the chief of the Wampanoags, a tribe native to New England. Massasoit befriended the Puritans at Plymouth in 1621 and attended the first Thanksgiving. Massasoit was also the name of an early Chicago hotel.

Matson Avenue
6146 N from 5936 W to 6094 W

This street may have been named for Canute R. Matson, a Norwegian immigrant who served in the Civil War and later held a number of political offices in Chicago. Matson was elected clerk of the city's Police Court in 1869 and 1871, justice of the peace in 1875, coroner in 1880, and sheriff in 1886.

It may be, however, that this street was named for General W. Matson, who

is said to have hired Abe Lincoln to argue a case against slavery.

Maud Avenue
1000 W from 1824 N to 1996 N

The best bet is that this street was named for Maud Long, daughter of Chicago Alderman Daniel Long, who served from 1889 to 1891. This avenue runs through Long's old 20th Ward on the Near North Side. A second possibility is that the street was named for Maud, Pennsylvania.

Mautene Court
1650 W from 1244 N to 1254 N

This street may have been named for an Indian chief.

Maxwell Street
1330 S from 500W to 1126 W*

Dr. Philip Maxwell, known locally as the "Falstaff of his profession," was a

physician who came to Chicago around 1832. He was a loud, boisterous joker, who when running for the state legislature argued that he should be elected because his arguments carried weight. He weighed 280 pounds.

Maxwell was a state representative from 1849 to 1852 despite, or perhaps because of the fact, that he always enjoyed a joke at anyone's expense. He told a visitor to Chicago one winter that he bathed daily in Lake Michigan, "as long as my weight will break the ice."

Sunday morning at the Maxwell Street Market, looking south on Halsted from O'Brien Street, October 1942.

Courtesy *Chicago Sun-Times*

May Street
1132 W from 902 N to 12256 S*

This street was named for Elizabeth May Curtiss, daughter of Chicago's tenth mayor, James Curtiss, who was born in Vermont in 1803 and served as mayor from 1847-1851.

Mayfield Avenue
5900 W from 1840 N to 6458 S*

Named after Mayfield, England.

Maypole Avenue
134 N from 1600 W to 5158 W*

William T. Maypole was a West Side alderman from 1896 to 1908.

McAlpin Avenue
6300 W from 6900 N to 7166 N

This street may have been named (and misspelled) for William McAlpine, the chief engineer of Chicago in 1851. Under McAlpine, a city water system was built that piped in fresh water from 600 feet out in the lake (reaching east from the shore at Chicago Avenue). Forty-eight miles of distribution pipe put in place at the time made it possible to serve a potential population of 100,000 people.

The street, however, may have been named for Patrick McAlpin, an early settler and a member of Holy Name Church in 1855.

McClellan Avenue
5600 W from 6150 N to 6250 N

This street was named for either land developer George R. McClellan or Civil War General George B. McClellan (1826-1885).

McClurg Court
400 E from 530 N to 678 N

Alexander C. McClurg was a spunky Chicago bookseller who played a hero's role in the Civil War.

The McClurg family monument in Graceland Cemetery, Clark Street at Irving Park Road.
G. Lane

McClurg was selling books for S.C. Griggs & Co. when the war broke out. He enlisted as a private in Company D of the 60th Regiment of the Illinois State Militia, fought in twenty major battles, and returned to Chicago four years later as an honored general.

Slight and delicate, McClurg hardly looked the warrior. He came to Chicago in 1859, in fact, because poor health had forced him to give up the study of law. But he came from a fighting family. His grandfather had come to America seeking political asylum after the Irish rebellion of 1798. And his father had built Fort Pitt Foundry in Pittsburgh, which furnished iron fixtures for the ship decks in the Union navy.

In the Civil War, young Alexander fought like a man possessed. One eyewitness recalled McClurg's bravery at the Battle of Jonesboro: The Union forces faced an "apparently impregnable" Confederate line that was "guarded by a battery pouring forth a most galling fire." The Union forces wavered. But then McClurg, without even waiting to draw his sword, rushed forward waving his handkerchief and shouting, "Forward!" "The coolness and promptness of the action were electric in their effect. The men followed him and, after one of the bloodiest charges of the Atlanta campaign, the position was taken, and victory was secured."

After the war, the Union begged McClurg to make a career of the military. But the mild-mannered storekeeper would have none of it. He returned to Chicago and to selling books.

McCook Avenue
6022 W from 5940 N to 5976 N

Major General Alexander McDowell McCook (1831-1903), of Ohio, commanded his first Civil War regiment at the first Battle of Bull Run. His father, seven brothers, and five cousins—known as "the fighting McCooks"—all fought in the Civil War.

McCormick Road
3300 W from 6231 N to 6363 N

This road and its northern extension through Lincolnwood was built in 1926 by the Chicago Sanitary District as an access road to its North Side Water Reclamation Plant. It was named for Robert R. McCormick (1880-1955), publisher of the *Chicago Tribune*, who was president of the Board of Trustees of the Chicago Sanitary District from 1905 to 1910.

McCrea Drive
3356 W in Garfield Park

Samuel H. McCrea was a West Park District commissioner from 1878 to 1884.

McCutcheon Terrace
944 W from 4900 N to 4924 N

Both this terrace and the McCutcheon School which stands nearby were named for the Pulitzer Prize winning cartoonist, John T. McCutcheon (1870-1949). Born in Tippecanoe County, Indiana, McCutcheon joined the staff of the *Chicago Tribune* in 1903 and remained with the paper until his retirement in 1945.

John T. McCutcheon, 1870-1949

Mary Eliza McDowell, 1854-1936

McDermott Street
1400 W from 2928 S to 2936 S

Named for Alexander Michael McDermott, who was a civil engineer and surveyor in about 1884.

McDonough Street
12000 W from 4000 N to 4900 N

(source unknown)

McDowell Avenue
1404 W from 4500 S to 4676 S

Mary Eliza McDowell (1854-1936), the great social worker, was once called the "garbage lady" of Chicago.

McDowell Avenue used to be Gross Avenue, and at 4630 S. Gross Avenue stood the settlement house run by Mary McDowell. On the recommendation of Jane Addams, the University of Chicago had asked McDowell to establish a settlement house near the stockyards. Not only did she fulfill that goal, but she promoted a nationwide investigation into the plight of women and children in industry. Through the settlement house, McDowell improved nutrition and hygiene in the stockyard neighborhoods, and she fought to reduce the infant mortality rate in an area where two out of three children died before the age of three.

Mary McDowell helped bring about meat inspection laws, and for twenty years she waged war against Packingtown's garbage dumps and the putrid "Bubbly Creek." Her protests resulted in new garbage disposal procedures in Chicago, for which she was dubbed the "garbage lady."

McFetridge Drive
1326 S in Burnham Park

William L. McFetridge (1894-1969) was president of the Chicago Park District and one of the most powerful labor leaders in the United States. From 1940 to 1960 he was president of the Building Service Employees International Union and its 315,000 members.

McLean Avenue
2034 N from 1400 W to 6460 W*

Named for John McLean, a United States senator from Illinois and the state's first congressman. He died in 1830.

McLeod Avenue
6246 W from 6000 N to 6124 N

James McLeod was a politically active land developer in about 1874.

McVicker Avenue
6032 W from 7347 N to 6258 S*

James Hubert McVicker (1822-1896) was a comedian. On May 2, 1848, he appeared in Chicago as the "first low comedian" in a theater owned by James B. Rice. Rice would later be elected mayor. *See Rice Street.*

Although McVicker worked as an actor in France and England and operated one of the best stock companies in the United States, he was probably best known in Chicago for the theaters he owned. In 1871 he spent $90,000 to build his second theater in Chicago, only to see it burn nine weeks later in the Fire of 1871. Shortly thereafter he spent $200,000 to build the Theatre Ludlow, and dubbed it the "best in the West."

Meade Avenue
6100 W from 7340 N to 6458 S*

Union General George Meade (1815-1872) was victorious in the Battle of Gettysburg in 1863. He graduated from West Point in 1835, fought in the Mexican-American War, and was the commander of the Army of the Potomac in the Civil War. *See Gettysburg Street.*

Joseph Medill, 1823-1899

Medford Avenue
6200 W from 6900 N to 7034 N

Named for Medford, Massachusetts.

Medill Avenue
2334 N from 1200 W to 7190 W

Joseph Medill (1823-1899) helped found the Republican Party and gave it its name. He was also a Chicago mayor who shunned the poor and the city's immigrants, yet he headed what's been called the first reform administration.

As a Cleveland, Ohio, newspaper owner, Medill visited Chicago in the winter of 1854-55. During that stay he bought an interest in the then financially troubled *Chicago Tribune*. He was thirty-two years old at the time.

While covering the 1856 Republican State Convention in Bloomington, Medill was so taken by the power of Abraham Lincoln's oratory that he forgot to take notes. During the Lincoln-Douglas debates of 1858, Medill threw the resources of the *Tribune* behind his close friend Abe Lincoln.

Medill was a founder of the Associated Press and mayor of Chicago

after the fire of 1871. In 1874, he bought a majority of the *Tribune* stock and ran the paper until his death. His last words before he died were said to be, "What is the news?"

Medina Avenue
6158 W from 5800 N to 5950 N

Named for either the Medina Club, home of the Masons of Illinois, or for the Medina River in England. Medina is also the name of the city in Arabia to which Mohammed fled in 622 and from which he converted Arabia.

Melrose Street
3232 N from 400 W to 7040 W*

Named for the Melrose Abbey, founded in 1136 in Melrose, Scotland.

Melvina Avenue
6200 W from 7156 N to 6458 S*

Named for Melvina, Wisconsin.

Memory Lane
5146 N from 8000 W to 8158 W

More than likely, the whimsical man or woman who named this street was inspired by the saying, "a stroll down Memory Lane."

Menard Avenue
5800 W from 6070 N to 6458 S

Menard Drive
5800 W in Columbus Park

Pierre Menard (1776-1844), a fur trader and merchant, became Illinois' first lieutenant governor in 1818. Elected to the first Illinois Senate in 1812, he was the senate's first president and remained in that position until Illinois became a state in 1818.

Mendell Street
1500 W from 1900 N to 2058 N

Named for Edward Mendell, a Chicagoan in the 1850s, who ran a printing business.

Mendota Avenue
6224 W at 6800 N to 5900 W at 7037 N

The *Mendota* was a passenger and freight steamboat that ran on the Mississippi River between St. Louis and Cairo in the 1840s. The boat was owned by George Springer, who moved to Chicago in 1848 and turned to investing in real estate. Mendota is an Indian word that means "mouth of the river." *See Luella Avenue.*

Menomonee Street
1800 N from 156 W to 558 W*

The Indian word *Menomonee* means "the wild rice men." It was the name of a tribe in Wisconsin and the name of a Potawatomie chief in Indiana in about 1836.

Mercer Avenue
6340 N from 6100 W to 6200 W

(source unknown)

Meredith Avenue
5626 W from 6200 N to 6256 N

George Meredith was an early resident of Austin.

Merrill Avenue
2132 E from 6700 S to 13758 S*

George W. Merrill was a South Side real estate developer. He was secretary of the Hook and Ladder Company of Chicago's volunteer fire department in 1837.

Merrimac Avenue
6234 W from 7156 N to 6258 S*

This street's name commemorates the Civil War naval battle of the ironclads, pitting the Union warship *Monitor* against the Confederate *Merrimack*— also called the *Virginia.* The *Monitor,* which had the prototype of the revolving turret, defeated the *Merrimack* on March 9, 1862, outside Hampton Roads, Virginia. The Indian word *Merrimac* means "sturgeon on swift water." *See Monitor Avenue.*

Merrion Avenue
2214 E from 9500 S to 9840 S

John Merrion, this street's namesake, was the grandfather of land developer Joseph Merrion. The younger Merrion subdivided the area through which this street runs in 1947. John Merrion was superintendent of the Short Line Railroad in South Chicago.

Metron Drive (Pvt.)
1550 E and 12800 S at Lake Calumet Harbor

The Metron Steel Corporation is located on this street.

Meyer Avenue
510 W from 1610 N to 1660 N

Adam Meyer was a North Side lakefront alderman from 1879 to 1883 and from 1890 to 1892.

Miami Avenue
6124 N from 5900 W to 6130 W

The Miami Indians once had a village on the present site of Chicago. Their village was here before the Potawatomies came into the area. The Indian word *Miami* means "people who live on the peninsula."

Michigan Avenue
100 E from 950 N to 12628 S

Michigan Avenue (Pvt.)
125 E from 13330 S to 13362 S

Named for the lake, this avenue ran right along the shore until the landfill for Grant Park pushed the shoreline east. *Michigan* is an Algonquin word for "great water."

Midway Drive
5900 S in Washington Park

See Midway Plaisance.

Midway Park
500 N from 5700 W to 5968 W

This street was named by real estate developer Henry Austin, who put stretches of green parkways in the middle of some of his streets.

Midway Plaisance
5900 S from 800 E to 1600 E

One mile long and 300 feet wide, this grass parkway began as the most popular feature of the 1893 Columbian Exposition. It was lined with the architecture of the world, everything from an Irish village to a Cairo street. There was a herd of reindeer with Lapp caretakers, African snake charmers, the wonderful White

The Ferris Wheel on the Midway Plaisance, at the World's Columbian Exposition, May 1, 1893.

Courtesy *Chicago Sun-Times*

City, and even an exhibit of 125 different weeds.

But the anchor of the Midway was the original Ferris Wheel. Built by George Washington Gale Ferris, a mechanical engineer from Galesburg, Illinois. The Ferris Wheel measured 250 feet in diameter, spun 36 cars, and could carry as many as 1,400 passengers on an axle 45 feet long and 32 inches thick.

You could "do" the Midway, visiting every show and enjoying every amusement, for $15.00.

Helen J. Mikols Drive
4700 W at 5536 S to 4800 W at 5636 S

Helen Mikols (1933-1984) was a Southwest Side civic leader who pushed for a new expressway on the Southwest Side—the Crosstown—a new Southwest Side rapid-transit line, and the revitalization of Midway Airport. Appropriately, this street runs into Midway Airport.

Mildred Avenue
900 W from 2600 N to 2958 N

Mildred Best was the mother of William Best, a subdivider in 1865. William Best was also a member of Best and Russell Company, which owned a brewery.

Millard Avenue
3632 W from 500 S to 111430 S*

Alden C. Millard was a real estate developer with the firm of Millard and Decker. This avenue passes through Millard and Decker's South Lawndale subdivision, which was developed in 1873.

Miller Street
1028 W from 700 S to 1942 S*

Samuel Miller was a charter member of the Cook County Board of Commissioners in 1831. He built the first bridge, a foot bridge, over the North Branch of the Chicago River at Kinzie and Canal streets in 1832.

Miltimore Avenue
5834 W from 5600 N to 5982 N

Named for Ira Miltimore, the builder of the first permanent public school in Chicago.

A machinist by trade, he oversaw the construction of a reservoir for fresh lake water at the corner of Lake Street and Michigan Avenue. And in 1845 he oversaw the construction of the school building, one so big that many locals called it "Miltimore's Folly."

Miltimore was an alderman of a ward located southwest of Randolph Street and the Chicago River from 1839 to 1842 and from 1844 to 1845.

Milwaukee Avenue
500 W at 200 N to 6543 W at 6556 N

This street as well as the city of Milwaukee toward which it goes take their names from an Algonquin Indian

village that was once located on the present site of Milwaukee, Wisconsin. The word means "fine land."

Minerva Avenue
1172 E at 6344 S to 1124 E at 6658 S

Named after Minerva, New York. Minerva was the Roman goddess of handicrafts and the arts.

Minnehaha Avenue
5400 W from 6300 N to 6558 N

This Indian word means "laughing water." Minnehaha was the heroine of Longfellow's poem, "Hiawatha." *See Hiawatha Avenue.*

Minnetonka Avenue
5626 W at 6500 N to 5458 W at 6944 N

This is an Algonquin word for "big water."

Mobile Avenue
6300 W from 7156 N to 6458 S*

Named after Mobile, Alabama.

Moffat Street
1832 N from 2000 W to 3136 W*

T.S. Moffat was a landowner and real estate promoter in about 1872.

Mohawk Street
532 W from 1306 N to 2058 N

Mohawk Street (Pvt.)
500 W from 816 N to 954 N

The Mohawks were one of the five nations of the Iroquois Confederacy who lived in what is now upper New York State. The name means "savage, ferocious."

Northwest Tower, corner of Milwaukee, Damen, and North Avenues.

G.Lane

Monitor Avenue
5832 W from 6064 N to 6258 S*

The *Monitor* was a Union warship in the Civil War. It defeated the Confederate warship *Merrimack* near Hampton Roads, Virginia, on March 9, 1862. The *Monitor* was an early ironclad, a warship covered with iron plates for protection. Its revolving turret gun became the prototype for modern warships. *See Merrimac Avenue.*

Monon Avenue
6234 W from 6934 N to 7068 N*

Named for Monon, Indiana. The meaning of this Indian word is uncertain.

Monroe Drive
100 S in Grant Park

Monroe Street
100 S from 86 E to 5574 W*

Named for James Monroe (1758-1831), the fifth president of the United States, who served from 1817 to 1825.

Monsignor McElligott Drive
10200 S from 2630 W to 2758 W

Msgr. Francis J. McElligott is a former director of cemeteries for the Roman Catholic Archdiocese of Chicago and a former pastor of St. John Fisher Church, which is located at 103rd and Washtenaw.

Montana Street
2432 N from 900 W to 5258 W*

Named for the state of Montana. Latin in origin, the word means "mountainous region."

Mont Clare Avenue
7132 W from 2500 N to 5526 N*

This street, the Montclare community area, and the Mont Clare Station on the Milwaukee Road line near Harlem and Fullerton probably all took their names from Montclair, New Jersey. One story has it that the street was named by a minister. Another story is that it was named by Mary Sayre Allen, the daughter of an early settler, who had visited Montclair, New Jersey, and liked the town so well she borrowed its name.

Monterey Avenue
11200 S from 1614 W to 1952 W

The Count of Monte Rey was the Viceroy of Mexico for whom the area of Monterey, California, was named in 1602. The street probably took its name from the California city.

Montgomery Avenue
2726 W from 4000 S to 4128 S

Montgomery Avenue
4128 S from 2600 W to 2638 W

Named for J. Montgomery, a South Side land developer who laid out the area through which this street runs.

Monticello Avenue
3632 W from 400 N to 6354 N*

Monticello was the Virginia estate of President Thomas Jefferson (1743-1826). *See Jefferson Street.*

Montrose Avenue
4400 N from 646 W to 8608 W*

Montrose Drive
4400 N in Lincoln Park

Montrose Harbor Drive
4400 N in Lincoln Park

Named for James G. Montrose (1612-1650), a Scottish nobleman and military leader.

Montvale Avenue
11334S from 1638 W to 1906 W

Named for Montvale, Tennessee.

Moody Avenue
6132 W from 7194 N to 6258 S*

Dwight Lyman Moody (1837-1899) was a successful shoe salesman who completed his life preaching and saving souls.

Moody came to Chicago in 1856 as a retail clerk. At one point he made $5,000 in eight months selling shoes. But he was also interested in providing Sunday school training for the city's youngsters. He soon turned to evangelizing in homes, tents, and missions. His travels took him across the U.S. and abroad. Although he was never ordained and had only a fifth-grade education, he became one of the most famous evangelists in American history, founding the Moody Bible Institute in 1889.

Moody refused to accept money for his work; and he gave the royalties from his hymn books to schools he founded for poor children. He raised millions for the YMCA and was an effective fund-raiser for victims of the Civil War and the Chicago Fire.

Moorman Street
1700 W from 1300 N to 1328 N

Named for John J. Moorman, a real estate subdivider.

Morgan Drive
5500 S in Washington Park

Morgan Street
1000 W from 752 N to 12928 S*

Thomas Morgan was an Englishman who in 1844 purchased the land between 91st and 115th Streets along the ridge in the area that would become Beverly Hills and Morgan Park. He built a home in the vicinity of 92nd Street and Pleasant Avenue and called it "Upwood," after his father's home in England. He farmed the land and bred livestock until his death in 1857. His heirs sold the land to the Blue Island Land and Building Company, which subdivided and developed it.

Morse Avenue
6944 N from 1108 W to 5476 W

Morse Avenue Circle Drive
6944 N in Loyola Park

Charles H. Morse was a member of the Rogers Park Building and Land Company, incorporated in 1873, which developed the community of Rogers Park. This street was named by the company. *See Touhy, Pratt, Lunt, and Greenleaf Avenues.*

Moselle Avenue
6300 W from 6800 N to 7086 N*

The Moselle River courses through northeastern France and West Germany. The well-known Moselle wines are made from grapes grown in the vineyards along this river.

Mozart Drive
2832 W in Humboldt Park

Mozart Street
2832 W from 6758 N to 8626 S*

Named for Wolfgang Amadeus Mozart (1756-1791), the Austrian composer.

Mulligan Avenue
6332 W from 5954 N to 6258 S*

When the Civil War broke out, James A. Mulligan rallied to the Union cause while some of his fellow Irish held back. Mulligan died a hero and was buried in Calvary Cemetery. His graveside monument is inscribed with his final orders, "Lay me down and save the flag!"

Mulligan was a respected Chicago lawyer. When war was declared, he issued a call: "Rally! All Irishmen in favor of forming a regiment of Irish volunteers to sustain the United States in and through the present war will rally!" The response was less than overwhelming, although two brigades

The Gazebo in Garfield Park, 1988.
G. Lane

were later formed, the Irish Brigade and the 90th Volunteers. Some Irish did not share Mulligan's anti-slavery views. Many of them worked in the lowest-paying jobs, and they feared that slaves, if freed, might replace them.

But on June 5, 1861, Chicago's Irish Brigade was mustered into the army with 937 men under Mulligan's command. They marched down Wabash Avenue, the Stars and Stripes and green flag of Erin flapping. In Lexington, Missouri, on Aug. 31, 1861, the brigade was promptly routed. Surrounded and outnumbered, they surrendered. They were soon freed in exchange for Confederate prisoners, but Mulligan himself was held prisoner for six more weeks.

Mulligan's Irish Brigade went on to fight in West Virginia, where he was wounded during the Battle of Kearnstown. But he insisted that his men protect the flag instead of carrying him. They did, and Mulligan was captured again. He died while in Confederate hands.

Mulligan's wife, Marian, later found her picture in his wallet. On the back was an inscription, written on the day he died: "Have been fighting since morning. God bless you, darling, and little ones. James."

Museum Drive
5700 S in Jackson Park

This drive runs in front of the Museum of Science and Industry.

Music Court Drive
112 S in Garfield Park

For many years music concerts were a standard attraction in the gazebo in Garfield Park's Music Court. The street leads to the court.

Muskegon Avenue
2838 E from 7726 S to 13213 S*

Muskegon, Michigan, was the source of this street's name. It is a Chippewa Indian word for "swampy" or "grassy bog."

Myrick Street
7852 S from 3750 W to 3848 W

William Franklin Myrick (1809-1889) settled in Chicago in 1836 and built the Myrick House, one of the earliest hotels, at what is now 29th Street and Cottage Grove Avenue. Myrick's tavern became a stopover for cattle drovers.

Myrtle Avenue
6200 N from 7132 W to 7744 W

The myrtle is a flower that grows on a bushy evergreen shrub. This street was named for the flower, or possibly for Myrtle, Mississippi.

N

Nagle Avenue
6400 W from 7154 N to 6258 S*

This street may have been named for Albrecht N. Nagel (1833-1895), a noted German medical writer and opthalmologist. The street runs through an area on the North Side that had a large German population.

Naper Avenue
6600 W from 5900 N to 6258 N

Named for Capt. Joseph Naper, who founded what is probably Chicago's oldest suburb, the Naper Settlement in 1831, now known as Naperville. He also helped found DuPage County.

Joseph Naper and his brother John sailed to Chicago to deliver a sailboat, then moved west to the Naperville area where they ran a sawmill. Threatened by the Black Hawk War of 1832, Naper sent the women and children of his settlement to Fort Dearborn, while he took command of the first militia in DuPage County. In response to the Indian uprising, he helped build Fort Payne near the settlement. The fort never saw battle.

The Naper Settlement, bigger than Chicago in the early 1830s, became the first town chartered in Cook County. In 1839, serving in the Illinois General Assembly, Naper proposed legislation that created DuPage County, detaching it from Cook. Naperville was the original county seat, although today it is Wheaton.

Naples Avenue
6400 W from 6036 N to 6152 N

Named for the southern Italian seaport of Naples, Italy.

Napoleon Avenue
6440 W from 5800 N to 5872 N

Named for Napoleon Bonaparte (1769-1821), military conqueror and ruler of France. *See Bonaparte Street.*

Narragansett Avenue
6400 W from 4761 N to 6458 S*

The Narragansett Indians were native to Rhode Island and lived around the bay of Narragansett.

Nashotah Avenue
6524 W from 5900 N to 6032 N

The Indian word means "twins" or "a pair." Nashotah, Wisconsin, is located on a pair of lakes.

Nashville Avenue
6600 W from 6532 N to 6458 S*

Nashville Avenue (Pvt.)
6600 W from 4000 N to 4140 N

Nashville, Tennessee was the site of a Union victory in December of 1864 that ended Southern resistance in Tennessee. The city was named for Revolutionary War general Francis Nash (1742-1777).

Nassau Avenue
6400 W from 6002 N to 6192 N

Nassau is the capital city of the Bahama Islands and also the name of counties in Florida and New York. It is usually assumed that a settler from back East named this street after the New York county.

Natchez Avenue
6434 W from 5528 N to 6458 S*

The Natchez Indian tribe lived around Natchez, Mississippi. The name means the "land between."

Natoma Avenue
6600 W from 6558 N to 6258 S*

Natoma was the name of an Indian girl in an opera written and produced by Victor Herbert in 1911.

Navajo Avenue
5300 W from 6200 N to 6458 N

The Navajo Indian tribe is native to the Southwest. The word means "a large area of cultivated land."

Navarre Avenue
6420 W from 5800 N to 6140 N

Navarre, once an ancient kingdom, is a northern province of Spain.

Neenah Avenue
6532 W from 6356 N to 6258 S*

Neenah, Wisconsin, is this street's namesake. *Neenah* is a Winnebago Indian word for "water."

Nelson Street
3032 N from 932 W to 6974 W*

Andrew Nelson (1818-1887) was a Chicago real estate investor and one of the first Lincoln Park commissioners. His son, John Nelson, a real estate subdivider, named this street in honor of his father in 1875. The elder Nelson, like many other Chicagoans, had taken a financial beating in the Chicago Fire of 1871.

Neola Avenue
6700 W from 6000 N to 6170 N

Neola is an Indian word for "maiden."

Nettleton Avenue
6800 W from 6026 N to 6161 N

Alfred Bayard Nettleton (1838-1911) was a lawyer, journalist, and soldier. As a Civil War general, he fought in more than seventy battles. He was the financial editor of the *Chicago Advance* and a commissioner of the World's Columbian Exposition of 1893.

Neva Avenue
7132 W from 6549 N to 5858 S*

Named for the Neva River in Russia.

Newark Avenue
6700 W from 5600 N to 6498 N

Named for Newark, New Jersey. The city was founded by Puritans in 1666 and named in honor of Rev. Abraham Pierson (1609-1678), who moved there from Newark-on-Trent, England. Some historians argue, however, that the city's name has a biblical origin of "New Ark."

Walter L. Newberry, 1804-1868

Newberry Avenue
828 W from 1204 S to 1730 S

This street was named for a Chicago businessman and philanthropist who was buried in a rum barrel.

Walter L. Newberry (1804-1868) came to Chicago in 1833 as a merchant; but he later turned to real estate, banking, and railroads. He was president of the Board of Education and the Chicago Historical Society. He is best remembered today for leaving half of his fortune ($2.1 million) to establish the Newberry Library, 60 West Walton Street, now one of the nation's finest privately endowed research libraries.

Newberry Library, 60 West Walton Street, in 1911.
Courtesy G. Schmalgemeier

Newberry died on a boat bound for Paris, and his body was sent back to Chicago in a rum barrel. The barrel served as his coffin when he was buried in Graceland Cemetery.

Newburg Avenue
6400 W from 5900 N to 6158 N

This avenue is believed to have been named for Newburgh, New York, the site of George Washington's final headquarters (1782-1783) in the Revolutionary War. It was here that Washington officially disbanded the Continental Army, and it was here that he rejected the idea that he should be crowned king.

Newcastle Avenue
6834 W from 6533 N to 5924 S

Newcastle, England, the source of this street's name, is located at the mouth of the River Tyne.

New England Avenue
6900 W from 6490 N to 6458 S*

This street was named for the New England region of the United States, which includes Maine, Vermont, New Hampshire, Massachusetts, Connecticut, and Rhode Island.

Newgard Avenue
1432 W from 6400 N to 6758 N

Named for Henry Newgard, the president of the North Shore Park District from 1916 to 1922.

New Hampshire Avenue
7000 W from 5628 N to 5746 N

Named for the state of New Hampshire.

Newland Avenue
6932 W from 6490 N to 5858 S*

Named for Newland, Virginia.

Newport Avenue
3432 N from 800 W to 7040 W*

Named for Newport, Rhode Island. The town was founded in 1639 by a group of religious refugees from Massachusetts.

Niagara Avenue
7000 W from 6000 N to 6292 N*

This avenue was named for Niagara Falls and the Niagara River in Canada and western New York. The Niagara area was of strategic importance to both the French and British in their attempts to control the Great Lakes in the eighteenth and early nineteenth centuries. The river connects Lake Erie and Lake Ontario. *Niagara* is an Indian word, meaning "bisected bottomland" or the "neck."

Nickerson Avenue
6900 W from 5800 N to 6150 N

Samuel Mayo Nickerson (1830-1914) was a distiller-turned-banker. Upon arriving in Chicago in 1858, Nickerson started making money by producing wines and whiskey. After achieving success in business, he urged the establishment of a national bank in Chicago and was a charter director of the First National Bank. He was the bank's president in 1867, and, after the Chicago Fire, he drew up the plans to rebuild the bank at Dearborn and Monroe. Nickerson was also a founder of the Union Stockyard Bank and a patron of the Art Institute of Chicago.

Nicolet Avenue
7044 W from 5730 N to 5862 N

Jean Nicolet (1598-1642) was a French explorer who discovered Lake Michigan while searching for China.

Nicolet, born in Cherbourg, France, came to Canada in 1618. His patron, Samuel de Champlain (see Champlain Avenue), the governor of New France and, some believe, the first European to see the Great Lakes, had stopped exploring on his own by that time. But Champlain liked to send promising young protégés to live among the Indians. Nicolet lived two years among the Indians of the Allumettes Island in the Ottawa River and another nine years among other tribes in that area.

Champlain sent Nicolet west to seek the "People of the Sea." They were then at war with the Hurons, and were said to be connected with an Oriental group described by Marco Polo.

So in 1634, Nicolet, traveling by canoe and clad in an Oriental damask robe, landed near Green Bay and fired pistols in the air while Indians came out of the woods and bowed before him. The Winnebagos called Nicolet the "Great Manitou," feasting him with beavers and wild deer.

The former Nickerson residence at 40 East Erie Street, now part of the American College of Surgeons.
G. Lane

Nicolet also traveled inland and is credited with discovering Wisconsin. In 1934 Green Bay celebrated the 300th anniversary of his arrival there.

Nina Avenue
7200 W from 5746 N to 6032 N

The *Nina* was one of the three ships Christopher Columbus (1451-1506) sailed when he discovered the New World in 1492.

Nixon Avenue
7032 W from 6500 N to 6548 N

Wilson K. Nixon was a piano salesman and land speculator who gave up reading for his health.

Nixon was born in Geneva, New York, in 1826 and grew up in Cincinnati, a sickly child, afflicted with an addiction to books. As a teenager, he toured Europe with his family for 1½ years, returning to Cincinnati to attend Woodward College, where he completed four years of course work in two years. But all that study wore him down. His doctors finally ordered him to stop reading so much and enter business.

Nixon started a grocery business, then turned to selling pianos. But after marrying the daughter of Miles Greenwood, a Cincinnati industrialist, he joined his father-in-law in the manufacture of iron products. During the Civil War, Eagle Iron Works manufactured Union muskets, cannons, and iron plating for ships.

Moving to Chicago in 1863, upon the advice of his wife's physician, Nixon turned to construction and real estate speculation. He and a partner purchased land at Clark and Washington streets and built one of the city's largest office buildings. It included a 1,600-seat concert room, "Smith and Nixon Hall," then the city's finest music room.

Within only a few years of his arrival, Nixon had asserted himself as one of Chicago's leading businessmen. He was praised for his puritan work habits and for fine character.

Noble Street

1400 W from 400 N to 1558 N*

Two brothers named Noble acted nobly when they helped keep Chicago from starvation.

In 1832 Mark and John Noble were raising cattle south of Chicago when other settlers, fearing Indian attacks during the Black Hawk War, took refuge in the city. This fearful immigration increased the city's population five-fold and drained its foodstores. When meat became scarce, the Noble brothers drove their 150 head of cattle to the city and butchered them, thus averting meat rationing for the troops of Fort Dearborn and the people of Chicago.

Nokomis Avenue

5300 W from 6300 N to 6482 N

Named for Nokomis, Illinois. This Indian word means "grandmother."

Nora Avenue

7032 W from 2900 N to 3962 N*

Named for Nora, a town in Sweden.

Nordica Avenue

7100 W from 6548 N to 5858 S*

(source unknown)

Normal Avenue

500 W from 1800 S to 12946 S*

Normal Boulevard

500 W from 5500 S to 7158 S

Normal Parkway

6734 S from 300 W to 458 W

The Cook County Normal School on the South Side was a pioneer in teacher training. It was once headed by Colonel Francis Wayland Parker, a founder of the Francis Parker School on the North Side in 1901. Parker once said he looked upon Chicago as the "storm center of civilization." At schools like the Normal School, also called the Chicago Normal Training School, teachers worked with actual students while learning to teach. The Normal School today is Chicago State University, located at 9501 S. Dr. Martin Luther King Drive.

Chicago Normal Training School in 1910. It is now Chicago State University at 9501 S. Dr. Martin Luther King Drive.

C.R. Childs, courtesy G. Schmalgemeier

Normandy Avenue

6700 W from 6558 N to 6458 S*

Named for the region of Normandy on the northwestern coast of France. This was the scene of the invasion of Europe by the Allies in 1944.

North Avenue

1600 N from 100 W to 7190 W

North Avenue Circle Drive

1600 N in Lincoln Park

North Boulevard

1600 N from 60 E to 68 W

When Chicago was incorporated in 1837, North Avenue was the city's northern boundary. By 1851 the city had annexed land as far north as Fullerton Avenue.

North Branch Street

800 W at 1132 N to 900 W at 1390 N

This street runs parallel to the east bank of the North Branch of the Chicago River.

Northcott Avenue

6900 W from 6000 N to 6154 N

John Northcott was a Chicago landowner in about 1870. He sold his land to a subdivider, and the subdivider named this street in his honor.

North Park Avenue

300 W from 1336 N to 1762 N

Named for North Park, Colorado, which contains the headwaters of the North Platte River.

North Shore Avenue
6700 N from 1030 W to 7768 W*

This street runs east as far as the shore of Lake Michigan on the North Side, hence its name.

North Water Street
400 N from 38 E to 558 E

This street is the first street north of the Chicago River, hence the name. It was one of the streets platted in the original subdivision of Chicago in 1830.

Northwest Highway
5400 W at 5000 N to 7800 W at 6888 N

This old Indian trail derived its name from its general direction--northwest out of the city.

Norwood Avenue
6000 N from 4324 W to 4350 W

Norwood Street
6032 N from 1200 W to 7756 W*

The neighborhood of Norwood Park was once a separate community. It was laid out and developed in 1868 by the Norwood Land and Building Association. The name comes from the 1867 novel *Norwood: or Village Life in New England* by Henry Ward Beecher, the clergyman, orator, and writer. The street was named for the community.

Nottingham Avenue
7100 W from 5720 N to 6458 S*

Named for Nottingham, England.

Nursery Street
1300 W from 2106 N to 2136 N

Joseph Sheffield, a settler in the 1830s, established a truck farm and nursery in the vicinity of this street. *See Sheffield Avenue.*

Oak Street
1000 N from 134 E to 648 W*

Named for the oak tree.

Oakdale Avenue
2932 N from 300 W to 6974 W*

Joseph Sheffield, a real estate developer from New Haven, New York, named this street for Oakdale Station, New York. *See Sheffield Avenue.*

Stephen A. Douglas, 1813-1861

Oakenwald Avenue
1100 E from 4000 S to 4598 S

Stephen A. Douglas (1813-1861), leader of the Democratic Party in the years before the Civil War, established the Oakenwald subdivision on seventy acres of lakefront between 31st and 35th Streets in 1852. He built his own home on the property in 1854. Oakenwald Avenue runs just south of the original subdivision and took its name from it. The name is German for oak wood or oak forest.

Oakland Crescent
1000 E from 4062 S to 4080 S

In 1851, businessman Charles Cleaver built a soap factory and a company town of wooden houses, called Cleaverville, in the vicinity of this street. He named the street Oakland in recognition of all the oak trees in the area. *See Cleaver Street, Oakwood Boulevard, and Oakwood Drive.*

Oakley Avenue
2300 W from 7568 N to 11866 S*

Oakley Avenue (Pvt.)
2300 W from 3900 S to 3950 S

Oakley Boulevard
2300 W from 1558 N to 1124 S

Charles Oakley (1792-1849) was one of the earliest Illinois politicians accused of patronage. As one of the first state-appointed trustees of the Illinois and Michigan Canal in 1844, he worked to obtain financing overseas and back East for the massive project. Oakley fought with Eastern bankers who accused him of turning the canal project into a patronage kingdom. *See Canal Street.*

Oak Park Avenue
6800 W from 6558 N to 6458 S*

This avenue is named for the western suburb of Oak Park. The village was first settled in 1833, but not called Oak Park until 1872 when it got its first railroad depot. It was only then that the name appeared on a sign at the depot and at the local post office.

On Oakley at Rice Street, St. Nicholas Ukrainian Catholic Cathedral (1913-15) in the Ukrainian Village neighborhood.

A. Kezys

Oakview Avenue
8700 W from 4500 N to 5556 N*

This street was presumably named for a view of oak trees.

Oakwood Boulevard
3946 S from 400 E to 926 E

Oakwood Drive
3946 S in Burnham Park

Oakwood Hall was the elegant home of Charles Cleaver, located at what is now the northwest corner of Oakwood Boulevard and Ellis Avenue. Cleaver built his company town, known as Cleaverville, around his soap factory in this area in 1851. *See Cleaver Street and Oakland Crescent.*

O'Brien Street
1244 S from 700 W to 742 W

This street was probably named for Alderman James O'Brien, who represented a ward along 12th Street, west of the Chicago River, from 1872 to 1877. He was also a subdivider and developer in about 1889.

Oconto Avenue
7332 W from 3000 N to 7558 N*

This is a Menomonee Indian word meaning "the place of the pickerel."

Octavia Avenue
7300 W from 3000 N to 7558 N*

Named for the railroad stop of Octavia, Nebraska. Octavia (69 B.C. to 11 B.C.)

was the sister of the Roman emperor Augustus and the wife of Mark Antony.

Odell Avenue
7332 W from 3000 N to 7558 N*

The tale of John P. Odell (1847-1910) reads like a Horatio Alger story. He started out in business with a high school diploma and a healthy ambition. He got a job as a cashier at Chicago's Union National Bank and worked his way up to the office of president. Odell was one of forty-five directors of the 1893 World's Columbian Exposition.

Ogallah Avenue
7542 W from 6414 N to 6678 N

The Ogallah Indian tribe was a branch of the Sioux. The name means "to scatter one's own."

Ogden Avenue
1 S at 1570 W to 2500 S at 4562 W

Ogden Avenue
1544 W at 1 N to 600 W at 1560 N

William Butler Ogden (1805-1877) was Chicago's first mayor.

Ogden arrived in town in the 1830s. He came to see what could be done with a muddy tract of land along State Street that one of his relatives had recently purchased for $100,000. After selling just a third of it for that price, he concluded this was his kind of town. He bought more land and made a fortune.

Ogden built Chicago's first drawbridge, first railroad (now called the

View in Washington Park in 1908. The park was designed by Frederick Law Olmsted.

C.R. Childs, courtesy G. Schmalgemeier

William Butler Ogden, 1805-1877

Chicago and North Western), and served as first president of Rush Medical College, now a part of Rush-Presbyterian-St. Luke's Medical Center on the West Side. He was also a charter member of the Chicago Historical Society.

As mayor, elected after the city's incorporation in 1837, he calmed fears during a financial panic and kept the city from defaulting on its debts.

Oglesby Avenue
2332 E from 6700 S to 13758 S*

Richard J. Oglesby (1824-1899) was a soldier in the Mexican-American War, a U.S. senator from Illinois, and governor of Illinois from 1865 to 1869 and from 1885 to 1889. During his term as senator, Illinois ratified the 13th and 14th amendments to the United States Constitution and repealed its racially discriminatory "Black Laws."

Ohio Street
600 N from 484 E to 5968 W*

Named for the state of Ohio. This Iroquois Indian word means "beautiful river."

Oketo Avenue
7400 W from 3000 N to 7558 N*

Arkaketoh was the chief of the Otoe Indians and the namesake of Oketo, Kansas. Oketo was the shortened version of his name, as used by the settlers.

Olcott Avenue
7500 W from 3000 N to 7558 N*

George C. Olcott (1858-1942) was the son of Orville Olcott, a Chicago pioneer and owner of a dry dock business. George C. Olcott was born in the family home near State and Van Buren streets. In 1900, he first published *Olcott's Land Values Blue Book*, an annual guide to property values in the Chicago area.

Oleander Avenue
7532 W from 3000 N to 7558 N*

Named for the oleander evergreen, a shrub with white to red flowers.

Oliphant Avenue
7800 E from 6536 N to 6762 N

This street may have been named for E.P. Oliphant, an officer in the Black Hawk War, 1832. *See Blackhawk Street.*

Olive Avenue
5632 N from 1400 W to 7840 W*

Named for the olive tree.

Olmsted Avenue
7400 W from 6520 N to 6858 N

Named for Frederick Law Olmsted (1822-1903), a noted American landscape architect and writer who designed Chicago's Garfield Park on the West Side (1869) and Jackson Park on the South Side (1871). He also designed New York City's Central Park, and he laid out the grounds for the World's Colombian Exposition in Chicago (1893).

Visionary Chicago architect Daniel Burnham once said of Olmsted that he "paints with lakes and wooded slopes; with lawns and banks and forest-covered hills; with mountainsides and ocean views."

Olmsted and Calvert Vaux laid out west suburban Riverside with streets that "wind like rivers."

When Olmsted designed the plan for Jackson Park in 1871, he disapproved of the site because it was laced with bogs and sand bars. "The place," he said, "was forbidding." When pushed to design

artificial hills along the lake, Olmsted told the South Park Commission, "There is but one object of scenery near Chicago of special grandeur or sublimity, and that, the lake, can be made by artificial means no more grand or sublime."

Olympia Avenue
7600 W from 5012 N to 6756 N

Named for the city and port of Olympia, the capital of Washington. Olympia in Greece was the site of the ancient Olympic Games held every four years from the eighth century B.C. to the fourth century A.D.

Onarga Avenue
7200 W from 6500 N to 6790 N*

Onarga is an Iroquois Indian word meaning "place of rocky hills."

Oneida Avenue
7700 W from 6414 N to 6470 N

This avenue was named after the Oneida Indians, one of the five nations of the Iroquois Confederacy. The word means "people of the stone."

Ontario Street
628 N from 472 E to 3960 W*

Named for Lake Ontario, the smallest and most easterly of the Great Lakes. The word is Iroquois and means "beautiful lake."

Opal Avenue
7832 W from 3200 N to 3564 N

Named for the precious stone.

Orange Avenue
7900 W from 3200 N to 5718 N*

This avenue was named for the citrus fruit.

Orchard Street
700 W from 1550 N to 3170 N*

This street was named for a nearby orchard by land developer John S. Wright. *See Wrightwood Avenue.*

***Signal of Peace* by Cyrus E. Dallin in Lincoln Park at the mouth of Diversey Harbor.**

G. Lane

Oriole Avenue
7600 W from 3001 N to 7658 N*

Named for the bird.

Orleans Street
340 W from 300 N to 2058 N*

This street was named for either New Orleans, Louisiana, or the French city of Orleans, on the banks of the Loire River. In 1429 Orleans was under seige by the English. They were turned back by Joan of Arc.

Osage Avenue
7932 W from 3200 N to 5724 N*

This street was named for either the Osage Indian tribe of Oklahoma (the word means "the strong") or for the osage orange tree.

Osceola Avenue
7432 W from 3000 N to 7556 N*

Osceola (1804-1838) was an Indian leader in the Seminole War, which began in 1835 when the United States tried to force the Seminoles out of Florida and west of the Mississippi River. Osceola, which means "rising sun," was captured. He died in prison.

Oshkosh Avenue
7800 W from 6500 N to 6764 N*

This street, as well as the city of the same name in Wisconsin, was named for Menomonee Chief Oshkosh (1795-1850). The word means "hoof" or "claw" or "nail."

Oswego Street
1650 W from 400 N to 420 N

Oswego is an Iroquois Indian word meaning "where the valley widens."

There is also a town of Oswego, Illinois, on the Fox River just south of Aurora.

DURING THE LONG WINTER MONTHS THE ELDERS OF THE TRIBE PASSED THE TIME THINKING UP STREET NAMES.

Otsego Avenue
7600 W from 6500 N to 6636 N

Named after a lake and city in New York. *Otsego* is an Indian word, possibly meaning "welcome waters" or "bodies of water."

Ottawa Avenue
7632 W from 3200 N to 7558 N*

This street, as well as the town of Ottawa, Illinois, on the Illinois River southwest of Chicago, were named for the Ottawa Indian tribe, whose name means "the traders."

Otto Avenue
9620 W from 5200 N to 5214 N

This street was named by Rosemont developer Arthur Adams. The reference of the name is unknown; Adams had no children.

Overhill Avenue
7700 W from 3200 N to 7558 N*

This avenue was named for a small village in West Virginia.

Owen Avenue
7700 W from 6900 N to 6986 N

Thomas Jefferson Vance Owen (1801-1835) was an Indian Agent who became the first president of the Town of Chicago when it was organized in August of 1833. He chaired the meeting during which incorporation was approved.

The son of Major Ezra Owen, an Indian fighter from Kentucky who traveled with Daniel Boone, T.J.V. Owen was appointed Indian Agent to Chicago in 1830. He got the job after helping a senator to be re-elected. As an Indian Agent, Owen finalized the 1833 treaty that forced the Indians to leave the Chicago area and move west of the Mississippi.

Oxford Avenue
7740 W from 6400 N to 6792 N*

Named for the city and university in England. Oxford University was founded in 1249.

Ozanam Avenue
7800 W from 3200 N to 7169 N*

Antoine Frédéric Ozanam (1813-1853) was a French historian and literary scholar who in 1833 helped found a charitable organization that was to become the St. Vincent de Paul Society.

Ozark Avenue
7732 W from 3200 N to 7558 N*

This avenue was named for the Ozark Mountains of Arkansas and Missouri. Ozarks was the name given by the French to the Quapaw Indians. The name was derived from the French words *aux arcs*, meaning "with bows."

P

Pacific Avenue
8000 W from 3200 N to 5314 N*

Named for the Pacific Ocean. The word means "peaceful." Portugese navigator Ferdinand Magellan (1480-1521) named this ocean the Pacific because it appeared to be relatively free of violent storms.

Packers Avenue
1324 W from 4200 S to 4600 S

Packers Avenue (Pvt.)
1324 W from 3952 S to 4658 S

This avenue honors the meat packers of the Union Stock Yards. At their peak the stockyards covered 500 acres and employed over 40,000 workers. The stockyards, designed as a large unified operation, opened their gates on Christmas day in 1865. The founders had purchased most of the land from former Mayor "Long John" Wentworth for $100,000.

Upton Sinclair's expose of the yards, *The Jungle* (1906), told of spoiled meats and rotten working conditions. A national uproar led to reforms in the meat packing industry. The yards were closed in 1971.

Page Avenue
8032 W from 3200 N to 3956 N*

Peter Page was an officer of the Young Men's Association of the City of Chicago in 1841. Walter L. Newberry was president. The association was the predecessor of the Chicago Public Library. *See Newberry Avenue.*

The Union Stock Yards, April 14, 1953.

Courtesy *Chicago Sun-Times*

Palatine Avenue
6300 N from 6400 W to 7768 W*

Named for Palatine, Illinois. The Palatine is one of the seven hills of Rome.

Palmer Boulevard
2200 N from 3000 W to 3130 W

Palmer Street
2200 N from 2200 W to 7190 W*

Potter Palmer (1826-1902), a dry-goods salesman, came to Chicago in 1852, opened a dry-goods store on Lake Street, and built a strong clientele on the principle of "square dealing." Palmer, unlike any other retailer in town, allowed customers to exchange goods or get their money back. He even permitted customers to take goods home and inspect them before making a purchase. His rivals said he would be out of business in months. But within a decade he owned the largest mercantile business in the Midwest.

On his physician's advice, Palmer retired in 1867, selling his business interests to his partners, Marshall Field and Levi Z. Leiter. He traveled Europe for a while before returning to Chicago with a fresh eye for business.

Palmer decided that Lake Street would not thrive much longer as Chicago's first street of commerce. He saw State Street, then a narrow plank road, as the shopping strip of Chicago's future. He bought a mile of State Street frontage, widened the street, and constructed a long row of buildings, including the first Palmer House at State and Quincy streets.

The original Palmer House was eight stories high with 225 rooms. It opened September 26, 1871 and closed thirteen days later, burned to ashes by the Chicago Fire. In fact, all of Palmer's buildings were destroyed.

The Potter Palmer mansion (1882) on Lake Shore Drive at Schiller, designed by Henry Ives Cobb and Charles Sumner Frost, was demolished in 1950.

Courtesy *Chicago Sun-Times*

Potter Palmer, 1826-1902

Undaunted and flush with good credit, Palmer arranged to borrow $1.7 million from an insurance company—possibly the largest individual loan ever recorded in the United States to that date. Within a few years he was back in the black.

Potter Palmer, also one of the founders of the Chicago Board of Trade, died on May 4, 1902.

Panama Avenue
8100 W from 3200 N to 5542 N*

Named for the Panama Canal.

Paris Avenue
8132 W from 3200 N to 5526 N*

This avenue was named for Paris, France. The city, in turn, was named for the Parisii, a Gallic people who by the end of the third century B.C. had settled in what is now Paris.

Park Place (Pvt.)
5520 S from 1344 E to 1508 E*

(source unkown)

Park Shore East Court
1536 E from 6200 S to 6274 S

This short street runs close by Jackson Park and the Lake Michigan shoreline, hence its name.

Park Terrace
60 W from 800 S to 1200 S

This street is in the middle of the Dearborn Park redevelopment of the old Dearborn Station rail yards.

Parker Avenue
2732 N from 3400 W to 5558 W*

John D. Parker arrived in Chicago in 1848 and watched the city's population grow from 17,000 to two million in about thirty-five years. He was a bookeeper, lumberman, house builder, and, by 1882, a land developer.

Parkside Avenue
5632 W from 5724 N to 6258 S

Laid out in 1872 by real estate subdivider Henry W. Austin, this street was originally known as Park Avenue, possibly because of its location near the Austin town hall and park. Parkside was the site of many of Austin's commercial buildings in the 1880s. *See Austin Avenue and Austin Boulevard.*

Parkview Terrace
3632 W from 3654 N to 3932 N*

This street was named for a mountain peak in Colorado.

Parnell Avenue
532 W from 2900 S to 12946 S*

A group of early Irish land developers named this street for Thomas Parnell (1679-1718), an Irish politician, poet, and essayist. This man is not to be confused with Charles Stewart Parnell, the famous Irish nationalist of the 1880s.

Patterson Avenue
3632 N from 600 W to 7748 W*

Thomas W. Patterson was a real estate subdivider in the firm of Patterson and Payson in about 1883.

Patterson Drive
1624 E in Jackson Park

L.B. Patterson was a commissioner of the South Park District from 1916 to 1924.

Patton Avenue
8414 W from 4536 N to 4624 N

Named for Army General George S. Patton, Jr. (1885-1945), the World War II hero, famous for his brilliant tactics in tank warfare.

Paulina Street
1700 W from 7742 N to 9156 S*

Paulina Taylor was the wife of real estate developer Reuben Taylor. He named the street.

Paxton Avenue
2200 E from 6700 S to 13758 S*

This avenue was named for either Andrew Paxton, a Chicago member of the Organization of the National Law and Order League, which aimed at restricting liquor traffic; or the town of Paxton, Illinois, the seat of Ford County in east central Illinois; or Sir Joseph Paxton (1801-1865), an English gardener and landscape architect who designed the "Crystal Palace" for England's Great Exhibition of 1851. The palace was a glass house that covered four times the area of St. Peter's Basilica in Rome.

Payne Drive
800 E in Washington Park

John Barton Payne, born in 1855 in Virginia, moved to Chicago in 1883 and practiced law. He was president of the South Park District in 1922.

Pearson Street
830 N from 208 E to 1760 W*

Pearson Street (Pvt.)
826 N from 516 W to 532 W

More than likely, these streets were named for Hirman Pearson, who was the city's treasurer from 1837 to 1839, and a West Side alderman from 1837 to 1838. The streets may, however, have been named for Judge John Pearson, who died in 1875, or Benjamin Pearson, the first milkman in Chicago.

Ebenezer Lutheran Church (1904-12) on Foster at Paulina Avenue in the Andersonville neighborhood.

G. Lane

Pensacola Avenue
4332 N from 1432 W to 5758 W*

Pensacola, which is also the name of a city in Florida, is derived from the Indian word *Pansfalaya,* meaning "the hair people."

Peoria Street
900 W from 824 N to 12930 S

Peoria Drive
800 W from 6200 S to 6442 S

Peoria is a French-Indian word of vague origins, perhaps meaning "man among men" or "he who comes carrying a pack on his back" or "carriers." The street is named after Peoria, Illinois. The Peoria Indians were one of five tribes in the Illinois Confederacy.

Perry Avenue
100 W from 5500 S to 12636 S*

Named for Oliver Hazard Perry (1785-1819), a United States naval officer who fought the British in the Battle of Lake Erie in the War of 1812. Perry and the American forces were victorious.

Pershing Place (Pvt.)
3920 S from 1900 W to 2028 W

Pershing Road
3900 S from 880 E to 3600 W

General of the Armies John J. Pershing (1860-1948) commanded the American Expeditionary Force in Europe during World War I.

Peshtigo Court
500 E from 500 N to 520 N

This street takes its name from the Peshtigo River in northeastern Wisconsin. The word is Indian and probably means "wild goose," or "snapping turtle."

Peterson Avenue
6000 N from 1600 W to 7760 W*

Pehr Samuel Peterson (1830-1903) was Chicago's Swedish Johnny Appleseed. His Rosehill Nursery grew at least sixty percent of all the trees planted along public streets in the three decades following the Chicago Fire of 1871.

Peterson was born in Sweden and came to Chicago in 1854. He leased land for his nursery west of Rosehill Cemetery, along what is now Peterson Avenue. Over the years he developed a technique that allowed him to plant larger trees than his competitors. He also planted all the trees at the World's Columbian Exposition of 1893 and was a founder of Rosehill Cemetery.

Phillips Avenue
2432 E from 7200 S to 9356 S*

Phillips Avenue (Circle Drive)
2426 E in Eckersall Park (8100 S)

Named for Louis H. Phillips, a South Side real estate developer.

Pierce Avenue
1532 N from 1600 W to 4124 W*

Ashael Pierce came to Chicago in 1833 and worked as a blacksmith. He and his brother M.J. Pierce later started the Pierce Brothers land development firm. In 1869 they developed about eighty acres of land. This street first appeared in that real estate subdivision.

Pehr S. Peterson, 1830-1903
Courtesy Swedish-American Museum

Pine Avenue
5500 W from 1 N to 1358 N

Named for a pine forest that once stood west of the city.

Pine Grove Avenue
500 W from 2700 N to 3954 N*

This street ran in the neighborhood of the Lake View House, a three-story wooden hotel built in 1854 in a forest of pine trees near the lake south of Irving Park Road. *See Lakeview Avenue.*

The Paderewski House at 2138 W. Pierce Street in the Wicker Park neighborhood, so called because the famous Polish pianist once played from the porch of this house.

G. Lane

Pioneer Avenue
8200 W from 3200 N to 5528 N

This avenue was named for either the Pioneer Association, a prestigious organization of early Chicago settlers, or for The Pioneer, the first locomotive of the Galena and Chicago Union Railway, now the Chicago and North Western Railroad. The Pioneer arrived in Chicago in 1848 and is now on display at the Chicago Historical Society.

Pippin Street
7652 S from 3700 W to 3910 W

This street may have been named for Pippin, Virginia. Pippin is a German personal name.

Pitney Court
1500 W from 3000 S to 3052 S

Franklin V. Pitney was an early landowner, a partner in the real estate firm of Broad & Pitney, and a founder of the Plymouth Congregational Church of Chicago.

Pittsburgh Avenue
8232 W from 3200 N to 5543 N*

Named for Pittsburgh, Pennsylvania.

Plainfield Avenue
8300 W from 3200 N to 5322 N*

Named for Plainfield, New Jersey.

Pleasant Avenue
2136 W at 8800 S to 1900 W at 9456 S*

The inspiration for this street's name was its hilly, wooded, and pleasant location. It runs through the Beverly Hills and Morgan Park neighborhoods.

Plymouth Court
30 W from 300 S to 1440 S

This street was named for Plymouth, Massachusetts, site of the first permanent European settlement in New England. The colony of Plymouth was founded in 1620.

Poe Street
1013 W from 1864 N to 1890 N

This street was named for Edgar Allan Poe (1809-1849), American poet and fiction writer.

Point Street
2648 W from 2000 N to 2154 N

This street cuts diagonally across two blocks making the area to the west of it appear as a triangle or point. The street may also have been named "Point" because it once tapered at both ends.

Polk Street
800 S from 1 W to 5262 W*

Named for James Knox Polk (1795-1849), the eleventh president of the United States, who served from 1845 to 1849.

Pollock Street
2608 W from 1 N to 42 N

(source unknown)

Ponchartrain Boulevard
5700 W from 6500 N to 6654 N

Possibly named for Lake Ponchartrain, just north of New Orleans, Louisiana.

Pontiac Avenue
8332 W from 3200 N to 4158 N

Pontiac (1720-1769) was an Ottawa Indian chief who was killed by an Illinois Indian. The meaning of his name is uncertain.

Pool Drive
5512 S in Washington Park

This street provides an access to the swimming pool in Washington Park.

Pope John Paul II Drive
4300 S from 2400 W to 3158 W

This one-mile stretch of 43d Street was named for Pope John Paul II in early 1980 to commemorate his visit to Chicago in 1979. In this new street's first six months, twenty-three of the pope's street signs were stolen.

Poplar Avenue
1000 W from 2700 S to 3066 S

Named for the poplar tree.

Portland Avenue
252 W from 4500 S to 4520 S

This avenue is named for the Island of Portland in the English Channel, famous for its cement. The island is a limestone peninsula connected to the mainland by a 200-yard-wide stretch of shingle.

Post Place
228 W from 200 N to 234 N

Justus Post, a colonel in the War of 1812, was a surveyor for the Illinois and Michigan Canal. He made his first survey of the proposed path of the canal in 1823. *See Canal Street.*

Potawatomie Avenue
8630 W from 4400 N to 5240 N*

The Potawatomie Indians lived in agricultural villages in summer, but moved to hunting grounds in winter. They lived in dome-shaped wigwams or large bark-covered houses in Wisconsin, Illinois, Indiana, and Michigan. Their name means "people of the place of the fire."

Potomac Avenue
1300 N from 1300 W to 5958 W*

Named for the Union's Army of the Potomac, which took its name from the Potomac River near Washington D.C. Potomac is a variation of Patowomek, an Indian village and tribe in Virginia. The word means "a place where something is brought."

Prairie Avenue
300 E from 1600 S to 13358 S*

The Henry B. Clarke House in the Prairie Avenue Historic District. Built in 1836, this is Chicago's oldest building.

G. Lane

Prairie Avenue (Pvt.)
300 E from 13200 S to 13274 S

Originally an old Indian trail linking Fort Dearborn and Fort Wayne in Indiana, this street is named for the vast Midwestern prairie. Prairie Avenue was once known as "Millionaire's Row." On Prairie Avenue between 16th and 22nd streets in the 1880s and 1890s, stood more than fifty mansions, including the homes of George Pullman, Marshall Field, John J. Glessner, and Phillip Armour. The elite began to move north, however, after Bertha Palmer, queen of Chicago society and wife of Potter Palmer, built a mansion on Lake Shore Drive. *See Palmer Street and Lake Shore Drive.*

Pratt Avenue
6800 N from 3200 W to 7569 W

Pratt Boulevard
6800 N from 1048 W to 3200 W

Paul and George Pratt were members of the Rogers Park Building and Land Company, which was incorporated in 1873. *See Touhy, Lunt, Morse, and Greenleaf Avenues.*

Prescott Avenue

5500 W from 6148 N to 6198 N

John A. Prescott was a builder and real estate subdivider.

Princeton Avenue

300 W from 2100 S to 12658 S*

Named for Princeton University in Princeton, New Jersey. Founded in 1746, Princeton is the fourth oldest university in the United States.

Prindiville Street

2246 N from 2700 W to 2738 W

This street was probably named for Capt. John Prindiville, who was known as the "storm king" in insurance, marine, and yachting circles. Born in Ireland, John Prindiville moved to Chicago in 1836. He commanded the brigatine *Minnesota* on the Great Lakes in 1850. In his later years he was an official of a Chicago yacht club and earned a living in the insurance business.

A more remote possibility is that this street was named for John's brother, Redmond Prindiville, another early Chicagoan.

Promontory Drive

2124 E in Jackson Park

Promontory Circle Drive

2124 E in Jackson Park

So named because this street travels a finger of land that juts into Lake Michigan.

Prospect Avenue

1721 W at 9500 S to 2000 W at 11054 S

Prospect Square

1800 W from 9100 S to 9132 S

These streets were named by the Blue Island Land and Building Company for Prospect, New York, the hometown of many of the company's partners.

Pryor Avenue

11156 S from 1600 W to 1933 W*

Roger Pryor, a real estate developer in about 1869, was a partner in the firm of Pryor and Hopkins.

Pulaski Road

4000 W from 6360 N to 11458 S*

This street's name was changed from Crawford Avenue, which honored an early West Side and Cicero settler named Peter Crawford, to honor Casimir Pulaski, a Polish hero in the American Revolution. But it took nearly twenty years of court battles and ethnic politics to change the name.

The battle began about 1933. At that time both Crawford and Pulaski were long dead.

Pulaski was born in Lithuania and fought as a Polish soldier, unfortunately against the Polish king. He was sentenced to prison, fled to France, met Ben Franklin, and decided to become an American Revolutionary. Pulaski fought courageously in the colonies, but didn't get along with his fellow officers, and he eventually resigned from the cavalry. Later, an act of Congress put him in charge of a light infantry unit known as Pulaski's Legion. The legion lost to the British at Egg Harbor, New Jersey, and again in South Carolina. Pulaski was killed in the siege of Savannah, Georgia, in 1779. He was 31, considered a hero, and credited with being the founder of the American cavalry.

As for Peter Crawford, an obscure Scottish pioneer and real estate speculator, he purchased 160 acres and founded the settlement of Crawford, which grew to become North Lawndale. In the 1840s he was a Chicago-area lumber dealer.

Ironically, in 1933, the year the Crawford-Pulaski war began, it was at the insistence of Mayor Ed Kelly that the name be changed to honor Count Pulaski.

Why? Politics.

In 1933 Kelly was running for mayor. One of his supporters, Emily Napieralski, was president of the Polish Women's Alliance. After the election, Kelly asked Napieralski what he could do to repay her for her support. She asked that a street be named after the great Polish General, Casimir Pulaski. Kelly agreed and chose Crawford to become Pulaski. This didn't sit well with businessmen along Crawford Avenue. It wasn't that they felt any great allegiance to old Peter Crawford. They were worried about having to change their business stationery—not to mention the confusion all this would cause their customers.

For the next nineteen years the battle raged in the courts and in the state legislature. But in 1952, the Illinois Supreme Court ruled that property owners along a street can't control the naming of the street.

Q

Quincy Street

220 S, from 1 W to 5574 W*

Named for John Quincy Adams (1767-1848), the sixth president of the United States, who served from 1825 to 1829.

Quinn Street

1000 W, from 2700 S to 3054 S

T. Quinn was a subdivider of the land through which this street runs.

R

Race Avenue
526 N, from 1200 W to 5968 W*

Named for William B. Race, who in 1874 subdivided an area in the vicinity of Ogden Avenue and 22nd Street.

Racine Avenue
1200 W, from 4746 N to 12258 S*

The best bet here is that this street was named after the city of Racine, Wisconsin. The city was named in 1835 for its primary river, the Racine, and the river was so named by early French explorers because it contained such a tangle of roots that canoe passage on it was almost impossible. *Racine* is the French word for root.

Another possibility is that the street was named for Jean Baptiste Racine (1639-1699), the French dramatist who is ranked among the greatest of French classical writers.

Railroad Avenue
900 S, from 5808 W to 5958 W

This street fronts the old Chicago & Great Western Railroad.

Railroad Place
1800 S, from 2400 W to 2422 W

This street fronts the Chicago, Burlington & Quincy Railroad right-of-way, since the early 1970s part of the Burlington Northern System.

Rainey Drive
5520 S in Washington Park

Named for Edward J. Rainey, a commissioner of the South Park District from 1905 to 1909.

Randolph Street
150 N, from 464 E to 3140 W

John Randolph (1773-1833) was a U.S. senator from Virginia from 1825 to 1827. A cousin of Thomas Jefferson, he started out in politics at age twenty-five as the president's floor leader in the House of Representatives. James Thompson, who laid out Chicago streets for the Illinois and Michigan Canal in 1830, was from Randolph County, Illinois, and probably named it for that reason.

Rascher Avenue
5432 N, from 1400 W to 8558 W*

Named for Charles Rascher, a real estate speculator, who published five Chicago atlases in the 1860s.

Raven Street
6300 N, from 6200 W to 6836 W

Ravens once were common in Chicago's woods.

Ravenswood Avenue
1800 W, from 3000 N to 7079 N*

The men who developed the community of Ravenswood were standing in a field in 1868 near what is now Leland Avenue and Clark Street, examining their property as the sun sank in the sky. A flock of ravens flew out of the woods, so the story goes, and one of the men exclaimed, "That's it: Ravenswood!"

Another possibility is that the street was named after Ravenswood, West Virginia, the hometown of one member of the Ravenswood Land Company. And others say that the woods in this area were the home of Chief Raven, an Indian leader.

Redfield Drive
3530 W in Marquette Park

Named for Robert Redfield, the attorney for the South Park District from 1909 to 1917.

Redwood Avenue
8024 W, from 5448 N to 5452 N

Named for the redwood tree.

Refectory Drive
1400 N in Humboldt Park

A refectory is a room for refreshment or a dining hall. A refectory, designed in the Prairie School style by architect Hugh M.G. Garden in 1907, overlooks a lagoon in the north central part of Humboldt Park.

Reilly Avenue
3716 W, from 7724 S to 7828 S

Named for Rev. Joseph Morris Reilly, a Roman Catholic priest who founded St. Denis Church at 83rd Street and St. Louis Avenue in 1951. He was the parish's first pastor.

Reserve Avenue
8730 W, from 4444 N to 5240 N

This street runs through what was once the reservation of Alexander Robinson, chief of the United Potawatomies. Robinson (1762-1872) was the son of a Scottish army officer and an Ottawa woman. His Indian name was Chechepinqua.

Robinson served as Indian interpreter under Dr. Alexander Wolcott, an Indian Agent at Fort Dearborn in 1823 and 1826. With Billy Caldwell, Robinson prevented his tribe from joining the Sauks in the Winnebago War of 1827 and

with Black Hawk in the war of 1832. At the Treaty of Prairie du Chien in July 1829, he was granted two sections of land on the Des Plaines River.
See Wolcott, Caldwell, and Sauganash Streets.

Reta Avenue
832 W, from 3500 N to 3558 N

Reta Benton was the wife of William H. Benton, a real estate speculator in the 1890s.

Rhodes Avenue
532 E, from 3100 S to 13247 S*

Named for J. Foster Rhodes, a real estate speculator and developer from Ohio. Rhodes was also a Chicago lawyer and builder in the 1870s and 1880s. He specialized in the construction of fireproof buildings, which were much in demand after the Chicago Fire of 1871. In 1874, he developed the Rhodes Subdivision, a section of land near Rhodes Avenue and 31st Street.

Rice Street
832 N, from 1800 W to 5968 W*

While many Chicago mayors have been accused of playing to the crowd, only one, John Blake Rice (1809-1874), was a professional actor.

Born in Maryland, Rice was not only an actor but a manager and owner of theaters in Bangor, Maine; Buffalo, New York; and Milwaukee, Wisconsin. More importantly, in 1847 Rice built the first real theater in Chicago, Rice's Theater, located on the south side of Randolph Street between State and Wabash. When it burned down in 1850,

Randolph Street at LaSalle, 1889, with a cablecar emerging from LaSalle Street tunnel under the Chicago River.

Courtesy *Chicago Sun-Times*

John B. Rice, 1809-1874

Rice spent $11,000 to build another, this one of brick. He is regarded as one of the founders of drama in Chicago.

Although early Chicago theater consisted mostly of local stock companies, Rice tried to stir up more interest in 1856 by promising to bring sixteen stars to town in six months. Among the actors employed by Chicago theater owners such as Rice and James McVicker were the Booths, including John Wilkes Booth, the actor who shot Abraham Lincoln.

Rice was elected Chicago's twentieth mayor on April 18, 1865, just a few days after Lincoln's assassination. He was mayor for four and a half years (1865-69), elected twice, both times defeating former Mayor Francis C. Sherman.

During Rice's term of office, the city was divided into twenty wards. He grappled with an exploding population that strained the public school system.

After leaving office, Rice turned to business interests, transforming his theater building into a business block. In 1872 he was elected to Congress, representing the first Chicago congressional district.

Richards Drive
1900 E in Jackson Park

Named for Harry S. Richards, who started his career with the South Park District in 1884 as a night watchman. In 1899 he was appointed assistant general superintendent; in 1911 he was appointed superintendent of maintenance and repair; and in 1926 he was promoted to general superintendent.

Richmond Street
2932 W, from 6756 N to 8258 S

The city of Richmond is the capital of Virginia.

Ridge Avenue
1200 W at 5600 N to 1900 W at 6382 N*

Ridge Boulevard
1900 W at 6400 N to 2200 W at 7558 N

For much of its length this street and boulevard run along the top of a ridge formed by prehistoric glaciers. It was part of the rim of the massive prehistoric lake that geologists call Lake Chicago.

Ridgeland Avenue
1732 E, from 6700 S to 9358 S*

In the 1870s this street was laid out along a line of sand hills by the real estate subdivider George Earle.

Ridgeway Avenue
3732 W, from 6354 N to 11372 S*

Thomas S. Ridgway (there was no "e" in his name) was a director of the McCormick Theological Society in Chicago for three years, the state treasurer of Illinois in 1874, and a trustee of Southern Illinois University for nineteen years. Ridgway (1826-1897) was a resident of downstate Shawneetown.

Another and perhaps more likely possibility is that the street was named for a Chicago real estate speculator, John Jacob Ridgeway.

Ridgewood Court
1368 E, from 5400 S to 5482 S

Ridgewood was the name of a small settlement in this area before the development of the suburb of Hyde Park. The settlement was named for Ridgewood, New Jersey, the home state of many early Chicagoans.

Ritchie Court
62 E, from 1300 N to 1326 N

The Rev. Arthur Ritchie came to Chicago from Boston in 1875 to accept the pastorate of the Church of the Ascension. The church was then located on this street. In 1884 Ritchie left Chicago to accept a position at St. Ignatius Church in New York City.

Riverdale Avenue
432 E at 13200 S to 548 E at 13346 S

This street runs through the Riverdale neighborhood at the far south city limits, just northeast of the suburb of Riverdale. The Little Calumet River runs through this neighborhood, which was first settled in 1836 but not called Riverdale until 1873.

Robinson Street
1700 W, from 3114 S to 3168 S

Alexander Robinson (1762-1872) was a chief of the united Potawatomies, Chippewas, and Ottawas. He was the son of a Scotch trader and an Ottawa woman. From 1823 to 1826 he served as an Indian interpreter at Fort Dearborn.

A second possibility is that the street was named for John Robinson (1793-1843), a U.S. senator from Illinois from 1830 to 1841.

Rochdale Place (Pvt.)
5474 S, from 1400 E to 1426 E

When this street was named in the early 1960s, it ran alongside a community of thirty-four homes founded on Rochdale cooperative principles. The modern cooperative was founded in 1844 by the Rochdale Society of Equitable Pioneers in Rochdale, Lancaster, England. The society envisioned an international wholesale and retail trade organization whose profits would be distributed to member-customers.

Rockwell Street
2600 W, from 7558 N to 11458 S*

Named for John A. Rockwell, a real estate man who in 1871 developed land along both sides of Rockwell Street, one block in either direction, north and south of Madison Street.

Holy Family Church (1857-60) and St. Ignatius College Prep (1869) on Roosevelt Road at Blue Island Avenue on the Near West Side.

Tom Gobby

Rogers Avenue
5212 W at 5218 N to 1328 W at 7666 N*

Philip Rogers (1812-1856) was the first white settler of the North Side community that would one day be called Rogers Park. An Irish immigrant, he came to Chicago from upstate New York in the 1830s, and in 1839 he built a cabin at the intersection of what now are Ridge and Lunt Avenues. From his truck farm earnings he purchased 1,600 acres before his death in 1856. His son-in-law, Patrick L. Touhy, and a consortium of real estate men went on to develop Rogers Park.

Roosevelt Drive
1200 S in Grant Park

Roosevelt Road
1200 S, from 128 E to 5958 W

Named for Theodore Roosevelt (1858-1919), the twenty-sixth president of the United States, who served from 1901 to 1909. A Republican, he was born in New York City, became a popular hero in the Spanish-American War, and was

The gate to Rosehill Cemetery (1859) in the Ravenswood neighborhood.

G. Lane

vice-president when William McKinley was assassinated in 1901.

Root Street
4134 S, from 1 W to 758 W

Named for James Porter Root (1840-1918), a Chicago lawyer-turned-politician.

Born in Madison County, New York, Root served as an assistant U.S. attorney in New York State before moving to Chicago. He opened a law practice in the high-rent Newhall Building at Randolph and Franklin Streets and simultaneously jumped into local Republican politics. In 1869 he was elected clerk of the Illinois House of Representatives. And in 1870 he was elected a state representative.

Roscoe Street
3400 N, from 400 W to 8158 W*

Named for the town of Roscoe, Pennsylvania.

Rose Street
9536 W, from 5200 N to 5212 N

Named for the flower.

Rosedale Avenue
5900 N, from 1200 W to 7824 W*

Named by John L. Cochran, the developer of Edgewater, for Rosedale, Pennsylvania, a suburb of his hometown of Philadelphia. *See also Berwyn and Edgewater Avenues.*

Rosehill Drive
5800 N, from 1601 W to 1776 W

Rosehill Cemetery, for which the street is named, is located on a rise of land owned in the 1850s by Hyram Roe, a tavern keeper. Roe's Hill became Rosehill.

Rosemont Avenue
6300 N, from 940 W to 4822 W*

This street was named by John L. Cochran, the developer of Edgewater, after Rosemont, Pennsylvania, a suburb along the Main Line, a commuter rail line running west from Philadelphia, Cochran's hometown. *See also Berwyn and Edgewater Avenues.*

Roslyn Place
2500 N, from 400 W to 462 W

Named for the town of Roslyn, New York.

Ross Avenue
200 W, from 6500 S to 6568 S

Dr. Joseph P. Ross, born in 1828, was one of the organizers of Cook County Hospital in 1866.

Ruble Street
652 W, from 1000 S to 2050 S*

Named for the monetary unit and silver coin of Russia.

Rumsey Avenue
8500 S at 3752 W to 8700 S at 3962 W

Named for Julian S. Rumsey (1821-1886), who was Chicago's Civil War mayor.

Rumsey moved to Chicago from Batavia, New York, in 1835 to work in a shipping business started by his uncles, George W. Dole and Walter L. Newberry. An early president of the Chicago Board of Trade, he was elected mayor in 1861. As mayor, Rumsey promptly led a committee of 100 Chicagoans to Washington, D.C. to appeal for compromise and peace between the North and South. But when the war came, he "gave the best of himself to arouse the patriotism of the community," reported the *Chicago City Manual* of 1911. "His administration was not memorable for much else."

Rundell Place

14 S, from 1000 W to 1168 W

Adeline Rundell was the second wife of Lemuel J. Swift, a partner from 1875 to 1884 in the real estate development firm of Dunlap & Swift. This street runs through one of their subdivisions.

Rush Street

65 E, from 401 N to 1138 N

Dr. Benjamin Rush (1745-1813) was one of four physicians to sign the Declaration of Independence. He was a great patriot who served as a surgeon in the Revolutionary War. He convinced Thomas Paine to write "Common Sense." Rush Medical College in Chicago, now Rush-Presbyterian-St. Luke's Medical Center, was named in his honor.

Russell Drive

536 E in Washington Park

Martin J. Russell, born in Chicago in 1845, was a newspaperman and a parks commissioner. A nephew of Colonel James A. Mulligan (*see Mulligan Avenue*), he served as a lieutenant under his uncle in the Civil War. Russell was city editor of the *Chicago Evening Post* in 1870, editorial writer of the *Chicago Times* in 1873, and editor of the *Chicago Herald* in 1883. He was a commissioner of the South Park District from 1880 to 1893.

Rutherford Avenue

6732 W, from 5342 N to 6258 S*

Thomas A. Rutherford in 1924 subdivided and sold for development a part of the West Side between Oak Park Avenue and Newland Avenue, north of Armitage Avenue. Rutherford Avenue runs just east of this subdivision.

Rush Presbyterian St. Luke's Medical Center at 1735 W. Congress Parkway.

G. Lane

S

Sacramento Avenue
3000 W, from 7558 N to 11258 S*

Sacramento Boulevard
3000 W, from 934 N to 1156 S*

Sacramento Drive
3000 W in Douglas Park

Sacramento Square Drive
442 N, from 3001 W to 3025 W

Named for the capital of California. The word is Spanish for "sacrament," and it refers to the blessed sacrament of the Lord's Supper.

Saginaw Avenue
2638 E, from 7500 S to 13034 S*

Saginaw is an Algonquin word for "mouth of a river." Saginaw, Michigan, was once the site of a Sauk Indian village.

St. Clair Street
200 E, from 500 N to 720 N

Named for General Arthur St. Clair (1734-1818), the first governor of the Northwest Territory, which included the future state of Illinois. Although St. Clair stood by Gen. George Washington during the bitter winter of 1776-77, he was later court-martialed for evacuating Fort Ticonderoga, popularly considered to be impregnable.

Born in Caithness County, Scotland, he began his military career as an ensign in the British army. He served the British in Canada, married a Boston girl, and bought 4,000 acres of land in Pennsylvania. As a brigadier general in the American army, he fought in the battles of Trenton and Princeton.

St. Clair served as a delegate to the Continental Congress of 1785-87, and as governor of the Northwest Territory for the next fifteen years. But he was an unpopular man on the frontier, considered by plain-speaking pioneers to be overbearing and paternalistic.

St. Georges Court
2260 N, from 2700 W to 2738 W

Named for St. George, the patron saint of England, who lived in the third century A.D. in Lydda, in Palestine. Legend tells of him rescuing a lady from a dragon. His feast day is April 23.

St. Helen Street
2114 N, from 2700 W to 2718 W

St. Helena (255 to 330 A.D) was a Roman empress, the mother of Constantine the Great, who was reputed to have discovered the true cross of Christ. Her feast day in the West is August 18.

St. James Place
2520 N, from 400 W to 470 W

Named for St. James, who died in 62 A.D. in Jerusalem, and was an apostle of Jesus, one of the original Twelve Apostles. He was a leader of the Jerusalem Christians. His Western feast day is May 3.

St. Joseph Avenue
5140 N, from 8500 W to 8562 W

This street is named for St. Joseph Ukrainian Catholic Church, 5000 N. Cumberland, which is nearby. The carpenter Joseph was the husband of Mary, the mother of Jesus.

St. Lawrence Avenue
600 E, from 4100 S to 13450 S*

Most likely named for the St. Lawrence River. And it was most likely named for St. Lawrence, the Roman deacon and martyr who is said to have been roasted to death on a gridiron in 258 A.D. He is one of the most venerated martyrs of the Catholic Church. His feast day is August 10.

St. Louis Avenue
3500 W, from 6256 N to 11658 S*

Named for Louis IX (1214-1270), king of France from 1226 to 1270, who was the most popular of the Capetian monarchs. He led the Seventh Crusade to the Holy Land in 1248-50 and died on another crusade to Tunisia. His feast day is August 25.

St. Mary Street
2170 N, from 2748 W to 2766 W

This street honors St. Mary Catholic Church, the first Catholic church in Chicago. Built of wood in 1833 near the southwest corner of Lake and State Streets, it was 25-by-35 feet in size. The Rev. John Mary Irenaeus St. Cyr was the first pastor. Old St. Mary's is now located at Wabash and Van Buren Streets.

St. Michael's Court
448 W, from 1600 N to 1758 N

This street was named for St. Michael Catholic Church, established nearby at Eugenie and Cleveland Streets in 1852. The church was named for Michael the Archangel, the patron saint of Michael

Diversey, a brewer who donated the land for the church. *See Diversey Avenue.* The present church was dedicated in 1869, was totally gutted by the Chicago Fire of 1871, and was rebuilt and rededicated in 1873. Michael the Archangel is celebrated as the protector of Christians, especially soldiers. His feast day is September 29.

St. Paul Avenue
1732 N, from 200 W to 5174 W*

Named for St. Paul, the apostle of the Gentiles, who was beheaded in Rome in about 67 A.D. He was converted to Christianity on the road to Damascus when he had a vision in which Jesus rebuked him for handing Christians over to prison and death. His feast day is June 29.

Sandburg Terrace
118 W, from 1530 N to 1556 N

Carl Sandburg said it first: "City of the Big Shoulders." And people have been saying it ever since. Sandburg (1878-1967), the poet and biographer, is best known for his poetic celebrations of Chicago and his biography of Abraham Lincoln.

Sandburg Terrace (Pvt.)
118 W, from 1226 N to 1528 N

Sanford Avenue
9700 W, from 5200 N to 5212 N

See Sprague Avenue.

Sangamon Street
932 W, from 904 N to 12930 S*

The Sangamon River, this street's namesake, in east central Illinois, was probably named by white settlers who corrupted the Indian word *sagamo*, meaning "chief" in some Algonquin dialects.

Carl Sandburg, 1878-1967

Sauganash Avenue
4140 W at 6000 N to 5548 W at 6864 N

Sauganash, whose English name was Billy Caldwell, was a chief of the Potawatomie Indians. In appreciation for his role in securing a treaty between his tribe and the U.S. government, the government in 1828 gave him approximately 1,600 acres along the Chicago River in what are now the Northwest Side communities of Edgebrook and Sauganash. This Indian reservation was a major hunting ground of the Potawatomies. In 1836, after the tribe was removed from the area, Sauganash sold most of the land to white farmers. *See Caldwell Avenue.*

Sawyer Avenue
3232 W, from 5558 N to 11476 S*

Named for Dr. Sidney Sawyer, the father of Ada Sawyer Garrett. The Garretts and their relations, the Butterfields, were among the largest landowners and real estate developers on Chicago's Northwest Side.

Dr. Sawyer, who was a resident of Chicago at least before 1840, married

Elizabeth Butterfield, one of three daughters of Justin Butterfield, an attorney with extensive land holdings. In 1846 the Sawyers' daughter Ada—for whom Ada Street was named—was born. In her later life, Ada Sawyer Garrett owned more Chicago real estate than any other woman except Edith Rockefeller McCormick.

Sayre Avenue
6958 W, from 6548 N to 6458 S*

William E. Sayre owned a 90-acre farm in the 1840s in what would eventually become the community area of Montclare. He built the first frame house there in 1840 and brought his produce to market over a dirt road that would become Grand Avenue. In 1872 the nucleus of the settlement of Sayre was created when the Chicago and Pacific Railroad laid track across the Sayre farm and established a station at what is today Sayre and Medill Avenues.

Schick Place
500 W, from 1250 N to 1270 N

William Schick was a North Side storekeeper in the 1880s who invested in real estate in the vicinity of Clybourn Avenue and Division Street.

Schiller Street
1400 N, from 72 E to 2158 W*

Johann Christoph Friedrich von Schiller (1759-1805), one of Germany's greatest literary figures, is considered the founder of modern German literature. This street may have been named by German subdividers; it honors the German population that was spread across the North Side, particularly in the neighborhood now known as Old Town.

School Street
3300 N, from 900 W to 8324 W*

From its earliest days, this street has

had the Nathaniel Hawthorne Elementary School located on it at the corner of Clifton (1226 W) at School Street.

Schorsch Street
3314 N, from 6602 W to 6622 W

This street honors three generations of a Northwest Side real estate and construction company. Albert J. Schorsch (1888-1970) started the family business in 1912 and brought in his six brothers over the years. Albert named Catherine Street in honor of his mother and Maria street in honor of his wife. Albert Schorsch, Jr. now runs the real estate business with his own sons.

Schraeder Drive
134 N in Garfield Park

(source unknown)

Schreiber Avenue
6432 N, from 1500 W to 7144 W*

In 1897, Dominick and Michael Schreiber were real estate speculators who subdivided an area between Ravenswood Avenue and Clark Street, north of Devon Avenue. Schreiber Avenue runs through this subdivision.

Schubert Avenue
2700 N, from 600 W to 7190 W*

Franz Peter Schubert (1797-1828) was an Austrian musician and composer of the early Romantic period. He is best known for his German songs for voice and piano.

Scott Street
1240 N, from 88 E to 574 W*

General Winfield Scott (1786-1866) was a leader in the Mexican-American War and a Whig nominee for president in 1852. He was the senior Union general in the early Civil War period. He also fought in the Black Hawk War of 1832.

Scottsdale Avenue
8100 S at 4670 W to 8450 S at 4600 W

When Raymond Lutgent began developing a new community on the far Southwest Side of Chicago in 1953, he named it for his son Scott. This subdivision was originally part of the Ashburn Flying Field, allegedly Chicago's first airfield. The retail anchor of the community today is the Scottsdale Shopping Center at 79th Street and Cicero Avenue. The street takes its name from the community name.

Sedgwick Street
400 W, from 1200 N to 2226 N

Named for Robert Sedgwick, a subdivider of the eastern portion of the land through which this street runs.

Seeley Avenue
2032 W, from 7546 N to 10773 S*

Seeley Avenue (Pvt.)
2028 W, from 3900 S to 3940 S

In 1879 Admiral Amos S. Seeley developed the land in the area bounded by Madison Street, Monroe Street, Hoyne Avenue, and Seeley Avenue.

Seipp Street
8540 S, from 2614 W to 2956 W

This street was named by Gallagher & Henry Builders of Oak Brook for August Seipp, a noted Chicago brewer, from whom the developers bought this Southwest Side land.

Conrad Seipp, 1825-1890

Seminary Avenue
1100 W, from 1906 N to 4364 N*

This street was named for the McCormick Theological Seminary which was located nearby from 1859 to 1975 on the Lincoln-Fullerton-Halsted campus which is today part of DePaul University. The seminary was founded in 1829 in Hanover, Indiana, as the theological department of Hanover College. It moved to New Albany, Indiana in 1840, and then to Chicago in 1859. Cyrus McCormick, the famed inventor of the reaper, was responsible for the seminary's coming to Chicago. He offered to endow four professorships for $25,000 each if the school would relocate in or near Chicago. Since 1975 the seminary has been located at 5555 S. Woodlawn Avenue in Hyde Park.

Seminole Street
5700 N, from 5600 W to 7940 W*

The Seminoles were a tribe of Indians living in Florida who once belonged to the Muskogee or Creek Confederacy. The name means "separatist" or "runaway." In the late eighteenth century, the Seminoles broke with the confederacy.

Seneca Street
236 E, from 500 N to 920 N*

The Senecas were a tribe of Iroquois Indians in upstate New York. *Seneca* is a corruption of an Indian word for "place of the stone."

Senour Avenue
1100 W, from 2500 S to 2632 S

Until the middle 1980s when the plant was closed, this street was the access road to the Martin Senour Paint Company manufacturing plant.

Serbian Road
5710 N, from 7846 W to 8050 W

This street runs alongside the Holy Resurrection Serbian Orthodox Cathedral at 5701 N. Redwood Drive. The cathedral was constructed in 1968 and serves a congregation of about 2,500 people. Chicago's Serbian community, which dates back to 1895, was first centered near the Loop, then in Wicker Park, and now in the northwest suburbs.

Shakespeare Avenue
2132 N, from 1400 W to 6926 W*

This street was named for William Shakespeare (1564-1616), the English playwright and poet.

***William Shakespeare* by William Ordway Partridge in Lincoln Park near Belden, was first seen at the World's Columbian Exposition of 1893.**

G. Lane

McCormick Theological Seminary, founded in 1863, on Halsted between Fullerton and Belden was Lincoln Park's foremost institution. These buildings were demolished in 1960.

Courtesy Commission on Chicago Landmarks

Shapland Avenue
9800 W, from 5200 N to 5224 N

See Sprague Avenue.

Sheffield Avenue
1000 W, from 2546 N to 3846 N

Joseph E. Sheffield (1797-1882) came to Chicago from Connecticut and established a truck farm and nursery in the 1830s. He bought up land along what is now Clark Street and sparked the beginnings of the Lincoln Park neighborhood. Sheffield was a founder and charter director in 1856 of the Chicago, Rock Island & Pacific Railroad, and a builder of the New Haven & Northhampton Railroad in Connecticut.

Shelby Court
966 W, from 1900 S to 1942 S

Possibly named for Shelby County, in south central Illinois. The county, in turn, was named by Kentucky settlers for General Isaac Shelby (1750-1826), an American frontiersman, soldier, and first governor of Kentucky.

Sheridan Road
400 W, from 2800 N to 3181 N

Sheridan Road
3900 N, from 600 W to 956 W

Sheridan Road
1000 W at 3900 N to 1400 W at 7734 N

Sheridan Road
6400 N, from 970 W to 1158 W

General Philip H. Sheridan (1831-1888), for whom Fort Sheridan was also named, was a Civil War cavalry commander and hero. His most infamous remark was: "The only good Indians I ever saw were dead." In 1884 he joined with a group of wealthy Chicagoans in constructing the Washington Park Race Track, the favorite gathering place of Chicago's high society for almost twenty years.

Sherwin Avenue
7332 N, from 1204 W to 7728 W*

Named for Ezra B. Sherwin, an early resident and trustee in 1881 of the village of Norwood Park, now a Chicago neighborhood. He lived in a house that still stands on Newcastle Avenue near Ardmore Avenue.

Shields Avenue
328 W, from 728 S to 5858 S*

General James Shields (1810-1879), an Irish immigrant, was shipwrecked off the coast of Canada. He became a soldier in the Black Hawk and Mexican Wars, and from 1849 to 1856 he was a U.S. senator from Illinois. Shields also became a justice of the Illinois Supreme Court. He had a reputation to uphold. So when criticisms were being whispered about that he was a bad state auditor, he apparently blamed Abraham Lincoln and his wife, Mary Todd Lincoln, for the gossip. Shields then challenged Lincoln to a duel, but Lincoln was able to talk his way out of the duel challenge, and the two men went on to become friends. Shields, a real estate speculator, came to Chicago in 1868.

Shore Drive
1800 E, from 5300 S to 5558 S

As the name indicates, this street runs parallel to the Lake Michigan shore, immediately west of Lake Shore Drive.

Short Street
1400 W at 2700 S to 1316 W at 2838 S

As the name says, this street is one of Chicago's shortest.

The Gary-Lyon monument and Willowmere pond in Graceland Cemetery, Clark Street at Irving Park Road.

G. Lane

Simonds Drive
800 W in Lincoln Park

Ossian Cole Simonds (1855-1931) designed much of the landscape in Graceland Cemetery. He was superintendent of the cemetery from 1881 to 1889, with full authority to develop it. He then assumed a position on the cemetery's board of managers. He became so well known for his naturalistic landscape at Graceland that Chicago's wealthiest families demanded his services. So he established a business near the cemetery, O.C. Simonds and Company, in 1903. He was gardener of Lincoln Park from 1908 to 1911.

Sioux Avenue

5400 W, from 6601 N to 7124 N

Named for the Sioux Indians, the largest group of Plains Indians. They called themselves the "Dakota," but the Chippewa called them *Nadoeisiw*, meaning "enemy." The French corruption of this word, *Nadwessioux*, was shortened to Sioux. Some historians believe the word meant "wanderers" and referred to the Sioux' nomadic ways.

Solidarity Drive

1250 S, from 600 E to 850 E

At the request of members of Chicago's Polish community, Mayor Jane Byrne renamed Achsah Bond Drive on March 2, 1980, to commemorate Polish labor leader Lech Walesa and his Solidarity trade organization. For years, this street leading to the Adler Planetarium had been known as "the Polish corridor" because statues of Nicolaus Copernicus and Thaddeus Kosciusko guard each end of it. Achsah Bond had been the wife of the first governor of Illinois.

Somerset Avenue

5600 N, from 6400 W to 6432 W

Somerset is a county in southwest England. This street, however, more than likely took its name from Somerset County, New Jersey, or Somerset County, Pennsylvania, birthplaces of many early Chicago settlers.

South Chicago Avenue

400 E at 6700 S to 3200 E at 9474 S

The South Chicago community, through which this street slices, is located on the far Southeast Side of Chicago.

Southport Avenue

1400 W, from 1952 N to 4158 N

In the 1840s, stagecoaches ran regularly between Chicago and Milwaukee, stopping in Kenosha, Wisconsin. In

Thaddeus Kosciusko, 1746-1817, by Alexander Chodinski on Solidarity Drive, was dedicated September 11, 1904. It originally stood in Humboldt Park.

G. Lane

Chicago the stages traveled along the street now called Southport. At that time, Milwaukee was referred to by stage teamsters as the "north port" and Chicago was the "south port."

South Shore Drive

2400 E, from 6700 S to 8334 S

South Shore Drive

7100 S, from 2400 E to 2542 E

This street runs along the south shore of Lake Michigan and through Chicago's South Shore community.

South Water Street

300 N, from 50 E to 154 E

South Water Street is one of Chicago's oldest streets. It once ran all along the south bank of the Chicago River, from Fort Dearborn west to where the river branches and goes south. It was the city's major market place. With the construction of Wacker Drive in the 1920s, the produce markets on South Water Street were displaced and relocated two miles to the southwest, to 14th and Morgan streets where they are today. See the next entry.

South Water Market

1435 S, from 1000 W to 1150 W

Moved to this location from South Water Street in 1926, the wholesale produce market retained its name from its former location. This is one of Chicago's principal wholesale produce markets.

Spaulding Avenue

3300 W, from 5858 N to 11476 S*

Jesse Spaulding (1833-1904) went from selling logs from a river raft to being a Chicago lumber king.

    Spaulding was a Pennsylvania farm boy whose first job was floating a raft down the Susquehannah River and selling lumber to dealers in Philadelphia and Baltimore. From there, he bought huge forests in Wisconsin and Michigan and shipped his wood by rail and barge—always with Chicago as his transportation hub—to dealers in Illinois, Iowa, Nebraska, Kansas, and Missouri.

    During the Civil War, Spaulding constructed, at his own expense, a South Side barracks for soldiers headed for the front and a North Side barracks for soldiers who returned.

Spokane Avenue

5340 W, from 6300 N to 6558 N

Named for the city of Spokane,

A morning in 1913 on the South Water Street Market. This market was moved in 1924 to make room for Wacker Drive.

Courtesy *Chicago Sun-Times*

Washington, which was named for the Spokane River, which in turn was named for the Indian tribe living on the river in 1805 when the explorers Lewis and Clark floated by. The word possibly means "children of the sun."

Sprague Avenue

9900 W, from 5200 N to 5224 N

This street and three others—Sanford, Shapland, and Stokes—run into a small, light-industrial subdivision of suburban Rosemont. Nobody seems to know how the streets got their names, but Rosemont mayor Donald Stevens knows something of their history. It seems,

Stevens said, that the land was sold off in thirty-foot lots by shady operators to visitors at the 1933 Chicago Century of Progress. But the land was virtually useless, so distant from rail lines and main roads that it was not developed until the late 1950s. Moreover, before dumping the lots at the fair, the sellers scraped off all the topsoil and sold it to the fair's organizers for use in landscaping.

State Street looking north from Madison Street in 1905.

Courtesy Chicago Historical Society
and *Chicago Sun-Times*

Springfield Avenue

3900 W, from 6358 N to 11056 S*

Springfield, Illinois, this street's namesake, is the state capital.

Stark Street

1100 W, from 2500 S to 2536 S

James L. Stark was a real estate subdivider on the North and South Sides in the 1870s. He was particularly involved in the development of the Northwest Side community of Ravenswood.

State Street

Baseline E & W, from 1168 N
to 12646 S

State Parkway

0 E & W from 1200 N to 1554 N

In the early 1800s, State Road was a main route south through the state of Illinois, hence the name. State Street later came to be "that Great Street," Chicago's busy, crowded, and exciting retail heart. Potter Palmer virtually made State Street, gambling on its future in the late 1860s by building the Field & Leiter department store there in 1868 and his grand Palmer House hotel there in 1870.

Today, State Street in the Loop is a semi-pedestrian mall, its ambiance diminished by the fumes and noise of buses. Just as State Street eclipsed the old Lake Street commercial district, the "Magnificent Mile" of North Michigan Avenue has in recent years drawn shoppers away from State Street and the Loop.

State Line Road
4100 E, from 10600 S to 11156 S

This street marks the boundary between Illinois and Indiana.

Stave Street
2540 W, from 2000 N to 2194 N

A. Stave was a cooper in Chicago's earliest days. The real estate subdivider W.P. Klemm, who bought Stave's land, named this street in his honor.

Stetson Avenue
154 E, from 232 N to 336 N

Eugene W. Stetson (1882-1959) was a New York financial magnate who began his career as a $40-a-month bank clerk in Macon, Georgia. He was a director of the Morgan Guaranty Trust Company and chairman of the executive committee of the Illinois Central Railroad. The street was named in his honor in 1955 when it was built beside the Prudential Building, the first air-rights structure in the Illinois Center development.

Steuben Street
11400 S, from 1700 W to 1770 W

Baron Frederick William Augustus von Steuben (1730-1794) was a German officer who fought alongside the colonists in the American Revolutionary War. He joined the revolutionary army under General George Washington in winter quarters at Valley Forge in 1778. He became the army's drill master.

Stevens Avenue
4028 W at 6000 N to 4000 W at 6030 N

George Stevens (1898-1980) founded his George Stevens Manufacturing Company in his garage in 1939. The company, now located at 6001 N. Keystone, manufactures machines for winding electrical coils. The street was renamed in Stevens' honor in 1979.

Stevenson, Adlai E., Expressway
400 E at 2500 S to 4832 W at 4300 S

Adlai E. Stevenson II (1900-1965) was a governor of Illinois, a two-time Democratic presidential candidate, and United Nations ambassador under Presidents Kennedy and Johnson.

Stewart Avenue
400 W, from 1600 S to 12658 S*

Gen. Hart L. Stewart, the man whose firm brought gas lighting to Illinois, was appointed the federal postmaster at Chicago in 1845 and served until April, 1849. In that year he and others founded the first gas light company in Illinois, the Chicago Gas Light and Coke Company.

On September 4, 1850, the first day of "town" gas service in Chicago, the city had only 260 gas lamps, including 36 in City Hall.

Stewart's company grew to become what is today the Peoples Gas Light and Coke Company, supplying natural gas to Chicago and its suburbs in northern Illinois.

Stockton Drive
67 W in Lincoln Park

Brigadier General Joseph Stockton was a hero of the Chicago Fire of 1871, credited with saving invaluable land title records by hauling them to safety and burying them in lakeshore sand. The records, belonging to a predecessor firm of the Chicago Title & Trust Company, listed the ownership of nearly every piece of property in Cook County and were of immense value in the reconstruction work that followed the fire.

General Stockton fought with General Ulysses S. Grant in the 72nd Regiment of the Illinois Infantry Volunteers, known as the Board of Trade Regiment, in the Civil War. Born in 1833,

The idle bed of the Illinois and Michigan Canal looking northeast from Central Park Avenue in 1935. The site was then being considered for a below-grade, high-speed highway route.

Courtesy *Chicago Sun-Times*

he came to Chicago from Pittsburgh when he was nineteen and was one of the planners and promoters of Lincoln Park. He was a commissioner of the Lincoln Park District from 1869 to 1892.

Stokes Avenue
10000 W, from 5200 N to 5224 N

See Sprague Avenue.

Stone Street
80 E, from 1200 N to 1326 N

Horatio O. Stone (1811-1877), a farm boy from New York, was a hardware store proprietor and real estate dealer in Chicago for almost forty years. Arriving in Chicago in 1834, he bought his first lot on Clinton Street for $90 that year and sold it the next year for $300. In 1871 he owned land between State Street and Lake Michigan, north of Division Street. Stone Street runs through this area.

Stony Drive
1632 E in Jackson Park

This street in Jackson Park feeds into Stony Island Avenue.

Stony Island Avenue
1600 E, from 5600 S to 12962 S*

When all of Chicago was a lake, the limestone ridge along which this street runs protruded above the waterline between what are now 92nd and 93rd Streets.

Stowell Street
1100 S, from 100 W to 139 W

(source unknown)

Stratford Place
3480 N, from 500 W to 632 W

Stratford-upon-Avon was the birthplace of William Shakespeare.

Streeter Drive
588 E, from 22 N to 216 N

In 1886 Captain George Wellington Streeter (1837-1921) claimed squatter's rights to all of the land north of Grand Avenue and east of Pine Street (Michigan Avenue). He continued to fight the city and the federal government for this land for the next thirty-five years. Back then, this property was little more than a huge sandbar, piled up around his rickety houseboat, the *Reutan*. But as the marsh land filled in, other squatters joined Streeter, and soon there was a new section in town—Streeterville. Streeter ultimately lost his claim and his land.

Strong Street
4932 N, from 3900 W to 7152 W*

D.O. Strong was a real estate speculator of the 1860s and 1870s who developed properties on both the North and South Sides of the city.

Sullivan Street
1306 N, from 400 W to 456 W

General John Sullivan (1740-1795) fought in the Revolutionary War, served as a member of the First and Second Continental Congresses and practiced law. In the war, he rallied a band of soldiers who captured Fort William and Mary from the British in his home state of New Hampshire.

Summerdale Avenue
5332 N, from 1400 W to 8756 W*

Summerdale was an early settlement in what now is Chicago's Lincoln Square community. The settlement stretched along this street between Western and Ravenswood Avenues.

Summit Avenue
800 W, from 8500 S to 8626 S

Named for the suburb of Summit, southwest of the city. It, in turn, was named for the "summit level" on the Illinois and Michigan Canal which passed through the area.

Sunnyside Avenue
4500 N, from 812 W to 8630 W*

Once there was a 300-pound woman named Gentle Annie Stafford who ran a house of prostitution in the Sunnyside Hotel at what is today the intersection of Sunnyside Avenue and Clark Street. Annie had class. She used to walk around at parties and ask, "Who's your favorite poet? Mine's Byron." In time, Annie moved out of the Sunnyside and it became respectable. The businessmen who made up the Ravenswood Land Company, which developed the community of Ravenswood, used to meet there.

Superior Street

732 N, from 432 E to 5968 W*

Named for Lake Superior, the largest of the five Great Lakes.

Surf Street

2900 N, from 330 W to 656 W

This street once began at the shore of Lake Michigan, where the surf swells and breaks.

Surrey Court

1300 W, from 2400 N to 2520 N

Surrey is a dairy farming county in southern England.

Sutton Place (Pvt.)

60 W, from 1300 N to 1348 N

(source unknown)

Swann Street

4642 S, from 122 W to 348 W*

M.M. Swan was a South Side real estate speculator in the 1850s.

A second possibility is that the street was named in honor of Sergeant Frank S. Swan, a hero of the U.S. Infantry in the Spanish-American War of 1898.

A third possibility is that the street honors Dr. Charles F. Swan, a prominent South Side surgeon in the 1870s.

T

Taft Avenue

11600 W, from 4200 N to 4400 N

Named for William Howard Taft (1857-1930), the twenty-seventh president of the United States, who served from 1909 to 1913. During his term the 16th Amendment to the Constitution was ratified, giving Congress the power to tax personal income.

Tahoma Avenue

5300 W, from 6400 N to 7040 N*

The Tahoma, more commonly called the Tacoma or Takoma, was a Northwestern Indian tribe. The name means "almost to heaven" or "tall peak," referring to Mt. Rainier in Washington State.

Talcott Avenue

5400 N at 6700 W to 6200 N at 7790 W

Lester Asahel Talcott, born in upstate New York in 1828, opened a foreign and domestic fruits and fancy groceries store in Chicago in 1851. He was a North Side real estate subdivider in the 1880s.

A less likely possibility is that the street was named for Mancel Talcott (1817-1878), an alderman from 1863 to 1867. He was a founder of the First National Bank of Chicago and a president of the Stock Yards National Bank.

Talman Avenue

2632 W, from 7424 N to 11458 S*

Named for Thomas P. Talman, a real estate subdivider and home builder in the 1870s.

Taylor Street

1000 S, from 2 W to 4256 W*

Two-flats in the 5500 block of S. Talman Avenue in the Gage Park neighborhood.

Taylor Street (Pvt.)

1000 S, from 5600 W to 5658 W

Named for Zachary Taylor (1784-1850), a hero of the 1846 Mexican-American War and the last Whig president. He was the twelfth president of the United States, serving from 1849 until his death in office in 1850.

Terra Cotta Place

2526 N, from 1730 W to 1758 W

The Northwestern Terra Cotta Company (1877-1956) had a factory on this street and clay quarries nearby in 1895, although its main offices were in the Rookery Building. This company was the principal supplier of terra cotta for such famous Chicago buildings as the Wrigley Building and the Railway Exchange Building on Michigan Avenue.

Thomas Street

1100 N, from 1336 W to 5958 W*

In all likelihood this street was named for Gen. Henry Thomas (1816-1870), a Union Army officer known as the "Rock of Chickamauga" for holding the Union

Army's left after the right collapsed in a battle near Chickamauga, Georgia in September, 1863.

A less likely possibility is that the street was named for a real estate subdivider, B.W. Thomas.

Thome Avenue
6300 N, from 1400 W to 4426 W*

G.H. Thome was a real estate subdivider in the Edgewater area.

Thompson Drive
2920 W in Douglas Park

Named for Harvey L. Thompson, a commissioner of the West Park District from 1882-1893.

Thorndale Avenue
5900 N, from 932 W to 7826 W*

This street was named by John L. Cochran, the subdivider of the Edgewater community, for Thorndale, Pennsylvania, a suburb of Philadelphia, his hometown. *See Berwyn and Edgewater Avenues.*

The Colvin house, at the northwest corner of Thorndale and Sheridan, one of the few remaining mansions on Sheridan Road in the Edgewater neighborhood.

G. Lane

Throop Street
1300 W, from 1698 N to 12258 S*

Amos G. Throop, a lumber merchant, was an alderman from 1849 to 1853 and from 1876 to 1880. He was active in the "Friends of Temperance in Illinois" society and sought, as he once wrote, to free the state "from the blighting curse entailed upon so many of our race by the unholy and demoralizing traffic in alcoholic drinks."

Tilden Street
426 S, from 506 W to 1064 W*

Samuel Jones Tilden (1814-1886) was governor of New York and the Democratic Party's presidential nominee in 1876. He was defeated in the general election by the Republican candidate, Rutherford B. Hayes.

A second possibility is that this street was named for Josiah S. Tilden, a South Side real estate subdivider.

Todd Street
500 W, from 2042 S to 2060 S

Named for Colonel John Todd, commandant of the Illinois Country in 1779.

Tonty Avenue
6150 W, from 6800 N to 7008 N

Henri De Tonti (1650-1704) was an Italian explorer known to the Indians as "the man with the iron hand." Although Italian, Tonti, whose name was Americanized as Henry Tonty, was an explorer in the service of France. He wore an artificial iron hand after his own hand was amputated. He was the chief lieutenant of the explorer Robert Cavalier, Sieur de La Salle, who first set eyes on the Chicago portage in 1682. *See LaSalle Street.*

Tooker Place
862 N, from 4 W to 34 W

Dr. Robert Newton Tooker, a professor of children's diseases, was a founder of the Chicago Homeopathic Medical College in 1857. He was also a noted real estate subdivider and owned the land through which Tooker Place runs.

Torrence Avenue
2634 E, from 9500 S to 13738 S

Joseph T. Torrence was a blacksmith, a blast furnace builder, a union fighter, a developer of Calumet Harbor, a promoter of the Chicago elevated train system, a Republican, and a wealthy man.

Torrence was born in Mercer City, Pennsylvania. At the age of nine, he left home to live with a relative and work for a blast furnace operator in Sharpsburg, Pennsylvania.

During the Civil War, Torrence became a major general under Ulysses S. Grant, and had his share of military experience. After being wounded four times and honorably discharged from the Union forces, he suited up again when Confederate raiders crossed into the North. He helped to capture the fabled General John Morgan.

During a major railroad strike in 1877, Torrence commanded the militia in Chicago. After 20,000 police and armed volunteers could not control the strikers, civil authorities gave him command of the city. It was then, according to the decidedly anti-labor publication, *America's Successful Men of Affairs,* that Torrence's "wise methods, vigorous measures and prompt and determined action overawed the mob and saved the city."

Later on General Torrence helped develop Calumet Harbor, worked in iron and steel operations in Hammond, Bridgeport, and Joliet, and was brigadier general of the Illinois' Guards First Brigade.

Elevated trains came into being in Chicago in part because of Torrence's push for main-line railroads without grade crossings, allowing traffic to travel under, not over, the tracks. He is considered a pioneer of elevated trains.

Torrence was also a founding father of East Chicago, Indiana. He helped lay out the town and held title to 1,000 acres of it.

Unlike many others who had streets named in their honor, the general never lived anywhere near the future Torrence Avenue. He lived on the Gold Coast at what was, even then, the fashionable corner of Lake Shore Drive and Bellevue Place.

Touhy Avenue
7200 N, from 1210 W to 7761 W*

Patrick L. Touhy (1839-1911) was a real estate mogul who helped found Rogers Park. He was with Mayor Carter Harrison, Sr. in 1893 on the day the mayor was assassinated. The headline on Touhy's obituary, October 18, 1911, mentioned those facts and also noted that his widow was worth $1 million. His wife's maiden name was Rogers, as in Rogers Park.

Born in Feakle, Ireland, in 1839, Touhy eventually immigrated to New York. After a stint in the carpet business there, he moved to Chicago and opened a grocery store in 1864.

Long before Touhy moved to Chicago, however, Philip Rogers, another Irishman, had settled on a ridge twenty-two feet above Lake Michigan that became known as Rogers' Ridge. In those days it was easy to get land named after yourself; you just bought it. By the time he died in 1856, Rogers owned 1,600 acres of the ridge and surrounding land, part of which is now Edgewater, most of which is Rogers Park.

One year after opening his grocery store, Patrick Touhy married Rogers' daughter Catherine and began to manage her father's 1,600 acres.

In 1869 Catherine inherited 800 of those acres from her brother. Touhy sold some of the land and developed the village of Rogers Park. He built a magnificent $18,000 home with a square tower in the middle of eighty acres of woods that ran east to the lake. The twenty-four-room mansion, near what is now the intersection of Clark Street and, yes, Touhy Avenue, was considered a symbol of luxurious living.

Touhy Avenue runs through Rogers Park. Several men to whom Touhy sold land also have streets named for them: Stephen Lunt, Luther V. Greenleaf, and Charles S. Morse. Other members of the Rogers Park Building and Land Co. who have streets named for them include Cyrus Leland and Paul and George Pratt.

As a wealthy land developer, Touhy became friendly with Mayor Harrison. They were together when Harrison was fatally shot by a disturbed young man who was angry because the mayor refused to appoint him city corporation counsel.

Touhy himself died of heart disease in 1911 in his home at 7051 N. Clark Street.

Transit Avenue (Pvt.)
4000 S, from 1300 W to 1358 W

The Union Stock Yard Transit Co., a private railroad, once ran along this street in the stockyards.

Tremont Street
5636 S, from 400 W to 546 W

The best bet is that this street was named for the town of Tremont, New Jersey. Historians often contend the street was named for the first Tremont Hotel, built in 1833 by Alanson Sweet at Lake and Dearborn Streets. But Tremont Street runs nowhere near the site of the old hotel.

Lake Street, west from Morgan.
G. Lane

Tripp Avenue

4232 W, from 6360 N to 8656 S*

Tripp Avenue (Pvt.)

4232 W, from 4300 S to 4658 S

Named for Dr. Robinson Tripp, sometimes affectionately called "Father Tripp," who bought a lot on Lake Street in the downtown area in 1853 and laid the first sidewalk in town.

Troy Street

3132 W, from 6558 N to 11358 S*

Named after Troy, New York, a city on the Hudson River.

Trumbull Avenue

3432 W, from 1052 N to 11324 S*

Trumbull Avenue (Pvt.)

3432 W, from 4136 S to 4258 S

Lyman Trumbull (1813-1896) was one of President Abraham Lincoln's staunchest political allies and one of his biggest headaches. Trumbull, in Lincoln's opinion, had an irritating way of insisting on a strict interpretation of the Constitution during a time of civil war. The senator from Illinois was openly critical, for example, of the president's willingness to order arbitrary arrests.

While a senator, Trumbull introduced a resolution which became the basis of the 13th Amendment abolishing slavery.

Trumbull was born in Colchester, Connecticut. As a young man, he rode on horseback to Belleville, Illinois, settled down, and practiced law. He was elected to the state legislature in 1840 and to the Illinois Supreme Court in 1848. He was elected to the U.S. Senate in 1855 and served in Washington for the next twelve years.

Lyman Trumbull, 1813-1896

Harper Memorial Library of the University of Chicago, on the Midway Plaisance.

G. Lane

U

Union Avenue

700 W, from 630 N to 12937 S*

This street name reflects the strong pro-Union sentiments of a majority of Chicagoans in the years before the Civil War.

University Avenue

1144 E, from 4400 S to 9858 S*

The University of Chicago, this street's namesake, was incorporated in 1890 and opened in 1892. It effectively put Hyde Park on the map. Dominic Pacyga says the opening of the University of Chicago was "the most important event in the history of Hyde Park" because it gave the neighborhood "a firm institutional, economic, and cultural base."

Urban Avenue

12 E, from 9100 S to 9168 S

(source unknown)

Van Buren Street
400 S, from 100 E to 5574 W*

Named for Martin Van Buren (1782-1862), the eighth president of the United States, who served from 1837 to 1841. He took office the same year Chicago incorporated as a city.

Vanderpoel Avenue
1800 W at 9136 S to 1700 W at 9858 S

Named for John H. Vanderpoel (1857-1911), a Dutch immigrant and artist-teacher. He was the first director of the School of the Art Institute of Chicago, taught there for thirty years, and his textbook, *The Human Figure*, published in 1909, is still used in art classes nationwide. A public school at 95th and Vanderpoel in the Beverly community, where Vanderpoel once lived, is named in his honor, as is the Vanderpoel Memorial Gallery of the Beverly Art Center.

Van Schaik Avenue
10400 S, from 2648 W to 2718 W

Chicago police officer Roger Van Schaik (1948-1979), an undercover narcotics investigator, was shot to death on the South Side on March 3, 1979, by an angry man bent on avenging his arrest three months earlier. Van Schaik's partner, William Bosak, *(see Bosak Avenue)* was also slain.

Van Schaik was born on the South Side, in the Roseland community, and was class valedictorian at St. Anthony's Grade School. He graduated from Fenger High School and joined the police force in 1969.

He was an excellent cop who received forty honorable mentions for service beyond the call of duty.

Van Vlissingen Road
1800 E at 9500 S to 2266 E at 10250 S

Arend Van Vlissingen, a real estate developer, laid out the subdivision of Van Vlissingen Heights along a railroad line in Chicago's South Deering community area in the early 1880s.

Vermont Street
12700 S at 600 W to 12772 S at 1020 W

Named for the New England state, Vermont, which in turn is derived from the French, meaning "green mountain." This is a continuation of Vermont Street, one of the oldest streets in adjoining Blue Island, Illinois.

Vernon Avenue
440 E, from 2720 S to 13450 S*

Named for William Vernon, an auditor for the Illinois Central Railroad, who was a personal friend of William F. Myrick, the subdivider of this South Side area. In 1917, Myrick laid out the Vernon Park subdivision, an area bounded by 93rd Street, 95th Street, South Parkway (now Martin Luther King Drive), and St. Lawrence Avenue. *See Myrick Street.*

Vernon Park Place
700 S, from 540 W to 1162 W*

Named after nearby Vernon Park (Lytle, Lexington, Loomis, and Cabrini Streets), which is now known as Victor Arrigo Park.

Victoria Street
5800 N, from 1200 W to 7832 W*

Victoria Street (Pvt.)
5716 N, from 4000 W to 4162 W

Named for Queen Victoria (1819-1901), queen of Great Britain and Ireland from 1837 to 1901 and empress of India from 1876 to 1901. She donated 1,000 books to Chicago after the fire of 1871.

The Vanderpoel house at 9319 S. Pleasant Avenue in the Beverly Hills neighorhood.

G. Lane

Vincennes Avenue

600 E at 3542 S to 2036 W
at 11888 S*

Once an Indian trail, Vincennes Avenue stretched along the high ground between Chicago and Vincennes, Indiana, and was named for that town. See also Governors' Parkway. The town, in turn, was named for Francois Margane, Sieur de Vincennes, a French Canadian explorer who built a fort on the Indiana site in 1731.

Along Vincennes Avenue in the 1830s, legend has it, was Horse Thief Hollow. At one time, according to South Side historian Bob White, Chicago had almost as many horse thieves as shifty politicians. And the thieves were said to have a hideout in one of the many ravines below Vincennes Avenue.

Indiana farmers going to market came down Vincennes in the early 1830s. They rumbled into town in covered wagons and camped overnight on the lake shore. The city's street urchins, trailing alongside the wagons, tried to steal the farmers' produce.

Vincennes was the last street in Chicago to have a streetcar. The "Green Hornet" made its final run down Vincennes Avenue on June 21, 1958. *See Governors' Parkway.*

Vine Street

624 W, from 1600 N to 1732 N

Named for the vine plants once found along this street.

Vintage Avenue (Pvt.)

1400 W, from 2900 S to 2950 S

This street was for many years an access road to the Old Rose Distributing Company, a wholesale distributor of wines and liquors that was then located on nearby Lock Street. At the company's request in 1958, the street was named Vintage by the city council. Old Rose, now located at 4130 S. Morgan Street, abandoned the Lock Street site in 1968.

Virginia Avenue

2632 W at 4500 N to 3116 W
at 5964 N*

Named for Mary Virginia Dunham, the daughter of John H. Dunham (1817-1893), a Chicago grocer, real estate developer, and banker. He founded the Merchants Loan and Trust Company.

"The Vincennes" apartments at Vincennes Avenue and 36th Street in 1913.

C.R. Childs, courtesy G. Schmalgemeier

W

Wabansia Avenue

1700 N, from 2300 W to 7190 W*

Waubansee, from which the name Wabansia is derived, was a Potawatomie Indian chief who died in 1846. He guarded the John Kinzie family, who were among Chicago's earliest white settlers. *See Kinzie Street.* His name meant "dim daylight."

Wabash Avenue

44 E, from 908 N to 12484 S*

Although the name for this street was probably taken from the Indian word meaning "gleaming white," it may be a corruption of Wabasha, a chief of the Mdewakanton Sioux. He was so impressive that many people thought he was much taller than he actually was.

Wabasha or Wapasha is believed to have been born in 1773 near present-day Winona, Minnesota. He was the second of two chiefs named Wabasha. His father was closely allied with the British. The son, however, sided with the Americans in disputes with the Winnebagos, Menomonees, and Sauks. Although the younger Wabasha, also known as La Feuille or The Leaf, never openly broke with the British during the War of 1812, he leaned toward the Americans. The British even tried his son-in-law Rolette for collusion with the Americans.

Wabasha was one of the chiefs at the great council of August, 1825, in Prairie du Chien, Wisconsin, between the federal government and tribes of the central north.

In 1832 he supported the Americans in the Black Hawk War against the Sauk tribe—a war started when Illinois volunteers killed two Sauk warriors sent, under a flag of truce, by Sauk War Chief Black Hawk to arrange a truce parley. *See Blackhawk Street.*

Stephen H. Long, an early nineteenth century explorer (for whom Long Avenue is named), visited Wabasha in 1817 and described him as one of the most honest and honorable of any of the Indians and a gifted orator.

Beltrami, an Italian traveler, said Wabasha needed only "an embroidered coat, a large portfolio . . . and spectacles" to appear a great statesman.

Wabash Avenue is not a continuous street, and most Chicagoans associate it with the Loop elevated tracks. But before the Chicago Fire it was a tree-lined strip of beautiful homes favored by the wealthy.

Wabash Avenue, north of the Chicago River, was known as Cass Avenue until 1930, when a bridge was built across the river.

Commission. Wacker was among those civic leaders who convinced the city to reclaim and preserve its lakefront. He was also a tireless campaigner against traffic congestion, and it was he who proposed relocating the South Water Street Market and rebuilding South Water Street into a double-deck drive. Hence, it was renamed Wacker Drive.

After serving as a director of the World's Columbian Exposition in 1893, Wacker helped to implement Burnham and Bennett's 1909 Plan of Chicago, which provided for a string of lakefront parks, Union Station, Soldier Field, and the Field Museum of Natural History.

Walden Parkway
1800 W, from 9730 S to 10654 S*

Named for Samuel D. Walden, a real estate subdivider in the 1880s. He developed the Walden Addition to Washington Heights, an area bounded by 96th Street, 99th Street, Wood Street, and Winchester Avenue. This parkway runs through the subdivision, now located in the Beverly neighborhood.

The Field Museum of Natural History, E. Roosevelt Road at S. Lake Shore Drive, constructed 1911-19.

G. Lane

Waldron Drive
1600 S in Burnham Park

Lieutenant Commander John Charles Waldron was a United States Navy pilot killed in World War II. This drive was named for him in 1948.

Wall Street (Pvt.)
1132 W, from 3600 S to 3658 S*

Although located on the South Side and far from Chicago's financial district, this street apparently was named for New York's Wall Street.

Wallace Street
600 W, from 2412 S to 12947 S*

John S. Wallace was a real estate subdivider in the 1860s who developed land in the area of what is now Wallace and 43rd Streets.

Wallen Avenue
6634 N, from 1600 W to 1760 W

Named for William L. Wallen, a real estate subdivider of the Edgewater community.

Charles H. Wacker, 1856-1929

Wacker Drive
340 N at 400 E to 200 N at 340 W . . . Also, 360 W, from 188 N to 424 S

This street was named for Charles H. Wacker (1856-1929), a Chicago brewer and chairman of the Chicago Plan

Waller Avenue
5700 W, from 1558 N to 144 S

Waller Avenue (Pvt.)
5700 W, from 900 S to 1158 S

Named for Robert A. Waller, who founded the Buena Park neighborhood on the North Side in the 1880s. He was a commissioner of Lincoln Park District from 1892 to 1894.

Walnut Street
234 N, from 640 W to 4758 W*

Named for the walnut tree.

Walter Burley Griffin Place
10432 S, from 1600 W to 1756 W

See Griffin Place.

Walton Drive
(In Calumet Park)

Named for Lyman A. Walton, a commissioner of the South Park District from 1903 to 1908.

Walton Street
932 N, from 265 E to 5968 W*

Walton Street (Pvt.)
980 N, from 516 W to 532 W

Isaak Walton (1593-1683) was an English writer and biographer, best known for his book, *The Compleat Angler.*

A second possibility is that this street was named for George Walton (1741-1804), a signer of the Declaration of Independence and a U.S. senator from Georgia.

Warner Avenue
4132 N, from 1400 W to 5358 W*

Named for L.A. Warner, a leading North Side real estate subdivider in the 1870s and 1880s.

Warren Avenue
23 N, from 640 W to 740 W*

Warren Boulevard
34 N, from 1500 W to 3358 W

Warren Drive
34 N in Garfield Park

Named for Lyman Daniel Warren (1848-1899), a Chicago real estate developer for most of his adult life, who first worked in his father's paint store, but found there was more money to be made in land.

A second and less likely possibility is that this street was named for Joseph Warren, a Boston physician and patriot who was slain at the Battle of Bunker Hill on June 17, 1775.

Warwick Avenue
3732 N, from 4000 W to 6358 W*

Richard Neville, Earl of Warwick and of Salisbury (1428-1471), was the most powerful noble of his time in England.

Waseca Place
11300 S, from 1630 W to 1722 W

Named for the town of Waseca, Illinois. The word is a corruption of the Dakota Indian word, *Washecha,* meaning "red earth."

Washburne Avenue
1232 S, from 1200 W to 2454 W*

Amid threats to the safety of Abraham Lincoln, Elihu Benjamin Washburne (1816-1887) was the only person to greet Lincoln when the new president secretly arrived in Washington, D.C., for his inauguration in 1861. Washburne was an Illinois congressman for sixteen years during the Civil War and Reconstruction, and president of the Chicago Historical Society. He lived in Galena and was a friend of Ulysses S. Grant.

Elihu Benjamin Washburne, 1816-1887

Washington Street
100 N, from 100 E to 440 W

Washington Boulevard
100 N, from 500 W to 5968 W

Named for George Washington, the first president of the United States, who served from 1789 to 1797. He was born at Westmoreland, Virginia, in 1732 and died at Mount Vernon, Virginia, in 1799.

Washington Park Court
432 E, from 4900 S to 5060 S*

Named after Washington Park, which is immediately south of this short street.

Washtenaw Avenue
2700 W, from 7558 N to 11458 S*

Washtenaw was the Algonquin Indian name for the settlement of Detroit, literally meaning "the place of the round or curved channel."

Washington Park Race Track around the turn of the century.

Fred Wagner, courtesy *Chicago Sun-Times*

Waterloo Court
646 W, from 3000 N to 3026 N

In the Battle of Waterloo in Belgium on June 18, 1815, the British under the Duke of Wellington defeated the French emperor Napoleon. This battle concluded the Napoleonic-era wars between France and the other European powers.

Watkins Avenue
1756 W at 11400 S to 2000 W at 11872 S

James Watkins was a farmer on what came to be the far South Side. He is one of the few black men for whom a Chicago street has been named.

Waukesha Avenue
5700 W, from 6500 N to 6944 N

Waukesha is a Potawatomie word for "fox." The street was named for the Wisconsin town of the same name.

Waveland Avenue
3700 N, from 600 W to 8356 W*

Joseph Sheffield, a North Side real estate subdivider, seized upon the name "Waveland" when he noticed how much of his land was submerged by Lake Michigan waves on stormy days. The street begins near the lake and runs several miles west of Sheffield's subdivision.

Wayman Street
320 N, from 600 W to 4758 W*

Named for William Wayman, a North Side real estate developer who was an alderman from 1854 to 1856.

Wayne Avenue
1332 W, from 2100 N to 6934 N*

This street was named by John L. Cochran, the developer of Edgewater, for a stop on the Main Line, a commuter rail line running out of his hometown of Philadelphia.
See Berwyn and Edgewater Avenues.

Webster Avenue

2200 N, from 300 W to 2158 W

Webster Drive

2200 N in Lincoln Park

Daniel Webster (1782-1852), the statesman and orator from Massachusetts, was a major spokesman for Northern Whigs during his twenty years in the U.S. Senate. Webster came to Chicago to visit the town in 1837, making his rounds in a carriage drawn by four cream-colored horses.

Weed Street

1532 N, from 622 W to 1068 W*

Named for Sarah M. Weed, the daughter of Thomas Morgan, the founder of Morgan Park. *See Morgan Street.*

Wellington Avenue

3000 N, from 300 W to 7558 W*

Named after Arthur Wellesley, first Duke of Wellington (1769-1852), a British soldier and statesman. He was one of those who pacified British India and who masterminded the defeat of Napoleon at the Battle of Waterloo in 1815.

Wells Street

200 W, from 1820 N to 6448 S*

Wells Street (Pvt.)

220 W, from 3700 S to 3864 S

Captain William Wells was a hero of Fort Dearborn about whom much Western-styled melodrama has been written.

Wells arrived at Fort Dearborn on August 13, 1812, from Fort Wayne, Indiana, leading thirty friendly Miami Indians along the Vincennes Trail. He died two days later in the Fort Dearborn Massacre, slain by unfriendly Potawatomie, while trying to lead a group of white settlers to safety.

Born in Kentucky, Wells was kidnapped by the Miami Indians at the age of twelve and raised by Little Turtle, a Miami chief. According to the historian A.T. Andreas, Wells left Little Turtle one day to rejoin the white men. "Father, I now leave you to go to my own people," Andreas reports Wells as saying. "We will be friends until the sun reaches the midday height. From that time we will be enemies. And if you want to kill me, then you may. And if I want to kill you, I may."

Word spread about a planned Potawatomie attack on Fort Dearborn, and Wells rode from Fort Wayne, Indiana, to the settlers' aid. As Wells led the settlers out of the fort and back down the path to Fort Wayne, the Indians struck at what is now 18th Street and Calumet Avenue.

"So that's your game, is it?" Wells growled through clenched teeth, as reported by the historians Paul Gilbert and Charles Lee Bryson. Wells spurred his horse and "rode alone into the face of danger." He shot seven or eight warriors before he himself was wounded in the face. But as he was about to die, Gilbert and Bryson tell us, he saw his niece nearby and had the presence of mind to gasp, "Goodbye and good luck. If you come through with this, just tell my wife that I died bravely."

By 1870, Wells Street had developed such a miserable reputation for debauchery, given its many brothels, that the city renamed it Fifth Avenue. But Chicago's Fifth Avenue never developed the class of New York's Fifth Avenue, and in 1918 the original name of Wells was restored.

Wendell Street

1028 N, from 152 W to 360 W

Named for John Wendell, a real estate subdivider in the 1860s.

Wentworth Avenue

200 W, from 1600 S to 12658 S*

Chicago Mayor John Wentworth (1815-1888) once told the voters, "You damn fools . . . you can either vote for me for mayor or you can go to hell." Setting the tone for Chicago politics, Wentworth was sarcastic and blunt. The city loved him. He stood 6 feet 6 inches tall and was known as "Long John."

A Dartmouth College graduate, Wentworth claimed an ancestral link to Thomas Wentworth, the Earl of Stafford, who was beheaded in 1641. "Long John" came to Chicago from New Hampshire in

DePaul University and St. Vincent's Church (1895-97) on Webster at Sheffield c. 1910.

Courtesy G. Schmalgemeier

John Wentworth, 1815-1888

On Leong Merchants' Assn.
Building sometimes called
Chinatown's City Hall on
Wentworth at 22nd Street.

G. Lane

1836 with thirty dollars in his pocket.
Within a month he was editor of the
Chicago Democrat, a weekly
newspaper. Within three years he
owned it.

Wentworth was a teacher, a lawyer,
a chief of police, a congressman for
twelve years, and a Republican mayor
who refused his salary. Wentworth once
tried to convince Abe Lincoln that he
needed a manager if he ever hoped to
live in the White House. Lincoln replied
that only events could make a president.

Locally, Wentworth was reputed to
own more real estate than anyone else in
the city. His first election as mayor was
violently contested. One person was
killed at the polls and others were
wounded.

While mayor (1857-58 and 1860-61),
Wentworth introduced the first steam fire
engine, named "Long John," and he
established the city's first paid fire
department.

Early in his first term, he led an
army of police officers down major city
streets and tore down every advertising
sign, awning, and sidewalk obstruction
that was in violation of an ordinance
previously ignored. Then he waged war
on "The Sands," leading thirty police
officers and dozens of righteous citizens
along the Near North Side lake shore,

razing the shanties of prostitutes,
gamblers, and dog-fight promoters.

In his inaugural speech for his
second term as mayor, Wentworth said,
"The best way to bring about the repeal
of an obnoxious law is to enforce it."

One of his last acts was to design
his own tombstone in Rosehill cemetery,
which bore no inscription. Wentworth
explained, "If there is no inscription on
my monument, people will ask whose
monument it is."

Wesley Terrace
9500 W, from 5200 N to 5212 N

Probably named for John Wesley
(1703-1791), English evangelical preacher
and founder of Methodism.

West Circle Avenue
7044 W, from 5700 N to 6087 N

This street and East Circle Avenue
together form a circle in Norwood Park.

West End Avenue
200 N, from 3800 W to 5968 W*

West End Drive
200 N in Garfield Park

This street begins and ends on what was
in the 1800s the far West Side of
Chicago.

Western Avenue
2400 W, from 7576 N to 11856 S

Western Boulevard
2400 W, from 3100 S to 5442 S

Most Chicago streets were named for pioneers, politicians, developers, and places inside and outside the city. But once in a while a street was named to tell you where you were.

Western Avenue is one such street. From 1851 to 1869 it told a traveler he was at the western edge of Chicago. In the early 1870s Chicagoans journeyed out to Western Avenue to picnic in the open fields nearby.

At 23.5 miles in length, Western Avenue is the longest street in the city.

Westgate Terrace (Pvt.)
614 S, from 1242 W to 1320 W

This half-block street was named for the Westgate Terrace development, built in 1968, through which it runs.

West Water Street
416 W, from 100 N to 182 N

This street runs along the west bank of the South Branch of the Chicago River.

Whipple Street
3032 W, from 6832 N to 11258 S*

Named for Henry Whipple (1824-1906), who was a real estate developer beginning in the 1840s. He was also a Methodist Episcopal minister.

Western Avenue looking north from Belmont in 1931.

Courtesy *Chicago Sun-Times*

Wicker Park Avenue

1800 W at 1301 N to 2000 W
at 1538 N*

Charles G. Wicker (1820-1889), a Chicago alderman from 1865 to 1869, once turned down a $25,000 bribe for his vote on a single issue. Wicker had argued that aldermen should be paid a sufficient salary so they wouldn't be tempted to take bribes. Newspapers of his time called him one of the few honest men in the council.

After coming to Chicago in 1839, Wicker started a wholesale grocery business on Lake Street and was known as a man of honor in his business dealings. He subdivided a tract of land along Milwaukee Avenue, laid out the streets and ditches, and gave it to the city. It's known today as Wicker Park.

Wieland Street

224 W, from 1400 N to 1556 N

Named for Christoph Martin Wieland (1733-1813), a German poet and philosopher. He is sometimes called the "German Voltaire."

Wilcox Street

132 S, from 2300 W to 4554 W*

Henry M. Wilcox developed five acres of land on the West Side after the Chicago Fire of 1871. The southern boundary of the development was Wilcox Street.

Wildwood Avenue

6100 W, from 6700 N to 6958 N

This street runs through what was once a wooded Potawatomie hunting ground.

Willard Court

1226 W, from 100 N to 1020 N*

This street honors Frances E. Willard (1839-1898), an American temperance leader and reformer. She was a woman who loved the outdoors, was a good shot, and liked to be called Frank.

Willard graduated from Northwestern Female College in 1859 and went on to become a nationally recognized leader for temperance and woman's suffrage. She helped found the Woman's Christian Temperance Union in 1874 and became its president five years later. Suburban Evanston was the national headquarters of the WCTU. In 1891 she was elected president of the World's WCTU and served in that capacity until her death in 1898.

Temperance, she believed, protected the home and the Christian life.

Frances E. Willard, 1839-1898

Willetts Court

3000 W, from 2500 N to 2534 N

Named for Martin Willetts, a real estate subdivider and builder in the 1880s, who developed parts of the North Side.

Williams Avenue

210 E, from 9110 S to 9154 S

Dr. Daniel Hale Williams (1856-1931), a black American surgeon, founded Provident Hospital in 1891, the first black hospital in the United States, in a two-story house at 29th and Dearborn Streets. At Provident, black patients were freely admitted and black nurses were trained. The hospital had an interracial staff and board of trustees.

In 1893 newspapers reported on an operation Dr. Williams performed, bringing him instant fame as the first physician to operate on the human heart. He was the best-known black physician in the country.

In 1929 Provident Hospital relocated to the Washington Park neighborhood. This historic hospital, in a new facility on 51st Street, closed its doors in 1988.

Willow Street

1740 N, from 212 W to 2058 W*

There once were a great many willow trees along this street.

Wilmot Avenue

2100 W at 1724 N to 2356 W
at 1978 N*

Named for David Wilmot (1814-1868), a congressman from Pennsylvania, who began the legislative effort to prohibit the expansion of slavery. He proposed in 1846 that slavery should be prohibited in any territory acquired through the peace treaty with Mexico.

Wilson Avenue

4600 N, from 732 W to 8770 W*

Wilson Drive

4670 N in Lincoln Park

John P. Wilson (1844-1922) drafted the laws under which the Sanitary District of Chicago was created. But he also helped establish Children's Memorial Hospital

John P. Wilson, 1844-1922

Wilson Drive (continued)

through an incentive clause in his will.

Wilson was crippled as a youth, and this halted his ambition to be a farmer. Instead, he became a lawyer and made a reputation as a real estate specialist when he successfully litigated land ownership questions after the Chicago Fire. Later on he was counsel for the World's Columbian Exposition in 1892 and 1893.

But it was Wilson's will that helped Children's Memorial Hospital. Wilson divided his estate of several million dollars among his three children, with an extra provision for the hospital. Specifically, he promised the hospital one-third of a million dollars if, and only if, it could raise twice as much money from other sources. If the hospital failed to raise the cash, it would receive only $50,000.

One daughter, Martha Wilson, who was a director of the hospital, left her sickbed in 1923 and personally set out to raise the money. After Thomas D. Jones contributed half of the amount needed, the goal was reached.

Ironically, by raising money to satisfy the will's conditions with regard to the hospital, Wilson's children were in effect taking money out of their own pockets. If the hospital had failed to raise the specified amount, more money would have gone to Wilson's children.

Wilton Avenue
932 W, from 2600 N to 3846 N*

Wilton is a borough of Wiltshire, England, known for its finely crafted Wilton rugs.

Winchester Avenue
1932 W, from 7546 N to 10058 S*

Winchester is a municipal borough of Hampshire County in the south of England.

Windsor Avenue
4532 N, from 800 W to 8500 W*

Windsor, a municipal borough of Berkshire, England, is the site of Windsor Castle, a principal residence of England's sovereigns since the days of William the Conqueror.

Winnebago Avenue
2200 W at 1700 N to 2356 W at 1890 N

The Winnebagos were the only tribe of Indians in the Chicago area who spoke the Sioux language. They formerly inhabited southwestern Wisconsin.

Winneconna Parkway
7800 S, from 400 W to 546 W

The name possibly was derived from the Algonquin Indian word *Ween-kam-ing,* meaning "a place where marrow is obtained." Alternately, the name might be a corruption of "Winnakenozzo," a band of Sioux Indians.

Winnemac Avenue
5032 N, from 1200 W to 8562 W*

Winamac, from which the word Winnemac was derived, was a powerful chief of the Potawatomie Indians. He was a signer of the 1795 Treaty of Greenville that surrendered the site of Chicago to the U.S. government. He took sides with the British in the War of 1812 and was killed by a Shawnee chief who had sided with the Americans. His name meant "catfish."

Winona Street
5100 N, from 840 W to 8562 W*

In Eastern Sioux dialect *Winona* means "first born child"—if the child is a girl. A Sioux village by the name of Winona once stood on the present site of Winona, Minnesota. The name is used in the legend of a Sioux maiden who committed suicide rather than agree to an arranged marriage.

The street also may have been named for Winona Tister, the daughter of a North Side real estate developer in the 1860s.

Winston Avenue
1500 W at 9500 S to 1300 W at 10198 S

Frederick Hampden Winston, who was born in Georgia in 1830 and came to Chicago in 1853, subdivided the land in this Washington Heights neighborhood. In 1868 Winston purchased the lands that would become Morgan Park from an early settler of that area. He later sold the land to the Blue Island Land & Building Company, the developers of Morgan Park. Winston was president of the Lincoln Park District from 1874 to 1886.

Winthrop Avenue
1100 W, from 4600 N to 6578 N*

John Winthrop (1588-1649) was the first governor of the Massachusetts Bay Colony. He was the colony's dominant intellectual and political leader.

Wisconsin Street

1900 N, from 200 W to 1147 W*

Named for the state of Wisconsin, which in turn took its name from the Wisconsin River. It is a Sauk word meaning "wild rushing channel."

Wisner Avenue

3500 W, from 2900 N to 2984 N

Albert Wisner was a real estate developer in this area in the 1880s.

Wolcott Avenue

1900 W, from 7546 N to 11858 S*

Dr. Alexander Wolcott (1790-1830) came to Chicago from Windsor, Connecticut, as an Indian Agent in 1820. He married Ellen Marion Kinzie, the daughter of one of Chicago's founders, John Kinzie. Their wedding was the first in Chicago. *See Kinzie Street.*

Wolfe Lake Boulevard

3825 E at 11820 S to 3500 E at 12790 S

This street runs along Wolf Lake in Hegewisch. Some Chicago history buffs say the lake was named in honor of a Chief Wolf of the Sioux tribe.

Wolfram Street

2832 N, from 800 W to 7042 W*

Named for Henry Wolfram, who in the early 1830s owned a farm bounded by what are now Halsted Street, George Street, Diversey Avenue, and Sheffield Avenue.

Wood Street

1800 W, from 2358 N to 10960 S*

Alonzo Wood was a real estate subdivider in the 1880s.

Woodard Street

3400 W, from 2810 N to 2942 N

Named for Tular J. Woodard, a real estate subdivider.

Rockefeller Chapel (1926-28) of the University of Chicago stands on the northwest corner of 59th and Woodlawn.

A. Kezys

Woodland Park (Pvt.)

3436 S, from 600 E to 666 E

The name of a small residential enclave laid out along this street by the statesman Stephen A. Douglas. *See Douglas Boulevard.*

Woodlawn Avenue

1200 E, from 4436 S to 10700 S*

Named for the South Side community of Woodlawn which goes from 60th to 67th Street and from Lake Michigan to King Drive. The South Side Realty Association named and developed much of the town of Woodlawn before it was annexed to Chicago in 1889. The area enjoyed phenomenal growth before and during the World's Columbian Exposition in Jackson Park in 1893.

Woodward Drive

3632 W in Garfield Park

(source unknown)

Wrightwood Avenue
2700 N at 400 W to 2600 N
at 7190 W*

John Stephen Wright, born in 1815, was the oldest of four brothers who engaged in Chicago real estate speculation between about 1835 and 1870. In 1853, Stephen Wright and a partner, James H. Rees, purchased some 300 acres of woodland on the shore of Lake Michigan about three miles north of Lake Street. In the financial panic of 1857 he lost all his holdings to his brothers and other creditors. Timothy Wright, the second oldest brother, owned much of the 300 acres of land—the heart of Wrightwood. Edward Wright, the youngest brother, served as Timothy's attorney and handled the subdivision's legal work.

Yale Avenue
232 W, from 5900 S to 12658 S*

This street is named after Yale University, founded in 1701 in New Haven, Connecticut. It is one of the oldest universities in the United States.

Yates Avenue
2400 E, from 10500 S to 13758 S*

Yates Boulevard
2400 E, from 7100 S to 9456 S*

Richard Yates (1815-1873) was a lawyer and a member of Congress whose anti-slavery sentiments led him to become a member of the Republican Party. He was present at the national convention at which Abraham Lincoln was nominated in 1860. He was governor of Illinois from 1861 to 1865. He also gave Ulysses S. Grant his first Civil War commission.

A stunningly handsome man and hypnotic speaker, Yates was said to be so zealous in recruiting troops during the Civil War that he had to be told to back off because he was recruiting too many.

When Democrats in the Illinois General Assembly in 1863 moved for a resolution urging an armistice and calling for a national peace convention, Yates used his powers as governor to suspend the assembly session.

Enormously popular with the voters, Yates later acknowledged a drinking problem but said it never affected his job performance.

York Road
12810 W, from 4800 N to 6400 N

Really more a suburban road than a Chicago street, this highway brushes the western edge of Chicago's O'Hare Airport before continuing south through west suburban York Township. The street takes its name from the township, which in turn got its name in the 1830s when pioneers from New York settled in the Hinsdale area.

New United Air Lines terminal at O'Hare International Airport.

David A. Miller

8th Street
800 S, from 1 E to 100 E

9th Street
900 S, from 1 E to 100 E

11th Street
1100 S, from 1 E to 100 E

11th Place
1130 S, from 120 E to 80 W

12th Place
1232 S, from 700 W to 3600 W*

13th Street
1300 S, from 124 E to 4400 W*

13th Place
1314 S, from 2600 W to 3600 W*

14th Street
1400 S, from 134 E to 4530 W*

14th Place
1432 S, from 32 E to 2624 W*

15th Street
1500 S, from 1 W to 4600 W*

15th Place
1532 S, from 500 W to 4600 W*

16th Street
1600 S, from 242 E to 4600 W*

17th Street
1700 S, from 1 W to 4400 W*

17th Place
1722 S, from 700 W to 800 W

18th Street
1800 S, from 328 E to 4400 W*

18th Place
1832 S, from 900 W to 4400 W*

18th Drive
1832 S, in Douglas Park

19th Street
1900 S, from 1 W to 4400 W*

19th Place
1920 S, from 710 W to 1200 W*

20th Place
2032 S, from 536 W to 1200 W*

St. Adalbert Church (1912-14) at 1656 West 17th Street in the Pilsen neighborhood, once solidly Polish, now predominantly Hispanic.

A. Kezys

The John J. Glessner house at the southwest corner of 18th and Prairie in the Prairie Avenue Historic District.

G. Lane

139

21st Street
2100 S, from 336 E to 4400 W*

21st Place
2132 S, from 400 W to 4400 W*

22nd Place
2232 S, from 200 W to 2900 W*

23rd Street
2300 S, from 416 E to 3700 W*

23rd Drive
2300 S, in Burnham Park

23rd Place
2332 S, from 200 W to 2900 W*

24th Street
2400 S, from 434 E to 4178 W*

24th Boulevard
2400 S, from 2800 W to 2936 W

24th Place
2432 S, from 368 E to 4378 W*

25th Street
2500 S, from 448 E to 4400 W*

25th Place
2532 S, from 34 W to 4400 W*

26th Street
2600 S, from 470 E to 4600 W*

26th Place
2620 S, from 33 W to 2631 W

27th Street
2700 S, from 522 E to 4400 W*

28th Street
2800 S, from 80 E to 4500 W*

28th Place
2832 S, from 132 E to 600 W*

29th Street
2900 S, from 626 E to 972 W*

29th Place
2920 S, from 468 E to 354 W*

30th Street
3000 S, from 516 E to 4600 W*

McCormick Place Exposition Center at 23rd Street and Lake Shore Drive, built in 1960, burned in 1967, and rebuilt and opened again in 1971.

Administration Building (1891) of the Illinois Institute of Technology at 33rd and Federal Streets, originally Armour Institute of Technology.

30th Place
3020 S, from 334 W to 354 W

31st Boulevard
3100 S, from 2400 W to 2734 W

31st Street
3100 S, from 628 E to 4600 W*

31st Drive
3100 S, in Burnham Park

31st Drive
3100 S, from 600 E to 1100 E

31st Place
3132 S, from 490 E to 2100 W*

32nd Street
3200 S, from 532 E to 4400 W*

32nd Place
3232 S, from 548 E to 168 W*

Charles L. Comiskey, 1858–1931

Comiskey Park at 35th and Shields Avenue, home of the Chicago White Sox since 1910.

G. Lane

33rd Street
3300 S, From 656 E to 4400 W*

33rd Boulevard
3300 S, from 100 E to 346 E

33rd Place
3332 S, from 634 E to 1856 W*

34th Street
3400 S, from 130 E to 3800 W*

34th Place
3432 S, from 800 W to 2450 W*

35th Street
3500 S, from 725 E to 3800 W*

35th Street (Pvt.)
3500 S, from 4000 W to 4500 W

35th Place
3532 S, from 800 W to 2800 W*

36th Street
3600 S, from 760 E to 3212 W*

36th Street (Pvt.)
3600 S, from 1000 W to 4500 W*

36th Place
3632 S, from 80 E to 3212 W*

36th Place (Pvt.)
3632 S, from 1200 W to 1236 W

37th Street
3700 S, from 814 E to 3058 W*

37th Street (Pvt.)
3700 S, from 1000 W to 1958 W

37th Place
3732 S, from 132 E to 3428 W*

37th Place (Pvt.)
3732 S, from 785 E to 236 W

38th Street
3800 S, from 916 E to 3800 W*

38th Street (Pvt.)
3800 S from 785 E to 238 W

38th Place
3832 S, from 400 W to 3600 W*

38th Place (Pvt.)
3832 S, from 700 E to 234 W

39th Place
3932 S, from 2500 W to 3200 W

40th Street
4000 S, from 974 E to 3200 W*

40th Street (Pvt.)
4000 S, from 4000 W to 4264 W

40th Place
4032 S, from 500 W to 3200 W*

41st Street
4100 S, from 1088 E to 3200 W*

41st Street (Pvt.)
4100 S, from 3816 W to 3958 W

41st Place
4117 S, from 1048 E to 3200 W*

42nd Street
4200 S, from 846 E to 4726 W*

42nd Street (Pvt.)
4200 S, from 3816 W to 3956 W

42nd Place
4232 S, from 1134 E to 3200 W*

Homes at the northwest corner of 37th and King Drive, 1988.

G. Lane

47th Place
4732 S, from 1400 E to 2456 W*

47th Place (Pvt.)
4746 S, from 3200 W to 3544 W*

48th Street
4800 S, 1440 E to 5158 W*

48th Place
4832 S, from 500 E to 2340 W*

48th Place (Pvt.)
4832 S, from 3030 W to 3458 W

49th Street
4900 S, from 1624 E to 5158 W*

43rd Street
4300 S, from 1168 E to 4936 W*

43rd Street (Pvt.)
4300 S, from 4200 W to 4984 W*

43rd Place
4332 S, from 43 W to 800 W

44th Street
4400 S, from 1153 E to 5158 W*

44th Street (Pvt.)
4400 S, from 1200 W to 4972 W*

44th Place
4432 S, from 1246 E to 4958 W*

45th Street
4500 S, from 1200 E to 5158 W*

45th Street (Pvt.)
4500 S, from 4210 W to 4520 W

45th Place
4532 S, from 460 E to 3825 W*

46th Street
4600 S, from 1267 E to 5158 W*

46th Street (Pvt.)
4600 S, from 4332 W to 4520 W

46th Place
4632 S, from 556 E to 3824 W*

47th Street
4700 S, from 1414 E to 5158 W

47th Drive
4700 S, in Burnham Park

The Field Museum in 1909, erected as the Fine Arts Building for the World's Columbian Exposition in 1893, was restored in 1933-34, and today houses the Museum of Science and Industry at 57th and Lake Shore Drive.

Courtesy G. Schmalgemeier

49th Place
4932 S, from 700 W to 2206 W*

49th Place (Pvt.)
4932 S, from 3000 W to 3156 W

50th Street
5000 S, from 1656 E to 5158 W*

50th Drive
5000 S, in Burnham Park

50th Place
5032 S, from 1620 E to 3760 W*

51st Street
5100 S, from 756 E to 6959 W*

51st Place
5132 S, from 300 W to 7154 W*

52nd Street
5200 S, from 1528 E to 7154 W*

52nd Place
5232 S, from 1514 E to 2144 W

52nd Place (Pvt.)
5232 S, from 4000 W to 4158 W

53rd Street
5300 S, from 1736 E to 7158 W*

53rd Drive
5300 S, in Burnham Park

53rd Place
5332 S, from 800 W to 5358 W*

54th Street
5400 S, from 1734 E to 7160 W*

54th Place
5432 S, from 1512 E to 5836 W*

55th Street
5500 S, from 1783 E to 6338 W*

55th Drive
5500 S, in Burnham Park

55th Drive
5500 S, in Gage Park

55th Drive
5500 S, in Washington Park

St. Gabriel Church (1887-88) at 45th and Lowe Avenue designed by Burnham and Root in the Canaryville neighborhood.

A. Kezys

55th Place
5532 S, from 1500 E to 4800 W*

56th Street
5600 S, from 1782 E to 7160 W*

56th Place
5632 S, from 332 W to 4800 W*

57th Street
5700 S, from 1536 E to 7160 W*

57th Boulevard
5700 S, from 1538 E to 1552 E

57th Drive
5700 S, in Washington Park

57th Drive
5700 S, in Jackson Park

57th Place
5732 S, from 1 W to 5708 W*

58th Street
5800 S, from 1432 E to 7160 W*

58th Place
5832 S, from 500 W to 4800 W*

59th Street
5900 S, from 1600 E to 7160 W*

59th Place
5932 S, from 242 W to 4000 W*

60th Street
6000 S, from 1552 E to 7158 W''*

60th Place
6032 S, from 242 W to 7158 W*

61st Street
6100 S, from 1568 E to 7158 W*

61st Place
6132 S, from 1432 E to 7158 W*

61st Place (Pvt.)
6132 S, from 814 E to 840 E

62nd Street
6200 S, from 1574 E to 7158 W*

62nd Place
6232 S, from 1418 E to 7037 W*

63rd Parkway
6259 S, from 800 W to 1000 W

63rd Street
6300 S, from 1564 E to 7158 W*

63rd Place
6332 S, from 1518 E to 7144 W*

64th Street
6400 S, from 1560 E to 7158 W*

64th Place
6432 S, from 856 E to 7158 W*

64th Drive
6432 S, in Jackson Park

65th Street
6500 S, from 1560 E to 7158 W*

65th Place
6532 S, from 1560 E to 4559 W*

66th Street
6600 S, from 456 E to 4800 W*

66th Place
6632 S, from 1560 E to 4559 W*

67th Street
6700 S, from 500 E to 2380 E

67th Place
6732 S, from 1556 E to 4000 W*

68th Street
6800 S, from 2380 E to 4524 W*

68th Place
6832 S, from 2000 W to 4000 W*

69th Street
6900 S, from 2380 E to 4410 W*

69th Place
6932 S, from 1532 E to 4146 W*

70th Street
7000 S, from 2380 E to 4150 W*

70th Place
7032 S, from 2380 E to 4000 W*

71st Street
7100 S, from 2580 E to 4000 W*

71st Place
7132 S, from 1974 E to 3552 W*

72nd Street
7200 S, from 2571 E to 3924 W*

72nd Street (Pvt.)
7200 S, from 4300 W to 4424 W

72nd Place
7232 S, from 2580 E to 3552 W*

73rd Street
7300 S, from 2674 E to 3824 W*

73rd Place,
7332 S, from 2518 E to 3552 W*

74th Street
7400 S, from 2732 E to 3552 W*

74th Street (Pvt.)
7400 S, from 3700 W to 3946 W

74th Place
7432 S, from 2640 E to 1300 W*

75th Street
7500 S, from 2788 E to 3554 W*

75th Place
7532 S, from 2738 E to 3936 W*

76th Street
7600 S, from 2864 E to 3936 W*

76th Street (Pvt.)
7600 S, from 4000 W to 4412 W

76th Place,
7632 S, from 2838 E to 3926 W*

77th Street
7700 S, from 2918 E to 4956 W*

77th Place
7732 S, from 2838 E to 4556 W*

78th Street
7800 S, from 3018 E to 4758 W*

78th Place
7832 S, from 2938 E to 4146 W*

79th Street
7900 S, from 3254 E to 4800 W*

79th Place
7932 S, from 3058 E to 4620 W*

63rd Street entrance to Jackson Park c. 1910.

C.R. Childs, courtesy G. Schmalgemeier

80th Street
8000 S, from 3158 E to 4428 W*

80th Place
8032 S, from 3226 E to 4156 W*

81st Street
8100 S, from 3158 E to 4760 W*

81st Place
8132 S, from 2958 E to 4454 W*

82nd Street
8200 S, from 3158 E to 4721 W*

82nd Place
8232 S, from 2958 E to 4736 W*

83rd Street
8300 S, from 3400 E to 4800 W*

83rd Place
8332 S, from 3156 E to 4716 W*

83rd Place (Pvt.)
8332 S, from 600 E to 720 E

St. Philip Neri Church (1926-28) at 2126 East 72nd Street in the South Shore neighborhood.

G. Lane

84th Street
8400 S, from 3358 E to 4446 W*

84th Street (Pvt.)
8400 S, from 600 E to 724 E

84th Place
8432 S, from 1752 E to 4756 W*

84th Place (Pvt.)
8432 S, from 732 E to 758 E

85th Street
8500 S, from 3356 E to 4756 W*

85th Place
8532 S, from 1752 E to 3956 W*

86th Street
8600 S, from 3356 E to 4756 W*

86th Place
8632 S, from 1752 E to 3918 W*

87th Street
8700 S, from 3328 E to 4756 W

87th Place
8732 S, from 322 E to 1750 E*

88th Street
8800 S, from 3328 E to 1924 W*

88th Place
8832 S, from 342 E to 1330 E*

89th Street
8900 S, from 3428 E to 2168 W*

89th Place
8932 S, from 200 E to 1356 E*

89th Place (Pvt.)
8932 S, from 1 E to 48 E

90th Street
9000 S, from 428 E to 2358 W*

90th Place
9032 S, from 1440 E to 1736 W*

90th Place (Pvt.)
9042 S, from 206 W to 344 W

91st Street
9100 S, from 3366 E to 2358 W*

91st Place
9132 S, from 1754 E to 1828 W*

92nd Street
9200 S, from 3328 E to 2168 W*

92nd Street (Pvt.)
9200 S, from 200 W to 362 W

92nd Place
9232 S, from 2356 E to 2400 W*

93rd Street
9300 S, from 3244 E to 2168 W*

93rd Street (Pvt.)
9300 S, from 200 W to 362 W

93rd Place
9332 S, from 1056 E to 1646 W*

93rd Place (Pvt.)
9312 S, from 216 W to 240 W

93rd Court
9363 S, from 3500 E to 3532 E

94th Street
9400 S, from 3530 E to 2356 W*

94th Street (Pvt.)
9400 S, from 200 W to 252 W

94th Place
9419 S, from 3012 E to 368 W*

94th Place (Pvt.)
9422 S, from 300 W to 368 W

95th Street
9500 S, from 3656 E to 2356 W

95th Place
9532 S, from 2524 E to 1750 W*

96th Street
9600 S, from 3658 E to 2356 W*

96th Place
9632 S, from 2728 E to 446 W*

97th Street
9700 S, from 3724 E to 2356 W*

97th Place
9732 S, from 2558 E to 1354 W*

98th Street
9800 S, from 3826 E to 2258 W*

98th Place
9832 S, from 2147 E to 1354 W*

98th Drive
9800 S, in Calumet Park

99th Street
9900 S, from 3882 E to 3958 W*

99th Place
9932 S, from 669 E to 2624 W

99th Drive
9900 S, in Calumet Park

100th Street
10000 S, from 3758 E to 3630 W*

100th Place
10032 S, from 662 E to 2624 W*

100th Drive
10000 S, in Calumet Park

101st Street
10100 S, from 4027 E to 2758 W*

101st Place
10132 S, from 650 E to 2624 W*

102nd Street
10200 S, from 4040 E to 3956 W*

102nd Place
10232 S, from 638 E to 3938 W*

103rd Street
10300 S, from 3926 E to 3958 W*

103rd Place
10332 S, from 766 E to 2640 W*

104th Street
10400 S, from 3951 E to 3958 W*

104th Place
10432 S, from 778 E to 3958 W*

105th Street
10500 S, from 3966 E to 3958 W*

105th Place
10532 S, from 758 E to 3558 W*

106th Street
10600 S, from 4059 E to 3958 W*

106th Place
10632 S, from 1 W to 2640 W*

107th Street
10700 S, from 4058 E to 3958 W*

107th Place
10732 S, from 200 W to 3908 W*

108th Street
10800 S, from 4058 E to 3868 W*

108th Place
10832 S, from 1 W to 3905 W*

109th Street
10900 S, from 4058 E to 3958 W*

109th Place
10932 S, from 1 W to 3858 W*

110st Street
11000 S, from 4058 E to 3958 W*

110th Place
11032 S, from 452 E to 3858 W*

111th Street
11100 S, from 4058 E to 4758 W*

111th Place
11132 S, from 536 E to 2356 W*

112th Street
11200 S, from 4058 E to 3158 W*

112th Place
11232 S, from 48 E to 3758 W*

113th Street
11300 S, from 3758 E to 4021 W*

113th Place
11332 S, from 48 E to 3660 W*

114th Street
11400 S, from 3828 E to 4010 W*

114th Place
11432 S, from 542 E to 3768 W*

115th Street
11500 S, from 3824 E to 4034 W*

115th Place
11532 S, from 926 W to 3628 W*

116th Street
11600 S, from 3824 E to 3628 W*

116th Place
11632 S, from 600 W to 3634 W*

117th Street
11700 S, from 3824 E to 3628 W*

117th Place
11732 S, from 162 E to 2556 W*

118th Street
11800 S, from 3824 E to 2558 W*

118th Place
11832 S, from 162 E to 2564 W*

119th Street
11900 S, from 2634 E to 2576 W*

119th Place
11932 S, from 1 E to 356 E*

120th Street
12000 S, from 2622 E to 1558 W*

120th Place
12032 S, from 1 E to 2250 E*

121st Street
12100 S, from 2622 E to 1556 W*

121st Place
12132 S, from 1 E to 2242 E*

122nd Street
12200 S, from 3222 E to 1556 W*

122nd Place
12232 S, from 1 E to 163 E*

123rd Street
12300 S, from 2624 E to 1558 W*

123rd Street (Pvt.)
12300 S, from 3032 E to 3064 E

124th Street
12400 S, from 2624 E to 756 W*

124th Place
12432 S, from 2 E to 166 E

125th Street
12500 S, from 1100 E to 756 W

125th Place
12532 S, from 167 E to 556 W*

126th Street
12600 S, from 3226 E to 756 W*

126th Place
12632 S, from 162 E to 556 W*

127th Street
12700 S, from 3222 E to 1021 W*

127th Place
12732 S, from 502 W to 530 W

128th Street
12800 S, from 3222 E to 542 W*

128th Place
12832 S, from 440 W to 856 W

129th Street
12900 S, from 2646 E to 3222 E*

129th Place
12910 S, from 1058 E to 1020 W

130th Street
13000 S, from 136 E to 3426 E

130th Street (Pvt.)
13000 S, from 301 E to 327 E

130th Place (Pvt.)
13014 S, from 643 E to 1171 E

131st Street
13100 S, from 452 E to 3556 E*

131st Street (Pvt.)
13100 S, from 600 E to 1166 E*

131st Place (Pvt.)
13114 S, from 230 E to 328 E

132nd Street
13200 S, from 500 E to 3544 E*

132nd Street (Pvt,)
13200 S, from 200 E to 1074 E*

132nd Place (Pvt.)
13210 S, from 300 E to 990 E*

133rd Street
13300 S, from 200 E to 3642 E*

133rd Street (Pvt.)
13300 S, from 136 E to 1168 E

133rd Place (Pvt.)
13332 S, from 700 E to 922 E

134th Street
13400 S, from 100 E to 4100 E*

134th Place
13432 S, from 300 E to 958 E*

135th Street
13500 S, from 900 E to 3624 E*

135th Place
13532 S, from 200 E to 260 E

136th Street
13600 S, from 200 E to 3356 E*

136th Place
13632 S, from 200 E to 340 E*

137th Street
13700 S, from 238 E to 2624 E*

138th Street
13800 S, from 200 E to 2512 E*

St. Simeon Mirotocivi Church (1968-69) at 114th Street and Avenue H, built by Serbian Americans on the far Southeast Side.

G. Lane

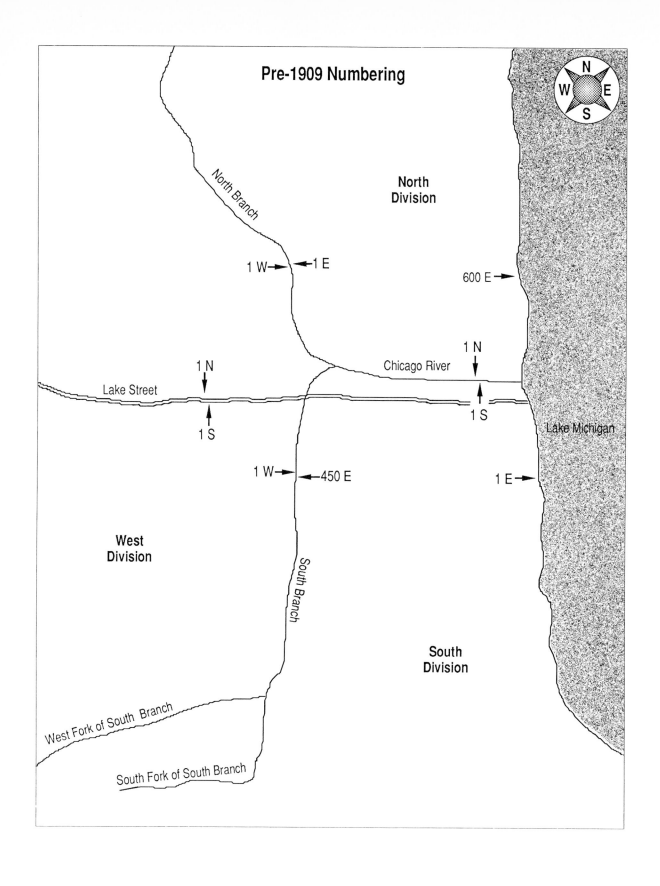

Pre-1909 Numbering

North Division

North Branch

1 W → ← 1 E

600 E →

1 N

Chicago River

1 N

Lake Street

1 S

1 S

Lake Michigan

1 W → ← 450 E

1 E →

West
Division

South Branch

South
Division

West Fork of South Branch

South Fork of South Branch

STREET NUMBERING CHANGES

by Gerrit E. Van Wissink

An understanding of the pre-1909 street numbering systems (note the plural usage) in Chicago is especially helpful to persons interested in the history of Chicago street names, to family genealogists, to garden variety historians, and even to the merely curious.

The importance of the adoption of the "Brennan" numbering system (named after Edward P. Brennan) on September 1, 1909 is that it brought order out of chaos. Chicago's pre-1909 street numbering systems were suitable for a small town of only a few thousand people in the mid-nineteenth century. But as the city's population doubled and redoubled, the geographically-based systems soon became inadequate.

The Pre-1909 Numbering Systems

The old numbering systems were inconsistent because the numbers ran differently in each one of the three "divisions" of the city. These "divisions" were based on the Chicago River, its two branches, the lake shore, and (in the absence of a West Branch of the river) on Lake Street, as follows:

a. The dividing line for north and south numbering was the main channel of the Chicago River, from Lake Michigan to "the forks," and then along Lake Street westward to the city limits. The numbers got larger the further north or south you were from the line.

This was a bit confusing because east of the South Branch, Lake Street was 1½ blocks south of the main channel of the river. This meant that the northeast corner of Lake and Halsted Streets (west of the S. Branch) would be 1 North, while the northeast corner of Lake and Franklin Streets (east of the S. Branch) would be numbered 29 South.

b. The dividing lines for east and west numbering were the branches of the river, and that's where the fun (or frustration) began. The North Branch ran north-northwest while the South Branch ran almost due south for about 1¾ miles before turning sharply to the west-southwest. These more-or-less diagonal dividing lines meant that numbers on the cross streets would not be the same as you walked north or south.

The worst inconsistency in the system was that the numbers ran differently in the South Division (south of the main channel and east of the S. Branch) than in the North Division (north of the main channel and east of the N. Branch). In the South Division, east numbers began at the lakeshore and got larger until you reached the South Branch.

This meant that in the South Division you could be on the east bank of the South Branch at approximately 550 E. 22nd Street, then cross the 22nd Street Bridge and be at 1 W. 22nd Street. At least when you crossed the North Branch, the numbers got larger the further away from it you went (east or west). Is it any wonder that strangers to the city were confused?

This inconsistency was also most apparent on the two streets named "Water." South Water Street ran parallel to the main river about one-half block south of it, and at the lakeshore it was numbered 1 E. South Water Street. But a block to the north, across the river, the numbering at the lakeshore was 654 E. North Water Street.

The "Brennan" Numbering System

Some have said the City of Chicago owes Mr. Brennan a prominent statue. I agree and suggest the northeast corner of State and Madison Streets for reasons that will soon become apparent.

Brennan's numbering system was deceptively simple, particularly since landfills on the lakeshore south of the river meant that buildings were being built beyond the lowest possible number! For his dividing lines he took U.S. Geodetic Survey Section Lines (used in legal descriptions for land titles). He used Madison Street to divide numbers North and South, and State Street for numbers East and West.

After much effort to pacify objections from the three divisions of the city, the new system was adopted. But it had to be implemented in two stages because of the longer time needed for adjustments in the central business district:

1. On September 1, 1909, these areas changed addresses:

    North of the main river and east of the North Branch (i.e., the North Division)

    West of the North and South Branches (i.e., the West Division)

    South of 12th Street and east of the South Branch (i.e., all of the South Division except the central business district)

2. The numbering change for the central business district (south of the main river, east of the South Branch, and north of 12th St.) took place on April 1, 1911.

149

When the final changes were made, another innovation was introduced: if streets of different names were on the same alignment (a uniform distance away from one of the new dividing lines), a single name was usually adopted. For a more detailed discussion of this, see the Appendix titled "Chicago Street Name Changes—A Selected Sample."

There were two other significant changes brought about by the 1909-1911 street numbering changes in Chicago:

It standardized the use of 800 numbers (or 8 "blocks" to a mile). The only exception to this is just south of the central business district where the mile-interval streets heading southward are 12th Street (Roosevelt Road), 22nd Street (Cermak Road), 31st Street, and then every 800 numbers after that.

Note: Some people still confuse a "block" (i.e., 100 numbers) with a "street." In many parts of the city, two or more streets occur within the range of 100 numbers. Instead of saying "It's four blocks from Touhy Avenue to Howard Street," it is much better to say, "It's 400 numbers . . . ." or "Touhy is six streets south of Howard Street."

The numbers grow uniformly larger as you go further from the intersection of State and Madison Streets. This avoids all the confusing inconsistencies discussed above.

© *1988 Gerrit E. Van Wissink*

STREET NAME CHANGES

A Selected Sample

by Gerrit E. Van Wissink

The names of many Chicago streets have been changed since 1833. Some of the reasons for those changes are:

a. The opening of a roadway to connect two streets that had different names. In 1920, for instance, when the "link" bridge joined Pine Street (north of the Chicago River) to Michigan Avenue (south of it), the name Pine Street was changed to Michigan Avenue.

b. A desire to avoid confusing numbered avenues (N-S) with numbered streets (E-W) by giving names to the less-numerous avenues. For instance, Sixtieth Street (6000 W) became Austin Avenue.

c. The need to eliminate duplications when Chicago annexed other towns that had used the same street names. This has not happened recently.

d. Chicago politicians have occasionally honored a group of voters by re-naming a street. In 1933 the City Council removed Peter Crawford's name from the north-south street at 4000 West and replaced it with that of the Revolutionary War hero Count Casimir Pulaski.

e. Fewer street names result if only one name is used when two or more streets run, un-connected, on the same alignment. For instance, Osgood Street in New Town and Kenmore Avenue in Edgewater-Uptown were aligned at 1050 West, and Kenmore survived. This was not always done consistently, especially if major streets were involved.

Here are some exceptions (and their exceptions) to reason "e" above:

1. At 1000 West: Morgan Street runs up to the North Branch of the Chicago River. Not far beyond it, Sheffield Avenue heads north, meeting end-to-end with Sheridan Road, which runs on for three miles.

2. At 1400 West: Loomis Street runs up to the North Branch; just beyond it Southport Avenue runs for several miles, and somewhat beyond that, it's Glenwood for several more miles.

3. At 800 West: Halsted Street runs northward beyond the North Branch until it is intercepted by Broadway which runs for several blocks on the same alignment before turning off. Beyond there, the same street is known as Clarendon Avenue for about a mile, and then it turns into Marine Drive for almost another mile.

151

A Sample of Street Name Changes

This list of street name changes is not complete; it's a selected sample from about 1900 to the present time. The card file in the City's Department of Maps and Plats is the final authority.

    I have included a few eliminations of street names where streets have disappeared due to the construction of large developments. These may have been shopping centers, modern office buildings, expressways, expanding industrial plants, and other civic improvements.

Airdre Place
4175 N.
is now Gordon Terrace

Alaska Street
1550 N.
is now Weed Street

Albert Street
1450 W.
is now Bishop Street

Aubert Avenue
4250 N.
is now Hutchinson Street

Austin Avenue
450 N.
is now Hubbard Street

Ayers Court
1225 W.
is now N. Willard Court

Beethoven Place
1250 N.
is now W. Scott Street

Best Avenue
950 W.
is now Wilton Avenue

Bixby Court
1450 W.
is now N. Bishop Street

Blucher Street
1300 N.
is now Potomac Avenue

Bunker Street
1100 S.
is now W. Grenshaw Street

Carl Street
1500 N.
is now W. Burton Place

Carlisle Place
1550 S.
is now W. 15th Place

Cass Avenue
50 E.; N. of main river
is now Wabash Avenue

Center Street
2000 N.; E. of the North Branch
is now Armitage Avenue

Central Avenue
2100 E.
is now Clyde Avenue

Centre Street
1200 W.; S. of the North Branch
is now Racine Avenue

Charlton Street
1550 W.
is now S. Justine Street

Colorado Avenue
diagonal, W. of Madison & Sacramento
is now Fifth Avenue

Congress Street Expressway
500 S.
is now Dwight D. Eisenhower Expressway

Conrad Street
1950 S.
is now W. 19th Place

Crawford Avenue
4000 W.
is now [second change] Pulaski Road

Eighth Street
800 S.
is now Polk Street

Evanston Avenue
diagonal, N. of Diversey Boulevard
is now Broadway

Fifth Avenue
200 W.; S. of main river
is now Wells Street

Fifty-fifth Street
5500 S.
is now Garfield Boulevard

Fifty-second Avenue
5200 W.
is now Laramie Avenue

Fifty-sixth Avenue
5600 W.
is now Central Avenue

Fortieth Avenue
4000 W.
is now [first change] Crawford Avenue

Garfield Avenue
2100 N.; E. of the North Branch
is now Dickens Avenue

Glengyle Place
5100 N.
is now Carmen Avenue

Graceland Avenue
4000 N.; E. of Clark St.
is now Irving Park Boulevard

Grand Boulevard
400 E.
became [first change] South Parkway

Horan Avenue
1850 W.
is now N. Honore Street

Humboldt Avenue
2200 N.; W. of the North Branch
is now Webster Avenue

Ignatius Street
6500 N.
is now Arthur Avenue

Indiana Avenue
500 N.; E. of the North Branch
is now Grand Avenue

Kenilworth Avenue
7200 N.; E. of Ridge Boulevard
is now Touhy Avenue

Lincoln Street
1900 W.
is now Wolcott Avenue

Market Street
350 W.
is now N. and S. Wacker Drive

Northwest Expressway
diagonal, NW. from Congress & Halsted
Streets
is now John F. Kennedy Expressway

Norwood Park Avenue
diagonal, NW. of Ainslie St. & Laramie
Avenue
is now Northwest Highway

Ontario Avenue
3200 E.
is now Brandon Avenue

Osgood Street
1050 W.
is now Kenmore Avenue

Penn Street
700 W.
is now Orchard Street

Perry Avenue
1500 W.; N. of the North Branch
is now Laflin Street

Pine Street
100 E.; N. of main river
is now Michigan Avenue

Pullman Avenue
diagonal, S. of Cottage Grove & 98th
Street
is now Cottage Grove Avenue

Robey Street
2000 W.; N. of 87th Street
is now Damen Avenue

Rockeby Street
900 W.
is now Fremont Street

Rogers Road
7200 N.; W. of Ridge Boulevard
is now Touhy Avenue

Seventh St.
700 S.
is now Balbo Drive

Seventy-second Avenue
7200 W.
is now Harlem Avenue

Sheldon Street
1400 W.
is now N. Loomis Street

Sixtieth Avenue
6000 W.
is now Austin Avenue

Sixty-fourth Avenue
6400 W.
is now Narragansett Avenue

Sixty-seventh Street
6700 S.
is now Marquette Road

South Parkway
400 E.
is now [second change] Martin L. King
Drive

South Water Street
300 N.
is now E. and W. Wacker Drive

Southport Avenue
1400 W.; N. of Foster Ave.
is now Glenwood Avenue

Southwest Expressway
diagonal, SW from 25th Street & S.
Lake Shore Drive
is now Adlai E. Stevenson Expressway

Temple Street
1300 W.
is now N. Throop Street

Thirty-ninth Place
3950 S.
is now Pershing Place

Thirty-ninth Street
3900 S.
is now Pershing Road

Tremont Avenue
2000 W.; S. of 91st St.
is now Damen Avenue

Twelfth Street
1200 S.
is now Roosevelt Road

Twenty-second Street
2200 S.
is now Cermak Road

Vedder Street
1250 N.
is now W. Scott Street

Walden Parkway
1900 W.; S. of 87th St.
is now S. Wolcott Street

Ziegfield Court
75 E.; N. of Van Buren St.
is now eliminated by construction of the
C.N.A. Financial Bldg. about 1970.